LOW-FAT
NO-FAT
COOKBOOK

KAREN BELLERSON

Avery Publishing Group
Garden City Park, New York

Text Illustrator: John Wincek
Interior Color Photographs: Victor Giordano
Photo Food Styling: BC Giordano
Front Cover Photograph: Foodpix
Back Cover Photographs: Victor Giordano
Cover Design: Phaedra Mastrocola
Typesetting: Elaine V. McCaw
In-House Editor: Joanne Abrams

Avery Publishing Group
120 Old Broadway
Garden City Park, NY 11040
1-800-548-5757

Library of Congress Cataloging-in-Publication Data

Bellerson, Karen J.
    Low-fat, no-fat cookbook : a tempting collection of over 190
contemporary and traditional recipes / Karen J. Bellerson.
        p.   cm.
    Includes index.
    ISBN 0-89529-782-5
    1. Low-fat diet—Recipes. I. Title.
RM237.7.B43 1998   97-27395
641.5'638—dc21   CIP

Printed in the United States of America

10 9 8 7 6 5 4 3 2 1

Contents

Dedicated with love to my children:
Dave, and his wife Robyn; Steven; Darin, and his wife Michelle.
May there always be rainy days and "warm fuzzies" in your lives.

Acknowledgments

Many thanks to my family and friends, especially Judy and Richard Murphy, for their generous help in sampling my recipes and giving me their *honest* critiques!

I am also indebted to Joanne Abrams, my ever-patient editor, for doing such a superb job of making sure that I said what I meant and meant what I said in every single recipe. Her know-how has been invaluable, and I want to thank her for graciously sharing it with me.

Preface

There is no love more sincere than the love of food.
—George Bernard Shaw

We are, as a society, becoming more and more knowledgeable about the subject of dietary fat, as well as about the enormous impact that the food we eat has on our overall health and well-being. My discovery of that impact is what prompted me to write my first book, *The Complete and Up-to-Date Fat Book,* as a means of enabling people to easily discover the amount of fat in the foods they were eating. When the book was published, many readers spoke to me about the problem of dietary fat, and I became aware of a simple fact: Although many people want to eat lower-fat foods and to defat their favorite dishes, they don't know how to begin. This motivated me to write this cookbook, in which I share the best of my low-fat recipes.

The recipes for this cookbook were created with certain objectives in mind. My number-one objective was that each recipe be low in fat. However, no matter how low-fat a dish is, if it doesn't have delicious flavor, you won't prepare it very often, if at all. So my number-two objective was that it be tasty. Third, as you well know, even when you gain the knowledge and awareness of the importance of eating healthy, nutritious food, you don't necessarily gain the time needed to prepare made-from-scratch recipes.

And if you don't have the time it takes to prepare a dish, you won't ever know how it tastes or how beautifully it can fit into a low-fat diet. Therefore, I made time an important factor in devising my recipes. I even considered the time it takes to *buy* the ingredients, in addition, of course, to the time it takes to put the ingredients together. When you want a recipe that's super-quick to make, look for the "Quick Dish" designation. These dishes are the perfect choices when you want to make a healthful, low-fat meal, but you're short on time. Be aware that in those sections in which *all* of the recipes are quick to make—in my collection of salad dressings, for instance—this designation has not been used. But in those areas in which dish preparation tends to be a bit more time-consuming—among the entrées, side dishes, and soups, for instance—the term "Quick Dish" will guide you to the fastest-to-make dishes in the collection. This book also includes an occasional recipe that takes slightly more time to make. But you'll find that the results are truly worth that extra bit of time!

Chapter 1 of *Low-Fat, No-Fat Cookbook* begins by looking at the basics of a healthy low-fat diet. It then shows you how you can quickly and easily replace many of the high-fat foods you may now be eating with healthier choices, enabling you to enjoy virtually all of your favorite dishes without guilt. In this chapter you'll also learn how to use herbs and spices to make your low-fat dishes flavorful and exciting. You'll even become acquainted with some handy kitchen tools that will help you get the fat out of gravies, soups, and a variety of other dishes.

Following these important basics, each chapter focuses on a specific meal of the day or a specific type of dish. The recipes begin with Chapter 2, which presents breakfast fare ranging from lusciously sweet Apple Cinnamon Pancakes to decadent Spiced French Toast With Peaches to savory Pastrami Breakfast Sandwiches. All of these dishes are easy to assemble and a delight to serve and eat.

Chapter 3 offers an exciting collection of sandwiches. No boring PB and J here! Instead, you'll find creations like Beef Teriyaki Steak Sandwiches, which can satisfy the most hearty of appetites; and Tiny Cranberry-Beef Sandwiches, which are dainty enough to serve at a special tea or as an appetizer.

Chapter 4 presents a wonderful assortment of easy-to-make dips, spreads, and snacks. Perfect for parties, these dishes are also healthy ways to satisfy hunger in between meals.

Chapter 5 offers scrumptious salads of all sizes and varieties, from a Simple Four-Bean Salad to an elegant Orange-on-Orange Salad With Chicken Tenderloins. The selection of salad dressings is so enticing that you will want to use these dressings as sandwich spreads and marinades, too!

There is nothing as heart-warming as a steaming bowl of homemade soup. So Chapter 6 presents six basic stocks and seven soups, each of which is guaranteed to make you feel warm and cozy on the next rainy day.

Chapter 7 is a mouthwatering collection of sauces, relishes, and toppings. Whether you want to add a crowning touch to a freshly baked potato or turn a dish of frozen low-fat yogurt into something really special, you're sure to find

what you're looking for among these recipes.

If you like the sound of Pork Tenderloin With Plum Sauce or Crispy Lemon-Lime Sesame Chicken, you're sure to love Chapter 8. And with over twenty-five recipes for alluring entrées, you'll find dishes that everyone else in your family will love, too!

Chapter 9 presents a wide assortment of vegetable dishes and other side dishes. Roasted Chili Corn on the Cob, Quick Mesquite Chicken Rice, and Roasted Rosemary and Garlic Potatoes are just a few of the colorful, nutritionally rich dishes that can help you turn even the simplest of main dishes into a meal to remember.

My Dad's Banana Puddin', Chocolate Chip Cheese Cake With Hot Fudge, and Heavenly Mixed Berry Trifle are just some of the deceptively rich-tasting desserts featured in Chapter 10. Every last one is so luscious, your only problem will be in choosing the one you want to try next.

Whether you're looking for a perfect pot of tea, a new delicious take on coffee, or a thick, frosty milk shake, Chapter 11 has a beverage that will meet your needs deliciously. Here are beverages that can enhance a main dish, serve as a grand finale to a meal, or make a refreshing between-meals snack.

As you glance through the pages of this book, you will see boxed insets that give you additional information about the selection and use of certain ingredients. If, for instance, you want to find the best potato for making potato salad, "The Popular Potato" on page 168 will identify the varieties best suited to your dish. New to the world of chilies? "Hot Peppers" on page 38 will guide you from selection to preparation. Other insets will tell you how to use yogurt successfully in hot dishes, how to make your green salads crisp and tantalizing, how to roast nuts and seeds for added flavor, and more. In addition, the recipes themselves will teach you new ways to prepare and enjoy delectable, elegant, easy-to-make dishes—dishes that are low in fat, but so sumptuously satisfying that no one but you will ever know just how healthy they are!

1

The Keys of Low-Fat Cooking

Contrary to what many people believe, adopting a low-fat diet is not a difficult task. Nevertheless, you will find that an understanding of certain concepts and the mastery of certain simple skills will help guarantee success each and every time you prepare a recipe that is already low in fat, or you try to reduce the fat in one of your own favorite dishes. This chapter will provide you with much of the information you need. First, you will learn what foods should and should not be included in a healthy diet. Then, you will learn about some valuable ingredient substitutions, you will learn how to read a food label so that you can make informed selections at the supermarket, and you will learn about the utensils that will prove useful in your fat-free cooking adventures. Finally, this chapter takes a detailed look at herbs and spices, to insure that although your food is low in fat, it's not low in flavor!

BUILDING A HEALTHY DIET

Most people know that for a diet to be healthy, dietary fat should be greatly reduced. But exactly which foods *should* be in a low-fat diet? To help us determine the best proportions of differ-ent foods, in 1992, the United States Department of Agriculture (USDA) developed the Food Guide Pyramid (see the figure on page 2), which shows the recommended number of servings in each food group. The lower a food group is positioned on the pyramid, the larger role that group should play in your diet. For instance, grains form the base of the pyramid, with six to eleven servings recommended daily. The next level of the pyramid is occupied by the vegetable group, with three to five daily servings recommended; and the fruit group, with two to four servings recommended. Moving upward, the next pyramid level is shared by the milk, yogurt, and cheese group (two to three recommended servings), and the meat, poultry, fish, beans, eggs, and nuts group (two to three servings). Note that the fat group, found at the peak of the pyramid, occupies the smallest space, indicating that you should include only small amounts of this category in your diet. Note, too, that in each range of recommended servings, the highest recommended number is not for everyone. Rather, the number of servings for which you should aim depends on your age, weight, and activity level.

What constitutes a serving? The following lists

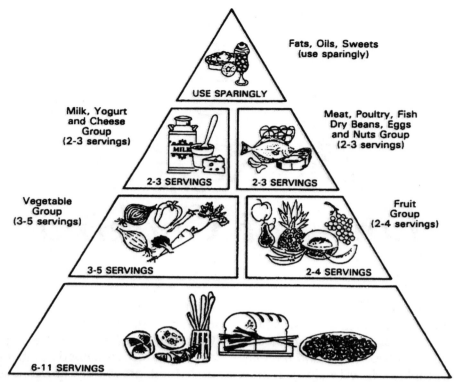

Fats, Oils, Sweets
(use sparingly)

USE SPARINGLY

Milk, Yogurt
and Cheese
Group
(2-3 servings)

Meat, Poultry, Fish
Dry Beans, Eggs
and Nuts Group
(2-3 servings)

2-3 SERVINGS   2-3 SERVINGS

Vegetable
Group
(3-5 servings)

Fruit
Group
(2-4 servings)

3-5 SERVINGS   2-4 SERVINGS

6-11 SERVINGS

Bread, Cereal, Rice and Pasta Group
(6-11 servings)

The Food Guide Pyramid

will show you what should be considered a serving in each of the pyramid's categories.

Breads, Cereals, Rice, and Pasta (6 to 11 servings)

1 slice bread
½ cup cooked rice or pasta
½ cup cooked cereal
1 ounce ready-to-serve cereal

Vegetables (3 to 5 servings)

½ cup chopped raw or cooked vegetables
1 cup leafy raw vegetables

Fruits (2 to 4 servings)

1 medium whole fruit
¾ cup juice
½ cup canned fruit
¼ cup dried fruit

Milk, Yogurt, and Cheese (2 to 3 servings)

1 cup milk or yogurt
1½ to 2 ounces cheese (about 1-x-2½-inch chunk, or 2 slices)

Meat, Poultry, Fish, Dried Beans, Eggs, and Nuts (2 to 3 servings)

2½ to 3 ounces cooked lean meat, poultry, or fish (about the size of a deck of cards)
1 to 1½ cups cooked beans or peas
2 to 3 eggs
4 to 6 tablespoons peanut butter

Fats, Oils, and Sweets (use sparingly)

While small amounts of this group can be part of a healthy low-fat lifestyle, these foods should be used as sparingly as possible.

America's Top Ten Fat Sources

Most of us know that Americans have far too much fat in their diets. But just where is all that fat coming from? Of course, fat comes from many sources. Here, though, are the ten most often consumed high-fat foods. If you eat any—or all!—of these foods, take heart. Virtually every food on the following list has a low- or no-fat substitute. The table found on page 6 will help you find delicious substitutes for these and many other high-fat foods.

The Ten Most Popular High-Fat Foods

- Margarine
- Whole milk
- Shortening
- Mayonnaise and salad dressing
- American cheese
- Ground beef
- 2-percent reduced-fat milk*
- Eggs
- Butter
- Vanilla ice cream

*Although a reduced-fat product, 2-percent milk is no longer considered *low* in fat, and contains 5 grams of fat per cup.

If you are just beginning to incorporate healthier foods into your diet, don't panic and throw out any higher-fat foods you may now have in your pantry. Save these products for the occasional treat, and try not to purchase them in the future. Remember that no food is a real "no-no," but that certain foods should definitely be enjoyed only once in a while. On those days when you really must indulge, simply plan ahead and eat lighter the rest of the day.

Like all habits, eating habits can't be changed overnight. It will take time for you to make a complete transition to healthy low-fat shopping, cooking, and eating. The next section will help you in this transition by guiding you in the substitution of low- and no-fat foods for those foods that are currently adding fat to your diet.

LOW-FAT TIPS AND SUBSTITUTIONS

Now that you've seen how each of the food categories fits into a healthy diet, you need to find ways of trimming the fat from the foods you presently eat and introducing yourself to healthier choices. If you're like most people, you already have a collection of recipes—family favorites that you don't want to discard just because they may call for some high-fat ingredients. Fortunately, by making just a few simple ingredient substitutions, it's easy to take a high-fat dish and turn it into an equally delicious but far healthier dish. Sound too good to be true? Just look at the following versions of the same stuffing recipe. The first version is the original high-fat recipe. The second is "defatted." Compare the nutritional data following each recipe, and see how by changing just one ingredient, I was able to make a delicious bread stuffing that is not just low in fat, but also far lower in calories than the original!

How can you start trimming the fat from your own favorite recipes and choosing healthier ingredients? Fortunately for anyone making the transition to a healthier diet, the grocery shelves are now carrying more and more low-fat and fat-free products. If you find that you're confused by all the advertising claims made on these new foods packages, don't despair. The inset "Reading the New Food Label," found on page 5, will help you see through the "hype" and easily identify the best foods available. Then refer to the table on page 6 for ideas on substituting these healthier ingredients for those ingredients you may now be using in your recipes, and for making wiser use of those ingredients that cannot be replaced.

Cranberry-Apple Stuffing

Original High-Fat Recipe	*New Modified Low-Fat Recipe*

Original High-Fat Recipe

2 tablespoons butter
1 medium onion, chopped
2 medium stalks celery, chopped
7 cups soft plain bread crumbs
3 cups diced apples
1 cup chopped dried cranberries
1 cup butter, melted
1 teaspoon ground thyme
1 teaspoon ground sage
Salt and freshly ground black pepper to taste

1. Place the 2 tablespoons of butter in a large skillet, and melt over medium heat.
2. Add the onions and celery, and cook until tender.
3. Remove the skillet from the heat, and stir in 1½ cups of the bread crumbs. Transfer the mixture to a large mixing bowl.
4. Add all of the remaining ingredients to the bread crumb mixture, and toss until well blended.
5. Place the stuffing mixture in a 2-quart baking dish, cover, and bake at 325°F for 30 to 45 minutes, or until golden on top. Serve hot.

Serves 10 to 12.

NUTRITIONAL DATA (PER SERVING)
Fat: 21 grams
Calories: 308
% of Fat From Calories: 61%

New Modified Low-Fat Recipe

½ cup fat-free chicken stock
1 medium onion, chopped
2 medium stalks celery, finely chopped
7 cups soft bread crumbs (made from fat-free bread)
3 cups diced apples
1 cup chopped dried cranberries
1 cup fat-free chicken stock
1 teaspoon ground thyme
1 teaspoon ground sage
Salt and freshly ground black pepper to taste

1. Place the ½ cup of chicken stock in a large skillet, and bring to a boil over high heat. Reduce the heat to medium.
2. Add the onions and celery to the stock, and cook until tender.
3. Remove the skillet from the heat, and stir in 1½ cups of the bread crumbs. Transfer the mixture to a large mixing bowl.
4. Add all of the remaining ingredients to the bread crumb mixture, and toss until well blended.
5. Place the stuffing mixture in a 2-quart baking dish, cover, and bake at 325°F for 30 to 45 minutes, or until golden on top. Serve hot.

Serves 10 to 12.

NUTRITIONAL DATA (PER SERVING)
Fat: <1 gram
Calories: 130
% of Fat From Calories: <1%

Reading the New Food Label

One of the best steps you can take when adopting a healthier lifestyle is to get in the habit of looking at the many foods offered in your supermarket and reading their Nutrition Facts labels. This will help you determine which foods will fit into your new low-fat diet. Confused by the new food label? The figure show below explains its components.

When interpreting the Nutrition Facts label, keep in mind that the guidelines shown are for healthy adults and children age two or over. While a low-fat diet is healthful for adults and older children, it may be harmful to children younger than two years of age. Also remember that the Daily Values listed on the label are for those people who eat 2,000 calories a day. If you are limiting your intake to less than 2,000 calories, this information will overestimate your needs.

Serving sizes are consistent across product lines, stated in both household and metric measures.

The list of nutrients covers those most important to the health of today's consumers, most of whom need to worry about getting too much of certain items (fat, for example), rather than too few minerals, as in the past.

The label states the number of calories per gram of fat, carbohydrates, and protein.

Calories from fat are show on the label to help consumers meet dietary guidelines that recommend people get no more than 30 percent of their calories from fat.

% Daily Value shows how a food fits into the overall daily diet.

The daily values on the label are based on a daily diet of 2,000 and 2,500 calories. Some are maximums, as with fat (65 grams or less); others are minimums, as with carbohydrates (300 grams or more). Individuals should adjust the values to fit their own calories intake.

Nutrition Facts

Serving Size ½ cup (114g)
Servings Per Container 4

Amount Per Serving

Calories 90   Calories from Fat 30

	% Daily Value*
Total Fat 3g	5%
Saturated fat 0g	0%
Cholesterol 0mg	0%
Sodium 300mg	13%
Total Carbohydrate 13g	4%
Dietary Fiber 3g	12%
Sugars 3g	
Protein 3g	

Vitamin A 80% • Vitamin C 60% • Calcium 4% • Iron 4%

*Percent Daily Values are based on a 2,000 calorie diet. Your Daily Values may be higher or lower depending on your calorie needs:

Nutrient		2,000 Calories	2,500 Calories
Total fat	Less than	65g	80g
Sat Fat	Less than	20g	25g
Cholesterol	Less than	300mg	300mg
Sodium	Less than	2,400mg	2,400mg
Total Carbohydrate		300g	375g
Fiber		25g	30g

Calories per gram:
Fat 9 • Carbohydrates 4 • Protein 4

The Nutrition Facts Label

Low-Fat Substitutions

High-Fat Ingredient	Low-Fat Replacement
Alcohol	Research shows that alcohol inhibits the body's ability to burn fat, so use or drink alcohol in moderate amounts only.
Avocado	Since over 70 percent of this fruit's calories come from fat, use this food sparingly.
Bacon, regular	Canadian bacon brushed with liquid smoke (a smoky tasting liquid seasoning available in the condiment section) and cooked in a nonstick skillet. Or use cooked turkey bacon or small amounts of a product such as Oscar Mayer Real Bacon Bits.
Beef, high-fat cuts	Lean cuts, such as eye of round, tenderloin, and sirloin tip steaks and roasts; flank steak; filet mignon; London broil; and extra lean (90% fat-free) ground beef. Keep in mind that "Select" cuts have less fat (and fewer calories) than "Prime" and "Choice" cuts. Choose meat with the least amount of marbling, and trim off all visible fat. Roast, bake, broil, grill, stir-fry, or stew to avoid adding extra fat. Also cook meat medium or well done to eliminate fat. When ground beef is called for, use extra lean (90% fat-free) ground beef, drain it in a colander, and pat dry with paper towels before adding to the recipe. If desired, choose one of the lean cuts mentioned above, and have it trimmed and ground. Or substitute ground turkey breast, being sure to check the label for fat content.
Bread, high-fat (croissants, biscuits, sweet rolls, butter-flake rolls)	French bread, Italian bread, pita pockets, English muffins, soft corn tortillas, fat-free flour tortillas, hard rolls, and bagels.
Butter, in baking	*See* Margarine or butter, in baking.
Butter, as spread or topping	Reduced-fat butter, jam, preserves, apple butter, peach butter, sweet potato butter, or butter-flavored spray.
Butter, for sautéing	Butter-flavored or plain cooking spray, broth, stock, low-fat or fat-free salad dressing, juice, wine, or flavored vinegars. Always use a nonstick skillet. For buttery taste, add butter-flavored salt or butter-flavored sprinkles to your dish.
Cheese, cottage, 4% fat	1%, 2%, or fat-free cottage cheese.
Cheese, cream	Reduced-fat or fat-free cream cheese. Better yet, make your own So-Simple Yogurt Cheese (page 53).
Cheese, hard	Reduced-fat or fat-free cheese. For best flavor and cooking results, try a blend of 2 parts fat-free cheese and 1 part reduced-fat cheese.

High-Fat Ingredient	Low-Fat Replacement
Chicken, dark meat with skin	White meat chicken without skin. If the skin is removed before cooking rather than after, the result will be only slightly less fatty. When baking the chicken, removing the skin after cooking helps retain moisture.
Chocolate, baking	Substitute cocoa powder or chocolate syrup whenever possible. (When using cocoa powder, substitute 3 tablespoons cocoa powder, 2 teaspoons sugar, and 1 tablespoon water or other liquid for 1 ounce baking chocolate.) If the recipe absolutely requires baking chocolate, use a smaller amount.
Coconut	Coconut-flavored extract or coconut water. (Coconut water, the liquid found inside the coconut, has only .5 gram of fat per cup!)
Cookies	Reduced-fat or fat-free cookies. Ginger snaps, vanilla wafers, animal crackers, and graham crackers are all good choices. Also try Chewy Coconut-Carrot Oatmeal Cookies (page 191).
Crackers	Reduced-fat or fat-free crackers (read the labels carefully for serving size), melba toast, breadsticks, crispbread, and oyster crackers.
Cream, sour	*See* Sour cream.
Cream soups	*See* Soups, cream.
Creamers, powdered nondairy	Nonfat dry milk powder or evaporated skim milk. Another good choice is fat-free liquid nondairy creamers, which come in a variety of flavors.
Desserts	Splurge on occasion, but more often enjoy fat-free or low-fat frozen yogurt or ice cream, sorbet, sherbet, angel food cake, or one of the fat-free or low-fat desserts in this book. Remember, too, that fruit makes a lovely, light, almost fat-free dessert!
Eggs, hard cooked	Discard the yolk, and use only the white.
Eggs, whole	For 1 egg, use 2 egg whites or appropriate amount of egg substitute (check the package label). For 2 eggs, use 1 whole egg and 1 or 2 egg whites, 3 egg whites, or appropriate amount of egg substitute. For 3 eggs, use 1 whole egg and 3 egg whites, or appropriate amount of egg substitute. For 4 eggs, use 2 whole eggs and 3 egg whites, or appropriate amount of egg substitute. Do not try to substitute all egg whites when the recipe calls for 5 or more eggs, as the results will be poor. Use an egg substitute instead.
Fish, high-fat (salmon, mackerel, sardines, herring, anchovies, tuna canned in oil)	Whiting, haddock, cod, halibut, pollack, and flounder, or tuna canned in water.

High-Fat Ingredient	Low-Fat Replacement
Frankfurters, regular	Reduced-fat or fat-free frankfurters. Read the labels; despite what most people think, chicken and turkey franks are not always the leanest choices. You can now find franks with less than 1 gram of fat per serving!
French fries	Oven-fry your spuds! (See Oven-Baked Spiced Potato Slices on page 172.)
Granola, traditional	Reduced-fat or fat-free granola.
Ice cream, premium	Low-fat or fat-free ice cream, sherbet, or frozen yogurt.
Lamb, high-fat cuts	Leg, loin roasts, and chops.
Luncheon meats, high-fat	Look for low-fat and fat-free products. Sliced turkey and chicken breast are always a good choice.
Margarine, as spread or topping	Reduced-fat or fat-free margarine. *See also* Butter, as spread or topping.
Margarine or butter, in baking	Applesauce, mashed sweet potatoes, apple butter, prune butter, low-fat yogurt, honey, buttermilk, preserves and jams, puréed fruit, mashed banana, mashed pumpkin, syrups, and reduced-fat margarine or light butter. For buttery taste, add butter-flavored extract to your batter.
Marinades, oil-based	Marinades made from fruit juices, low-fat or nonfat yogurt, soy sauce, wine, teriyaki sauce, tomato juice, vegetable purées, flavored vinegars, or buttermilk.
Mayonnaise, as salad dressing	Fat-free or light mayonnaise; a mixture of 1 part light and 2 parts fat-free mayonnaise; fat-free mayonnaise mixed with nonfat plain yogurt; low-fat or fat-free cottage cheese; and buttermilk.
Mayonnaise, as sandwich spread	Fat-free or light mayonnaise, mustard, or low-fat or fat-free ranch or Thousand Island dressing.
Milk, evaporated	Evaporated skim milk.
Milk, whole and 2%	Skim milk, 1% milk, or buttermilk.
Nuts	All nuts are high in fat. While some nuts are healthier than others, to reduce fat, you should use less of all nuts. For optimum flavor and crunch, see the inset "Toasting and Roasting Nuts and Seeds" on page 77. If crunch is all you're after, try sprinkling on a crunchy cereal.
Oil, vegetable	All oils are 100 percent fat, and contain the same amount of fat and calories. Some oils are healthier than others, though. Choose

High-Fat Ingredient	Low-Fat Replacement
Oil, vegetable (continued)	those lower in saturated fat, such as canola, safflower, sunflower, corn, and olive, and use smaller amounts of all oils. When sautéing, use cooking sprays in place of oils.
Olives	High in fat—they are, after all, the source of olive oil—olives should be used sparingly.
Pasta, egg	Eggless pasta products.
Peanut butter	Use a reduced-fat product, or less of the regular. Try mashing it with banana to get more coverage with less fat.
Pizza with meat toppings	Replace the meat with Canadian bacon, or substitute green pepper, onion, and other chopped vegetables.
Popcorn	Air pop and spray with butter-flavored spray, or use light butter-flavored microwave popcorn.
Pork, high-fat cuts	Leaner cuts, such as center-cut ham (at least 97% fat-free), tenderloin, sirloin, and Canadian bacon.
Potato chips	Fat-free or low-fat potato chips, tortilla chips, and pretzels.
Potatoes, baked, with sour cream or butter	Good toppings include fat-free, 1%, or 2% cottage cheese; low-fat or fat-free plain yogurt; buttermilk; fat-free or reduced-fat margarine or butter; low-fat or fat-free sour cream; or Healthy Sour Cream (page 106). Or fluff with skim milk and sprinkle lightly with Parmesan cheese.
Refried beans	Reduced-fat or fat-free refried beans. (See Healthy Refried Beans on page 159.)
Salad dressings, oil-, sour cream-, and mayonnaise-based	Low-fat and fat-free commercial or homemade dressings. When using commercial dressings, try mixing a bottle of fat-free with a bottle of low-fat for more flavor. When eating out, always ask for your dressing on the side. Then, instead of pouring it on your salad, dip your fork in it before spearing a bite of salad.
Snacks	Pretzels, toasted bagels, cold sweet potato wedges, frozen (peeled) bananas, cored and sliced apples sprinkled with cinnamon sugar and cooked in the microwave, or any of the many snack recipes in this book. Remember that fruit is a fat-free snack that is so good for you!
Soups, cream	Low-fat homemade cream soups enriched with buttermilk or skim milk, and thickened with puréed vegetables, evaporated skim milk, flour, cornstarch, and/or arrowroot.
Sour cream	Fat-free or low-fat sour cream, 1% cottage cheese, nonfat plain yogurt, or Healthy Sour Cream (page 106).

High-Fat Ingredient	Low-Fat Replacement
Tortilla chips	Baked low-fat or fat-free tortilla chips.
Tortillas, fried flour or corn	Tortillas softened by steaming, sprayed lightly with a butter or cooking spray, and baked for crispness.
Turkey, dark meat with skin	Turkey breast without skin.
Turkey, whole, self-basting	Plain (unbasted) turkey. (A self-basting turkey has been injected with oils.) Remove the skin before eating or using in recipes.
Veal, ground	Veal is, for the most part, a lean meat choice. But since ground veal packages do not indicate if the meat was trimmed before grinding, it is best to choose sirloin or top round cuts and have your selection trimmed and ground.
Vegetable oil	*See* Oil, vegetable.
Vegetables, marinated in oil	Steamed, grilled, or roasted vegetables.
Waffles	Low-fat homemade waffles, or reduced-fat commercial products like Downyflake's Crisp & Healthy Waffles.
Whipped topping	Commercial fat-free or low-fat whipped topping, nonfat vanilla yogurt, or Fat-Free Whipped Cream (page 117).
Yogurt	Low-fat or nonfat yogurt. To maximize health benefits, look for the phrase "live or active cultures" on the label.

A GARDEN OF HERBS AND SPICES

Fats *do* add flavor to foods. And when you remove some or all of the fat, you also remove some of the flavor. Fortunately, you can replace that lost flavor with healthier options. This is why herbs and spices are so important in low- and no-fat cooking.

If you haven't already discovered the wonderful impact a pinch of the right herb or spice can have on a dish, you are in for a real treat! You will find that there is no easier or healthier way to enrich the foods you eat than by boosting their flavors with fat-free herbs and spices!

Although at one time in history, some herbs and spices were available only to the wealthy, today, even the most exotic of seasonings can be found in most supermarkets. Many produce departments even carry packaged fresh herbs. You can also find herbs and spices sold in bulk at both co-ops and health foods stores, where the cost of these products is usually lower. For the freshest seasonings, though, you might consider growing herbs in your own garden, or even in pots on a sunny kitchen windowsill.

What Are Herbs and Spices?

Herbs are actually the aromatic leaves, stems, and flowers of plants that are grown in temperate regions. Examples of common herbs are basil, oregano, and thyme. Spices are the aromatic products of the seeds, buds, fruit, flowers, bark, or roots of plants that are grown in more tropical regions. Common spices include black pepper, cinnamon, and ginger. Herbs may be used fresh or dried, and are available whole, ground, or crushed. Spices are always used dried, and come either whole or ground.

Storing Herbs and Spices

To make sure that you get the most flavor from your seasonings, it is important to store them properly and to replace them when necessary. Dried herbs and spices retain their flavor best when kept in tightly closed containers in a cool, dark place, away from the heat of the stove. But even the best-stored seasonings lose their flavors over time, and should be checked at least once a year for freshness. Periodically smell and taste your seasonings to see if they have retained their full-bodied aroma and flavor. Also check to see if their color has faded. Faded color is a reliable sign that flavoring power has diminished, and that the product should be replaced.

Using Herbs and Spices

Herbs and spices are easy to use. And as you use them more and more, you will get a feel for how and when they should be added to your dishes. By following certain guidelines, however, you will be more likely to enjoy pleasing results from the start.

When seasoning with fresh herbs, use scissors to snip the herbs into the desired size. Although dried herbs and spices are available already ground, for the best flavor, you may want to buy certain seasonings whole, and grind them directly before use. A perfect way to grind your own spices is through the use of a small coffee grinder. To prevent each spice from being affected by any spice previously ground, wipe out the grinder before or after each use. Then fill it with a half slice of bread made into crumbs, grind for a minute or two, and discard the bread crumbs —along with any residue left by previously ground spices. A mortar and pestle is another great tool for grinding spices.

When you first start using herbs and spices, experiment with small amounts until you become familiar with their flavor and strength. Keep in mind that these ingredients are meant to enhance the natural flavors of foods, not to mask them. Start with no more than ¼ teaspoon at a time, unless you are using a stronger spice or herb, such as cayenne pepper, chili powder, or cloves. Strong spices and herbs should be used in very small amounts in the beginning— no more than ⅛ teaspoon until you become familiar with their flavor and pungency. Also remember that the more spice used in baked goods, the drier your finished product will be.

Be aware that dried herbs are more highly concentrated than fresh. So when substituting fresh herbs for dried in a recipe, use three to four times the amount called for.

To obtain the full flavor of your seasoning, it is important to add it at the proper time. For best results:

☐ When making slow-cooking meats, vegetables, sauces, and soups, add crumbled or powdered herbs and spices at the same time you add the salt and/or pepper—forty-five to sixty minutes before the end of the cooking time. When using whole spices, add them at the start of cooking.

☐ When making quick-cooking vegetables, sauces, and gravies, add the seasonings when cooking begins.

☐ When making ground meat dishes such as hamburgers, meatballs, and meat loaves, add the seasonings directly to the meat mixture before cooking.

☐ When making cold foods, such as salads, salad dressings, and dips, blend the herbs and spices into the dish several hours—even a day!— before serving. This allows the flavors to "marry" and blend, giving optimum flavor.

Making the Best Match

Naturally, part of the success enjoyed when using herbs and spices depends on correctly matching the seasonings to the food. Below, you will find a listing of some of the herbs and spices—as well as other flavorings, like lemon

Herb and Spice Terms

As you scan cookbooks, you may see certain terms used to describe herb and spice mixtures. The following are some of the most common of these terms.

Blend. This is a mixture of spices, herbs, seeds, and/or other flavorings, either ground or whole, that are used to prepare a specific type of dish. Popular blends include poultry seasoning, curry powder, Cajun seasoning, and pickling spices.

Bouquet Garnis. This mixture of different herbs and/or spices—for instance, marjoram, thyme, parsley, and bay leaves—is fastened in a bunch with string or tied inside a small piece of cheesecloth. The mixture is then added to soup, stew, or a similar dish during cooking, and removed before serving.

Fines Herbes. This combination of equal amounts of three or four finely chopped herbs, such as parsley, basil, tarragon, and chives, is used to season savory dishes.

Salad Herbs. These herbs, used to season salads, include tarragon, oregano, chervil, dill, thyme, basil, marjoram, rosemary, parsley, and savory.

Sweet Herbs. These are herbs whose leaves, seeds, and/or roots have a fresh mellow flavor, unlike the sharp, pungent, and sometimes bitter flavors of cumin, bay leaf, oregano, and rosemary. Sweet herbs include chervil, anise, mint, and cilantro.

---

peel and leeks—most commonly used in cooking and baking. Included is a description of the flavor or aroma you can expect from each. I have also listed the most common uses. But don't let that deter you from being creative! Let your experience as well as your taste buds be your guide.

If you are just beginning to use herbs and spices, don't feel that you have to go out and purchase all of the following seasonings. A good beginning collection may include only the ten most popular spices: black pepper, celery salt or seeds, chili powder, cinnamon, garlic salt or powder, nutmeg, paprika, parsley flakes, onion salt or powder, and oregano. Experiment with these spices, and add more along the way.

Allspice is the dried unripe fruit of an evergreen tree native to the West Indies. Also known as pimento and Jamaica pepper, it is a mildly sharp spice that gives you the blended flavors of cloves, nutmeg, and cinnamon. Use it in baked goods, stews, chowders and other soups, meat and poultry dishes, relishes, fruit and vegetable salads, puddings, pickling mixtures, vegetables, eggnog, syrups, apple butter, applesauce, and mincemeat.

Anise, a plant native to the Mediterranean region, has a licorice-like aroma and flavor. The seeds are used in baked goods; teas; desserts; and cheese, beef, pork, and fish dishes. Fresh anise leaves are delicious in salads and candies.

Basil is one of my favorites. An Old World herb, it has a fresh and spicy flavor that combines those of mint and anise. A wonderful seasoning for tomatoes and tomato dishes, basil can also be used with beef, pork, veal, and lamb dishes, as well as chicken, turkey, duck, and fish. It is also great with potatoes, mushrooms, peas, spinach, squash, eggplant, asparagus, beets, broccoli, cabbage, and carrots; in salads of all kinds; and in cornbread, egg dishes, pasta dishes, and sauces (especially pesto).

Bay leaf is the green pungent and aromatic leaf of the laurel tree. Use it in vegetable and fish soups, tomato sauces and juice, poached fish, meat, stews, stuffings, marinades for game, dried bean dishes, rice, egg dishes, beets, potatoes, and salads. Note, though, that the bay leaf has a strong flavor, so use it sparingly.

Capers are the small unopened flower buds of a bush found in the Mediterranean. With the sharp flavor of pickles, capers are delicious in salads, meat gravies, fish sauces, chicken dishes, and potatoes.

Caraway seeds are the fruit of a Eurasian herb. With a characteristic sharply pungent flavor, these seeds make flavorful additions to breads, cookies, beef and lamb stews, pork roasts, stuffings, vegetable salads, cream cheese spreads and dips, sauerkraut, cabbage dishes, pickling spice, slaw, soups, and goulashes. Keep in mind that these seeds have a strong flavor that can turn bitter if cooked too long.

Cardamom is an Indian herb with seeds that have a pleasant aroma with a slightly gingerish, sharp flavor. Use them sparingly in meat, poultry, and fish dishes; marinades; baked goods; fruit salads; salad dressings; dips; spreads; sauces; gravies; hot beverages; pickles; and East Indian, Mexican, and Spanish dishes.

Cayenne pepper, the ground fruit of any of several varieties of capsicum (pepper), is a hot and biting spice. Add it sparingly to pizza, spaghetti, meat, and barbecue sauces. Also use it in chilies, dips, sausage mixtures, egg dishes, salad dressings, curries, and marinades.

Celery, besides being a versatile vegetable, is useful for its leaves and seeds. Celery flakes, seeds, and salt all have a tart, fresh celery flavor. Use them in salad dressings, dips, egg and cheese dishes, fish dishes, sauces, soups, pickling spices, and stews, and as a substitute for celery, when you are "fresh" out of it!

Chervil, a Eurasian herb, has a pleasant aroma with a slight anise-like flavor. Use it in soups; egg and cheese dishes; green salads; potato salads; meat, poultry, veal, and fish dishes; and mushroom dishes. Add chervil towards the end of the cooking time, as it loses its flavor if cooked too long.

Chili powder, a spicy blend of ground chili and other seasonings, has a characteristic hot, pungent aroma and flavor. Add it to Spanish and Mexican dishes, salad dressings, dips, relishes, sauces, egg and cheese dishes, soups, stews, and meat, poultry, and fish dishes. Use this spice cautiously.

Chives are a Eurasian herb with a delicate onion flavor. Use them in green salads, potato dishes, soups, sauces, egg and cheese dishes, and fish and poultry dishes. For best flavor and color, use this herb fresh or frozen, as color and taste fade when chives are dried.

Cilantro, also referred to as Chinese parsley or leaf coriander, is a Eurasian herb with a mild sweet aroma and flavor. Use it in Mexican, Mediterranean, and Asian dishes, and in many soups and stews.

Cinnamon is another of my favorites. The inner bark of a tropical tree, this spice has a sweet and deliciously pungent aroma and flavor. Use it in baked goods; cooked fruit and fruit salad; beverages such as punches, teas, coffee, eggnog, and hot chocolate; pork, lamb, and chicken dishes; sweet potatoes; baked beans; carrots; squash; and syrups.

Cloves, the buds of the clove tree, have a strong and pungently sweet aroma and flavor. They are used either whole or ground in baked goods, curries, fruit dishes, meat and poultry dishes, sauces, relishes, pickling spices, soups, punches, teas, ciders, sweet potatoes, baked beans, squash, and marinades. They are also used whole to stud baked ham. Use cautiously, as the flavor can become hot.

Coriander. *See* Cilantro.

Cumin, the seeds of a Mediterranean herb, has a slightly bitter aroma and flavor, similar to that of the caraway seed. Add it cautiously to potato salads, egg salads and other egg dishes, soups, sauces, dips, rice dishes, meat and poultry dishes, bean dishes, salad dressings, cheese spreads and other cheese dishes, and Mexican and Spanish dishes. Also use it as a pickling spice.

Curry powder is a blend of many ground spices, including cardamom, cloves, dill, cayenne, ginger, black pepper, red pepper, cumin, mustard, and turmeric. The particular spices and the proportions used may differ with each manufacturer. Use it in meat, poultry, and fish dishes; soups; dips; salad dressings; cheese spreads and other cheese dishes; chutneys; egg dishes; and curries; and as a pickling spice.

Dill, an herb native to Eurasia, has a mild aroma and flavor. Add either the leaves or the seeds to sauces; salads and salad dressings; dips; egg and cheese dishes; poultry, fish, lamb, pork, and beef dishes; potato salad and other potato dishes; tomatoes; cucumber salads; chowders and other soups; bean dishes; green salads; zucchini; pickles; stuffings; cabbage; broccoli; cauliflower; sauerkraut; slaw; and breads.

Fennel seeds, which come from a Eurasian plant, have a mild anise-like aroma and flavor. Add them to baked goods, soups, salads, stews, sauces, marinades, poultry and fish dishes, sausages, potatoes, and carrots; or use them as a pickling spice.

Filé, made from powdered sassafras leaves, is used as a thickening and flavoring agent in Creole dishes.

Garlic, an edible bulb, has a characteristic aromatic flavor. For best results, use it fresh. Or try garlic powder or salt. Use garlic in meat, poultry, and fish dishes; soups; sauces; stews; vegetables; salads and salad dressings; dips; marinades; breads; and cheese dishes. Remember that garlic is known for its strong flavor and should be used sparingly.

Ginger, the root of a tropical southeast Asian plant, has a pungently sweet aroma and flavor with a "bite." Common to all Oriental cuisines, from Japan to India, ginger is a delicious addition to meat, poultry, and fish dishes, including curries and sausage; vegetables; pickles; salad dressings; baked goods; spiced and stewed fruits; marinades; puddings and custards; chutney; carrots; cranberries; and baked beans. Use it sparingly, as it is deceptively hot.

Horseradish, the root of a Eurasian plant belonging to the mustard family, has a characteristically strong aroma and flavor. Grated and mixed with vinegar or lemon juice, horseradish makes a spicy condiment. It is also used to enhance sauces, dips, slaws, and chutneys. Use this food cautiously, as it is extremely hot!

Italian seasoning is a versatile blend of herbs. Containing marjoram, thyme, savory, rosemary, sage, basil, and oregano, this blend may be used in pasta sauces; pizza; fish, poultry, and meat dishes; gravies; soups; stews; and salad dressings.

Leek, an edible plant related to the onion, has a mild sweet onion aroma and flavor. Use leeks as you would onions in soups, stews, salads, and vegetables. Leeks may also be served as a cooked side dish.

Lemon peel has a potent lemon fragrance and flavor. Add it to baked goods, frostings, puddings, fruit salads, and other fruit dishes. When using bottled lemon juice, try adding lemon peel to enhance the flavor of the dish.

Lemon verbena, an aromatic New World shrub, is valued for its sweetly scented, lemon-flavored leaves. Use it in vegetable marinades, fruit salads, salad dressings, jellies, punches, and custards, and to brighten the flavors of fish and poultry dishes. Keep in mind that a little goes a long way!

Mace is an aromatic spice made from the covering of the nutmeg kernel. With a strong nutmeg-like aroma and flavor, mace can be added to soups, sauces, fish, cakes, cookies, chocolate puddings, cooked fruits, egg and cheese dishes, pickles, and jellies. Use mace sparingly, as its flavor can be overpowering.

Marjoram, an aromatic plant, has a definite strong flavor, similar to that of both oregano and sage. Use it sparingly to flavor meat, poultry, and fish dishes; soups; egg and cheese dishes; stews; sauces; stuffings; mushrooms; rice; potatoes; green salads and salad dressings; peas; carrots; beans; eggplant; spinach; tomatoes; and zucchini.

Mint, an aromatic plant, has a strong, fresh, sweet aroma and flavor that leave a cool refreshing aftertaste in your mouth. Available in several varieties, including spearmint and peppermint, this herb can be used in lamb and veal sauces, frozen desserts, fruits and fruit drinks, teas, jellies, cakes, cookies, candies, marinades, puddings, potatoes, peas, carrots, spinach, and rice. Also use it as a garnish for cold beverages and desserts.

Mustard seeds, which come from a family of Eurasian plants, have a sharply pungent aroma and flavor. The whole mustard seeds are used in the making of pickles, chutney, salad dressings, dips, relishes, marinades, baked beans, sausages, egg dishes, and potato dishes. The seeds are also ground into a powder, which may be used to prepare many of the same foods, including the popular hot dog condiment.

Nutmeg, available either whole or ground, is the aromatic seed of an evergreen tree. Only the inside of the seed, with its characteristically sweet and spicy aroma and flavor, is used for nutmeg. The seed's protective web is ground for mace. Use to season baked goods, sauces, stewed fruits, eggnog, soups, egg dishes, rice pudding, sweet potatoes, carrots, squash, spinach, cauliflower, green beans, lima beans, meatballs, and poultry. For best results, buy nutmeg in its whole form and grate it as you need it.

Onions, the edible bulbs of a plant, are a popular vegetable and flavoring, prized for their strong characteristic aroma and flavor. Onions can be used fresh, or in the form of dehydrated flakes, bits, powder, and salt. Use this versatile seasoning in meat, poultry, and fish dishes; breads; soups; vegetables; salads and salad dressings; stuffings; and more.

Orange peel has a strong sweet orange aroma with a surprisingly bitter flavor. Add it to baked goods; fish, chicken, and meat dishes; vegetables; fruits; and fruit salads.

Oregano, actually a type of marjoram, has a sharp aromatic aroma and flavor. Use it in Italian, Spanish, and Mexican dishes; in roast lamb, egg, seafood, poultry, duck, and meat dishes; and in salad dressings, soups, dips, cheese dishes, breads, potatoes, tomatoes, mushrooms, eggplant, and zucchini.

Paprika, a seasoning made from ground sweet red peppers, has a mild sweet aroma and flavor. Use it to flavor Hungarian goulash; fish, egg, chicken, and veal dishes; cheese dishes; potatoes; dips; and salads. Also use it as a garnish to add a wonderful red color to otherwise bland-looking dishes. Be aware that different types of paprika vary in taste. For instance, Spanish paprika is milder than Hungarian paprika.

Pepper, the ground berries of certain plants, is the most widely used spice worldwide, with a characteristic aromatic flavor. Use it in soups; sauces; meat, poultry, fish, and game dishes; vegetables; salads and salad dressings; marinades; and almost any food except sweets. Note that black pepper is stronger than white, but that white is preferred when making white sauces. When using either type, freshly grind the pepper for best flavor.

Poppy seeds have a mildly sweet, nutty aroma and flavor. Add them to baked goods, salads and salad dressings, and pasta.

Poultry seasoning is a blend of sage, pepper, savory, marjoram, thyme, onion powder, and celery salt. Use it to flavor chicken and duck, pork stuffings, dumplings, chowder, egg dishes, and rice dishes.

Rosemary, an aromatic shrub, has a sweet, pungent aroma similar to that of tea, and a sharp, bittersweet flavor akin to that of the pine needles it resembles. Use it to season lamb, fish, beef, pork, and poultry dishes; egg and cheese dishes; soups; jams; jellies; fruit and green salads; stuffings; potatoes; cauliflower; peas; spinach; lima beans; tomatoes; sauces; breads; and dumplings. Use this herb sparingly, as it is strong.

Safflower, an annual plant with orange-yellow flowers, is also called Mexican saffron, and is used as a substitute for saffron. It is, however, not as strong in flavor or coloring properties as saffron, so that more must be used to achieve the desired effect. It may also be used to enhance soups, salad dressings, sauces, and pasta salads.

Saffron, the aromatic stigma of the saffron plant, has a strong aroma, but a delicate, bitter flavor. Use the threads to add flavor and a distinctive orange-yellow color to poultry, meat, and fish dishes; breads; egg dishes; rice dishes; and soups. Saffron has the dubious honor of being the most expensive spice in the world.

Sage, the leaves of the aromatic sage plant, is minty until dried, and then becomes pungent and slightly bitter. Use it in meat, poultry, and fish dishes; sausages; egg and cheese dishes; soups; stuffings; potatoes; tomatoes; cornbread; marinades and salad dressings; and green salads. Use this herb sparingly, as its flavor is strong and can become bitter as it cooks.

Savory, native to Mediterranean regions, comes in two types. Summer savory has a peppery thyme flavor and is used in bean dishes, chowders and other soups and stews, sauces, meat dishes, green salads and salad dressings, breads, rice, and stuffing. Winter savory has a stronger piney flavor, and is used in dishes containing strong game meats and in pâtés.

Sesame seeds are actually the hulled fruit of a tropical herb, and have a sweet nut-like flavor. Add them to baked goods, poultry and fish dishes, salads, candies, stuffings, dips, vegetables, soups, and noodles.

Shallots, a type of onion, have a subtle onion aroma and flavor. Use shallots in soups, sauces, and salads.

Sweet cicely, an aromatic herb, has a sweet licorice-like aroma and flavor. Use it in salads, cabbage dishes, sweet potatoes, carrots, fruit juices, desserts, and iced beverages. Note that this herb is known as the "sugar saver," as it reduces the amount of sugar needed in your recipes.

Tarragon is an aromatic herb with a sweet licorice-like aroma and a surprisingly bitter flavor. Add it sparingly to poultry, fish, and meat dishes; egg and cheese dishes; green salads and salad dressings; sauces; soups; stews; pickling spices; tomatoes; mushrooms; beets; spinach; potatoes; and artichokes.

Thyme is a Eurasian herb with a warm, pungent aroma and flavor. Add it sparingly to season meat, poultry, lamb, and seafood dishes; chowders and other soups and stews; stuffings; egg and cheese dishes; salads and salad dressings; and vegetables. When using fresh thyme, use the leaves only, as the stems are tough.

Turmeric, the powdered rhizome of a tropical plant, is bright yellow in color, and has a peppery aroma and a ginger-like, bitter flavor. Use it sparingly to add color, aroma, and flavor to curries, sauces, pickles, salad dressings, marinades, relishes, cheese and egg dishes, Cornish hens, venison and other game meats, and fish dishes.

HELPFUL KITCHEN TOOLS

It isn't necessary to buy a cabinet of new equipment to switch to low-fat cooking. But you will find that a few simple tools and gadgets will help you more easily reduce the fat in many of your dishes.

Egg Separator. Although this gadget has been around for a long time, it bears mentioning for those who aren't familiar with it. An egg separator may be plastic or metal, and looks somewhat like a ¼-cup measuring cup that has slit-like openings around the side. You simply place it on the edge of a bowl, and crack the egg into the separator. The yolk falls into its center, and the egg white falls through the slits into the bowl below. This is easier than using the shell of the egg, and there's no need to fish out pieces of egg shell.

Fat Separator. This is a specially designed pitcher with a spout that extends from the bottom. Simply place your gravy, broth, or other liquid in the pitcher, and allow it to sit for a few minutes. The fat will rise to the top, allowing you to pour out your defatted liquid from the bottom. This is great for separating the fat from meat drippings!

Fat-Skimming Ladles. These ladles are designed with slots near the top edge of the bowl, allowing you to skim fat—which rises to the top—from stocks, stews, sauces, and soups. The fat lands in the bowl of the ladle, while the defatted liquid remains in the pot.

Nonstick Cookware. Nonstick cookware will enable you to sauté, bake, and perform a variety of other cooking operations without oil or butter, and without fear of the food sticking to the pan. Just coat the pan lightly with nonstick cooking spray before each use.

Yogurt Sieve. Although this specially designed sieve is not a necessity for making So-Simple Yogurt Cheese (see page 53), it does make the process easier.

MEASUREMENTS AND EQUIVALENTS

Although most recipes clearly state the amount needed of each ingredient—1 cup diced green pepper or a pinch of pepper, for instance—it's not always an easy matter to first translate the listed amounts into a realistic shopping list, and then measure that amount for use. How many green peppers must you buy to yield 1 cup? What exactly is a pinch? The tables of measurements and conversions that begin on page 18 should help

you easily plan your purchases and then make accurate measurements that insure success.

ABOUT THE RECIPES

When creating the recipes for this book, I had three primary objectives—that the dishes be low in fat, that the dishes be delicious, and that the dishes be quick to prepare. In this day and age, with most homes having working parents, short-cuts are sometimes necessary if you want to enjoy a wholesome home-cooked meal. For this reason, my recipes often contain some commercially prepared food—bottled salad dressings, jarred sauces, and so on. My recipes show that these foods, when chosen wisely, can be part of a healthful low-fat diet. In some cases, I mention ingredients by brand name because I have found that these products give me the best nutritional and culinary results. If a particular brand is unavailable, feel free to substitute a comparable product. Just be aware that this may cause the calorie and fat counts to change.

Each of the recipes in this book is followed by nutritional data per serving, including the number of fat grams, the number of calories, and the percentage of calories from fat. The information used to compute these analyses came from *The Complete and Up-to-Date Fat Book* and from nutritional information provided by manufacturers.

When computing the nutritional analysis for each recipe, I used the following guidelines:

• Substitute and optional ingredients were not included in the analysis.

• Variations were not included in the analysis.

• When the recipe includes a marinade, the entire marinade was included in the analysis.

• Since there is some controversy regarding how many alcohol calories evaporate during cooking, I simply used the calorie content of the full amount of alcohol in the analysis.

• When one recipe includes another recipe that appears within the book—a sauce recipe, for instance—the second recipe has, of course, been included in the analysis.

A FINAL WORD
BEFORE YOU BEGIN COOKING

It really is no wonder that as much as I love food, I would write a cookbook. I am not referring only to the actual eating of the food, which happens to be one of the great joys of life. I love *all* aspects of food.

The multitude of wonderful colors created by nature—the rich vibrant reds, oranges, yellows, and purples, and the soft mellow golds and peaches—makes foods so alluring to the eye. And the intense aromas! Some foods have such tantalizing fragrances that they actually seduce the senses until your mouth waters and you're overcome by hunger.

The splendid diversity of textures offered by different foods is another aspect that I love. Crunchy, creamy, crispy, soft, smooth—these textures give each food its own unique "mouth feel," adding to the pleasure. And the variety of flavors is limitless, as all foods may be served alone, combined with other foods, or enhanced by herbs and spices. When I cook—and especially when I create a new recipe—I often feel like a scientist or chemist. I add a splash of this, a pinch of that, and a smidgen of something else, all in the quest of making a nutritious, richly flavored, satisfying dish.

As you read through the recipes in this book, don't let a particular herb, spice, or other flavoring keep you from trying a recipe. Our tastes are as individual as we are. Simply replace that ingredient with one that you prefer, and make the recipe your own creation. After all, what you are seeking is gloriously nutritious and delicious food. So let's get cooking!

BASIC EQUIVALENTS AND CONVERSIONS

TABLE OF MEASUREMENTS

Measurement	Equivalents		
Pinch or dash	= less than ⅛ teaspoon		
1 teaspoon	= ⅓ tablespoon		= ⅙ fluid ounce
1 tablespoon	= 3 teaspoons		= ½ fluid ounce
2 tablespoons	= ⅛ cup		= 1 fluid ounce
4 tablespoons	= ¼ cup		= 2 fluid ounces
8 tablespoons	= ½ cup		= 4 fluid ounces
12 tablespoons	= ¾ cup		= 6 fluid ounces
16 tablespoons	= 1 cup	= ½ pint	= 8 fluid ounces
⅛ cup	= 2 tablespoons		= 1 fluid ounce
¼ cup	= 4 tablespoons		= 2 fluid ounces
½ cup	= 8 tablespoons		= 4 fluid ounces
¾ cup	= 12 tablespoons		= 6 fluid ounces
1 cup	= 16 tablespoons	= ½ pint	= 8 fluid ounces
2 cups	= 1 pint		= 16 fluid ounces

Measurement		Equivalents		
4 cups	= 2 pints	= 1 quart		= 32 fluid ounces
8 cups	= 4 pints	= 2 quarts		= 64 fluid ounces
16 cups	= 8 pints	= 4 quarts	= 1 gallon	= 128 fluid ounces
½ pint	= 1 cup			= 8 fluid ounces
1 pint	= 2 cups			= 16 fluid ounces
2 pints	= 4 cups	= 1 quart		= 32 fluid ounces
4 pints	= 8 cups	= 2 quarts		= 64 fluid ounces
8 pints	= 16 cups	= 4 quarts	= 1 gallon	= 128 ounces
½ quart	= 2 cups	= 1 pint		= 16 fluid ounces
1 quart	= 4 cups	= 2 pints		= 32 fluid ounces
2 quarts	= 8 cups	= 4 pints		= 64 fluid ounces
4 quarts	= 16 cups	= 8 pints	= 1 gallon	= 128 fluid ounces
½ gallon	= 8 cups	= 4 pints	= 2 quarts	= 64 fluid ounces
1 gallon	= 16 cups	= 8 pints	= 4 quarts	= 128 fluid ounces

FOOD EQUIVALENCY AMOUNTS

Ingredient	Amount	Equivalent Amount
Breads		
Bread	1 pound loaf	= 12–16 slices
	1 slice	= ½ cup soft crumbs
		= ¼ cup dry bread crumbs
Dairy and Eggs		
Butter or Margarine	1 pound	= 2 cups
		= 4 sticks
		= 32 tablespoons
	8 ounces	= 1 cup
		= 2 sticks
		= 16 tablespoons
Cheese, Cottage	1 pound	= 2 cups
Cheese, Cream	3 ounces	= 6 tablespoons
	8 ounces	= 1 cup
Cheese, Hard	1 pound	= 4–5 cups shredded

Ingredient	Amount	Equivalent Amount
Egg Whites	8–10	= 1 cup
Eggs, Whole	3–4	= 1 cup
Nonfat Dry Milk	1 pound	= 5 quarts liquid skim milk
Flour and Cornmeal		
All Purpose Flour	1 pound	= 4 cups (sifted)
	1 ounce	= ¼ cup (sifted)
Cake Flour	1 pound	= 4¾–5 cups (sifted)
Cornmeal	1 pound	= 3 cups
Whole Wheat Flour	1 pound	= 3½–3¾ cups (unsifted)
Fruit		
Apples	1	= 1 cup sliced
	1 pound	= 3 cups peeled and sliced
		= 1⅔ cups cooked
		= 1¼ cups puréed
Apricots	1 pound	= 3 cups dried
		= 6 cups cooked
Bananas	1 pound (3–4)	= 1¾ cups mashed
Candied Fruit	1 pound	= 3 cups chopped
Cherries	1 pound	= 2 cups (without pits)
Cranberries	1 pound	= 2 cups (without pits)
Dates	1 pound	= 1½ cups finely chopped
Grapes	1 pound	= 2½ cups
Lemon	1 medium	= 2–3 tablespoons juice
		= 1 tablespoon grated rind
Orange	1 medium	= ⅓–½ cup juice
		= 2 tablespoons grated rind
Raisins	1 pound	= 2½ cups
Strawberries	1 pint	= 1½ cups sliced
Meat and Poultry		
Chicken, whole	3½ pounds	= 3 cups cooked diced
Meat	1 pound	= 5 cups cooked diced
Meat, ground	1 pound	= 5 cups cooked
Nuts		
Any type, chopped	¼ pound	= 1 cup
Almonds (in shell)	1 pound	= 1¼ cups shelled
Pecans (in shell)	1 pound	= 2 cups shelled and chopped

Ingredient	Amount	Equivalent Amount
Walnuts (in shell)	1 pound	= 1½–1¾ cups shelled and chopped

Sugar, Sweeteners, Miscellaneous

Ingredient	Amount	Equivalent Amount
Brown Sugar	1 pound	= 2¼–2½ cups, firmly packed
Chocolate Chips	6 ounces	= 1 cup
Cocoa Powder	1 pound	= 4 cups
Confectioner's Sugar	1 pound	= 3½ cups
Honey	1 pound	= 1⅓ cups
Molasses	1 pound	= 1⅓ cups
Syrup	1 pound	= 1⅓ cups
White Sugar, granulated	1 pound	= 2 cups

Vegetables

Ingredient	Amount	Equivalent Amount
Cabbage	1 pound	= 2½ cups cooked
		= 4½ cups shredded
Carrots	1 pound	= 2½ cups diced raw
		= 3 cups shredded
		= 2 cups cooked
Celery	1 medium bunch	= 4½ cups chopped
Green Pepper	1 large	= 1 cup diced
Mushrooms	¼ pound	= ¼–½ cup cooked sliced
Onions	1 medium	= ½ cup chopped
Potatoes	1 pound (3 medium)	= 2½ cups sliced
		= 2 cups mashed
Spinach	1 pound	= 1½ cups chopped cooked
Split Peas	1 pound	= 2½ cups cooked
String Beans	1 pound (3 cups)	= 2½ cups cooked
Tomatoes	1 pound (3 medium)	= 1½ cups cooked

OVEN TEMPERATURE TABLE

Description	Temperature in Fahrenheit	Description	Temperature in Fahrenheit
Cool Oven	200–225	Moderate Oven	350–375
Very Slow Oven	250–275	Hot Oven	400–425
Slow Oven	300–325	Very Hot Oven	450–475

METRIC CONVERSION TABLES

Common Liquid Conversions

Measurement	=	Milliliters
$1/4$ teaspoon	=	1.25 milliliters
$1/2$ teaspoon	=	2.50 milliliters
$3/4$ teaspoon	=	3.75 milliliters
1 teaspoon	=	5.00 milliliters
$1^1/4$ teaspoons	=	6.25 milliliters
$1^1/2$ teaspoons	=	7.50 milliliters
$1^3/4$ teaspoons	=	8.75 milliliters
2 teaspoons	=	10.0 milliliters
1 tablespoon	=	15.0 milliliters
2 tablespoons	=	30.0 milliliters

Measurement	=	Liters
$1/4$ cup	=	0.06 liters
$1/2$ cup	=	0.12 liters
$3/4$ cup	=	0.18 liters
1 cup	=	0.24 liters
$1^1/4$ cups	=	0.30 liters
$1^1/2$ cups	=	0.36 liters
2 cups	=	0.48 liters
$2^1/2$ cups	=	0.60 liters
3 cups	=	0.72 liters
$3^1/2$ cups	=	0.84 liters
4 cups	=	0.96 liters
$4^1/2$ cups	=	1.08 liters
5 cups	=	1.20 liters
$5^1/2$ cups	=	1.32 liters

Converting Fahrenheit to Celsius

Fahrenheit	=	Celsius
200—205	=	95
220—225	=	105
245—250	=	120
275	=	135
300—305	=	150
325—330	=	165
345—350	=	175
370—375	=	190
400—405	=	205
425—430	=	220
445—450	=	230
470—475	=	245
500	=	260

Conversion Formulas

LIQUID When You Know	Multiply By	To Determine
teaspoons	5.0	milliliters
tablespoons	15.0	milliliters
fluid ounces	30.0	milliliters
cups	0.24	liters
pints	0.47	liters
quarts	0.95	liters
WEIGHT When You Know	Multiply By	To Determine
ounces	28.0	grams
pounds	0.45	kilograms

2

Breakfast Time

Does the morning rush at your house keep you and your family from enjoying a healthy, satisfying breakfast—or, for that matter, from having any breakfast at all? You may never skip breakfast again, for the recipes in this chapter are so quick and easy to prepare that you'll always have time for a delicious start-the-day-right meal that gets everyone in your house going strong. Just add a glass of skim milk, fruit juice, or one of the luscious beverages from Chapter 11, and you'll have a winning breakfast in minutes.

This chapter begins with recipes for several scrumptious low-fat pancakes. Yes, *low-fat*! By replacing whole milk with buttermilk and making other healthy substitutions, it's easy to make truly tantalizing low-fat creations. You'll also find a healthier version of golden French toast. Crowned with Maple-Cinnamon Syrup or another sweetly tempting topping from Chapter 7, these are satisfying delights, indeed.

When time is at a real premium, treat your family to Apple Cheese Broil or Pastrami Breakfast Sandwich—two hot and tasty Quick Dishes that are sure to please. Prefer something sweet and fruity? Try Quick and Simple Breakfast Fruitosia, full of the goodness of oranges, apples, and yogurt. Or whip up Berry-Oatmeal Breakfast Drink and enjoy a wonderfully nutritious breakfast beverage.

Whether you long for a stack of steaming, syrup-topped pancakes or a quick savory bite, this chapter has the morning meal you're looking for—with all the flavor that will lure your family out of bed, but without all the fat that can slow them down. Breakfast, anyone?

Orange Pancakes

Yield: *20 large pancakes, or 40 small pancakes*

1½ cups all purpose flour

2 tablespoons sugar

1 teaspoon baking powder

½ teaspoon baking soda

1 teaspoon butter-flavored sprinkles

1 teaspoon cornstarch

2 egg whites, slightly beaten

1 cup nonfat buttermilk

1 cup orange juice

1 teaspoon Vanilla Butter & Nut extract or vanilla extract

These pancakes are yummy served with blackberry jam.

1. Place the flour, sugar, baking powder, baking soda, butter-flavored sprinkles, and cornstarch in a medium-sized bowl, and stir to mix well. Set aside.

2. Place all of the remaining ingredients in a medium-sized bowl, and whisk together until well mixed. Add the egg mixture to the flour mixture all at once, and stir with a spoon until blended. The batter will be slightly lumpy.

3. Allow the batter to sit for 5 minutes. If you prefer a thinner batter, you may add more buttermilk.

4. Lightly spray a nonstick griddle or skillet with cooking spray, and preheat over medium to medium-high heat. Spoon the pancake batter onto the hot griddle using 2 tablespoons for large pancakes, or 1 tablespoon for dollar-sized pancakes. Cook for 1 to 2 minutes, or until the surface is bubbly and the bottom is golden brown. Turn the cakes, and cook the second side until golden brown. Serve hot, accompanied by blackberry jam, if desired.

NUTRITIONAL DATA (PER PANCAKE)
Large Pancake

Fat: .8 gram	Calories: 46	% Calories from fat: 16%

Dollar-Size

Fat: .4 gram	Calories: 23	% Calories from fat: 16%

Apple Cinnamon Pancakes

You don't need apples for these tasty delights—just apple juice! Not only are these pancakes delicious served hot with Cinnamon Sauce (page 112), but they make a great snack served cold spread with apple butter.

1. Place the flour, baking powder, baking soda, salt, and spices in a medium-sized bowl, and stir to mix well. Set aside.

2. Place all of the remaining ingredients in a small bowl, and whisk together until well blended. Add the apple juice mixture to the flour mixture all at once, and stir with a spoon until blended. The batter will be slightly lumpy.

3. Lightly spray a nonstick griddle or skillet with cooking spray, and preheat over medium to medium-high heat. Spoon the pancake batter onto the hot griddle using about 2 tablespoons of batter for each cake. Cook for 1 to 2 minutes, or until the surface is bubbly and the bottom is golden brown. Turn the cakes, and cook the second side until golden brown. Serve hot, accompanied by warm Cinnamon Sauce, if desired.

Yield: 15 pancakes

1½ cups all purpose flour

2 teaspoons baking powder

¼ teaspoon baking soda

¼ teaspoon butter-flavored salt or plain salt

½ teaspoon ground cinnamon

¼ teaspoon ground ginger

¼ teaspoon ground nutmeg

2 egg whites, slightly beaten

1½ cups unsweetened apple juice

1 tablespoon reduced-fat margarine, melted and cooled

2 tablespoons honey

1 teaspoon butter-flavored extract

NUTRITIONAL DATA (PER PANCAKE)

Fat: .5 gram   Calories: 65   % Calories from fat: 7%

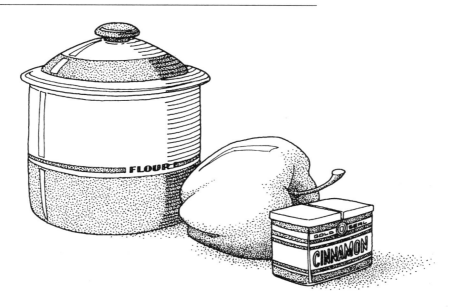

Extra-Light Cottage Cheese Pancakes

Yield: *15 pancakes*

2 cups 2% small curd cottage
cheese

1 tablespoon lemon juice

1 large egg

2 egg whites

¼ cup sugar

¾ cup all purpose flour

*These pancakes are absolutely delicious served with warm
Strawberry Sauce (page 111) or Mixed Berry Sauce (page 112)!*

1. Place the cottage cheese and lemon juice in a blender, and process
on medium speed until smooth, occasionally scraping the sides of the
blender. Add the egg, egg whites, and sugar, and process until the mixture becomes light and fluffy.

2. Transfer the cheese mixture to a medium-sized bowl, and add the
flour, gently blending it in with a fork. Be sure not to overmix, or the
pancakes will be tough. The batter should be slightly lumpy.

3. Lightly spray a nonstick griddle or skillet with butter-flavored cooking spray, and preheat over medium-high heat. Spoon the pancake
batter onto the hot griddle using about 2 tablespoons per pancake.
Cook for 1 to 2 minutes, or until the bottom is golden brown and
slightly crisp. This batter does not spread or bubble like other pancake
batter, so watch it carefully. Turn the cakes, and cook the second side
until golden brown. Serve hot, accompanied by Mixed Berry or
Strawberry Sauce, if desired.

NUTRITIONAL DATA (PER PANCAKE)

Fat: 1 gram   Calories: 65   % Calories from fat: 14%

Spiced French Toast With Peaches

This is one of our favorites for a leisurely weekend breakfast!

1. Drain the peaches, reserving the juice. Cut each peach slice lengthwise into halves or thirds to make thinner slices.

2. Place the reserved peach juice and the peach slices in a small saucepan, and cook over low heat until warm, stirring occasionally. Keep warm until needed.

3. Place the egg, egg whites, milk, extract, and spices in a medium-sized bowl, and whisk together until frothy. Pour the mixture into a shallow dish.

4. Lightly spray a nonstick griddle or skillet with cooking spray, and preheat over medium-high heat. Working with 1 slice at a time, dip both sides of each bread slice in the egg mixture and place on the griddle. Cook for about 2 minutes, or until the bottom is lightly browned. Turn the toast, and cook the second side until lightly browned. (To keep the dipping mixture well blended, stir it with a fork or whisk after dipping every 2 slices.)

5. Transfer the French toast to individual serving plates, and top with the warm peaches and juice. Serve hot, topping each slice with a fine dusting of powdered sugar, if desired.

Yield: *10 slices*

1 can (1 pound) "lite" peach slices in juice, undrained

1 egg

2 egg whites

1 cup skim milk

1 teaspoon butter-flavored extract

1 teaspoon ground cinnamon

¼ teaspoon ground nutmeg

10 slices honey bran cracked wheat bread (preferably 1 day old)

3 tablespoons powdered sugar, sifted (optional)

NUTRITIONAL DATA (PER SLICE WITH PEACH TOPPING)
Fat: 1.6 grams   Calories: 115   % Calories from fat: 13%

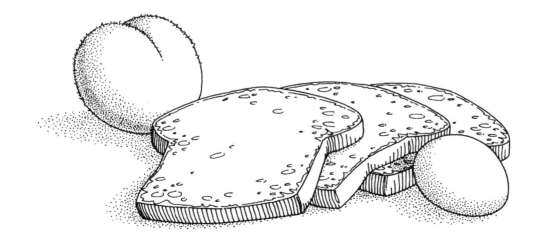

Maple Ham and Waffles With Apples

Yield: *4 servings*

1 tablespoon reduced-fat
  margarine

2 medium golden Delicious
  apples, cored and thinly sliced

2 teaspoons butter-flavored
  sprinkles

¼ teaspoon ground nutmeg

⅓ cup light maple-flavored syrup

1 package (5.5 ounces) Louis
  Rich Carving Board Thin-Sliced
  Honey Glazed Ham, cut into
  bite-sized pieces

8 Downyflake Crisp & Healthy
  Apple and Cinnamon frozen
  waffles

This scrumptious breakfast dish takes no more than 15 minutes to make! For a real treat, serve it with Maple-Cinnamon Syrup (page 113).

1. Place the margarine in a large nonstick skillet, and melt over medium-high heat. Reduce the heat to medium, and add the apple slices. Sprinkle the butter-flavored sprinkles and nutmeg over the apples. Pour the syrup over all, and toss to mix. Cook for 4 to 5 minutes, or until the apples are crisp-tender, stirring occasionally.

2. Add the ham pieces to the apple mixture, and gently stir, blending well. Cook for 5 minutes, or until the ham is heated through. Remove the skillet from the heat, and cover to keep warm.

3. Prepare the waffles according to package directions. To serve, place 2 waffles side by side on each individual serving plate. Spoon the apple and ham mixture over the top of each. Serve hot, topping each with Maple-Cinnamon Syrup, if desired.

NUTRITIONAL DATA (PER SERVING)
Fat: 4.4 grams   Calories: 285   % Calories from fat: 14%

Apple-Peanut Butter Muffins

Quick Dish

Yield: *4 servings*

4 whole wheat and honey English
  muffins, split and lightly toasted

2 tablespoons plus 2 teaspoons
  reduced-fat peanut butter

4 small red Delicious apples,
  cored and thinly sliced

I love this easy-to-make open-face sandwich, which can be served as a nutritious quick breakfast or a snack.

1. Arrange a split English muffin on each of 4 individual serving plates. Spread a thin layer of peanut butter over each muffin half.

2. Layer some of the apple slices over the peanut butter. Garnish with the remaining slices, and serve.

NUTRITIONAL DATA (PER SERVING)
Fat: 5 grams   Calories: 253   % Calories from fat: 18%

Apple Cheese Broil

There really is a reason for the old saying, "An apple a day keeps the doctor away." According to research, it has to do with the pectin— the soluble fiber—in the apple, which helps to reduce levels of LDL (the bad cholesterol). Try this for a quick, delicious, pectin-loaded breakfast!

1. Arrange the cinnamon bread on a flat surface, and spray lightly with the butter spray. Arrange a slice of cheese over each piece. Follow with a layer of sliced apples, and sprinkle with the brown sugar. Finally, top with the shredded cheese.

2. Place the topped bread slices under a preheated broiler, and broil for about 2 minutes, or until the cheese melts. Serve hot.

NUTRITIONAL DATA (PER SERVING)

Fat: 2 grams   Calories: 156   % Calories from fat: 11%

Quick Dish

Yield: *4 servings*

4 slices cinnamon bread, with or without raisins, lightly toasted

I Can't Believe It's Not Butter spray

4 slices (¾ ounce each) fat-free sharp Cheddar cheese

2 large red Delicious apples, cored and thinly sliced

2 tablespoons brown sugar

1 ounce shredded reduced-fat sharp Cheddar cheese

Pastrami Breakfast Sandwich

This sandwich will really give you a "hot" start to the day!

1. Toast the English muffins, and immediately arrange 2 halves on each individual serving plate. For each serving, arrange a cheese slice on 1 muffin half. Layer 2 slices of pastrami over the cheese, followed by a splash of Tabasco sauce. Top with the second muffin half.

2. Arrange the apple wedges next to the sandwich, and serve immediately.

NUTRITIONAL DATA (PER SERVING, INCLUDING APPLE)

Fat: 3.5 grams   Calories: 315   % Calories from fat: 10%

Quick Dish

Yield: *4 servings*

4 sourdough English muffins, split

4 slices (¾ ounce each) fat-free Cheddar cheese

8 deli-thin slices (1 ounce each) turkey pastrami, heated

Dash Tabasco sauce

4 red Delicious apples, cored and cut into wedges (garnish)

Berry-Oatmeal Breakfast Drink

Yield: *4 servings*

2½ cups skim milk

1 package (12 ounces) frozen (unthawed) unsweetened berries (your favorite type)

¼ cup sugar

1 teaspoon coconut-flavored extract

1 teaspoon vanilla extract

½ teaspoon ground cinnamon

¼ cup quick-cooking oats

Nutmeg (garnish)

My husband, David, had his doubts when I first concocted this drink, but one taste and he loved it! He will have some for breakfast, refrigerate the remainder, and "reblend" it for a nutritious snack later in the day.

1. Place all of the ingredients except for the oats and nutmeg in a blender, and process on medium-high speed until well blended.

2. Add the oats to the blender mixture, and process until smooth and frothy, occasionally scraping the sides of the blender container.

3. Divide the mixture among 4 tall chilled glasses, garnish with a sprinkling of nutmeg, and serve immediately.

NUTRITIONAL DATA (PER SERVING)

Fat: .5 gram   Calories: 179   % Calories from fat: 3%

Cinnamon-Apple Oatmeal

Yield: *4 servings*

1⅓ cups apple juice

1⅓ cups water

3 tablespoons brown sugar

1 teaspoon ground cinnamon

1⅓ cups quick-cooking oats

1 large red Delicious apple

8 ounces light nonfat Creme Caramel or Candy Apple Yogurt

Ground cinnamon (optional)

This is a wonderfully different way to serve an old favorite! If desired, substitute Caramel Creme Cheese Sauce (page 116) for the yogurt.

1. Place the juice, water, brown sugar, cinnamon, and oats in a medium-sized saucepan, and stir to combine. Bring to a boil over medium-high heat, stirring occasionally. Reduce the heat to medium and cook uncovered, stirring occasionally, for 1 minute, or until the oatmeal is of the desired consistency. (For a thinner oatmeal, use more water.)

2. Core the apple, and cut 4 thin slices from it. Set the slices aside, and shred the remainder of the apple.

3. Divide the oatmeal among 4 individual serving bowls, and top each with some of the shredded apple. Spoon equal amounts of the yogurt over the apple, and garnish with an apple slice. If desired, sprinkle with the cinnamon. Serve hot.

NUTRITIONAL DATA (PER SERVING)

Fat: 3 grams   Calories: 272   % Calories from fat: 10%

Strawberry-Banana Breakfast Treat

This is a fast, yummy, nutritious way to begin any day!

1. Place the bananas and yogurt in a small bowl, and stir until well blended. Divide the mixture between 2 individual serving bowls.

2. In each bowl, stir in ½ cup of cereal. Top with 1 teaspoon of preserves, if desired, and serve.

Quick Dish

Yield: *2 servings*

2 medium bananas, peeled, sliced in half lengthwise, and cut into ¼-inch slices

12 ounces light nonfat strawberry or strawberry-banana yogurt

1 cup Ralston Strawberry Muesli Cereal with pecans

2 teaspoons strawberry preserves (optional)

NUTRITIONAL DATA (PER SERVING)

Fat: 2 grams   Calories: 290   % Calories from fat: 6%

Quick and Simple Breakfast Fruitosia

As great as this is for breakfast, it is delicious for any time of the day! For a change of pace, try different flavors of yogurt.

1. Place the orange and apple pieces in a medium-sized bowl, and mix well. Set aside.

2. Place the yogurt in a small bowl, and stir in the coconut extract. Spoon the yogurt over the fruit, and toss until well blended.

3. Spoon the fruit mixture into individual serving bowls, top with the granola, and serve.

Quick Dish

Yield: *2 servings*

2 small navel oranges, peeled, sectioned, and cut into bite-sized pieces

1 medium apple, cored and cut into bite-sized chunks

8 ounces light nonfat vanilla yogurt

2 teaspoons coconut-flavored extract

¾ cup Kellogg's Low-Fat Granola (with or without raisins)

NUTRITIONAL DATA (PER SERVING)

Fat: 2 grams   Calories: 282   % Calories from fat: 6%

3

Supremely
Super Sandwiches

Ever since the Earl of Sandwich requested that meat be placed between two slices of bread so that he could eat at the gaming table, the sandwich has enjoyed great popularity. In fact, one survey estimated that more than 11 billion sandwiches are now eaten each year! And no wonder. In addition to its convenience, the sandwich is perhaps the most versatile of all dishes. According to the occasion and to personal preferences, it can be cold or hot, dainty or king-sized, open-faced or double-decker, simple or sophisticated.

This chapter has sandwiches to suit any and every occasion and taste—all low in fat, and all totally delicious. Looking for a stick-to-your ribs sandwich? Try Beef Teriyaki Steak Sandwiches or Barbecue Turkey Hoagies. Hot and hearty, these will satisfy the largest of appetites. Want something hot and spicy? Hot and Zesty Sausage Sandwiches nearly sizzle on the plate! Tiny Cranberry-Beef Sandwiches, as the name implies, make great light entrées or appetizers. Or try Light Egg Salad Sandwiches for a healthy and refreshing twist on an old favorite. And the old grilled cheese sandwich pales in comparison with the warm smoky flavor of Smoky Bacon and Cheese Sandwich, a Quick Dish that's a snap to make, but satisfyingly flavorful.

So whether you're looking for a one-dish meal, an accompaniment to your favorite soup, or a savory tidbit to satisfy a middle-of-the-night craving, you're sure to find a perfect match within the following pages. From Chicken Pita Tacos With Salsa to Feisty Franks, these are sandwiches that satisfy. Your only problem may be in deciding which one to try first!

Barbecue Turkey Hoagies

Yield: *8 servings*

¾ cup Turkey Stock (page 93) or other fat-free turkey stock, divided

1 small onion, chopped

1 large clove garlic, minced

¾ cup catsup

¼ cup chili sauce

⅛ cup white vinegar

2 teaspoons liquid smoke

¾ cup water

⅓ cup brown sugar, packed

1 pound smoked turkey breast, shredded

4 small (6-inch) soft hoagie rolls, halved lengthwise

I Can't Believe It's Not Butter spray

1 small sweet red onion, thinly sliced

Leaf lettuce

These hoagie sandwiches make a quick and delicious entrée on those busy days. Cabbage Slaw With Poppy Seed Dressing (page 70) is a great accompaniment.

1. Place ¼ cup of the turkey stock in a medium-sized nonstick skillet with lid, and bring to a boil over high heat. Reduce the heat to medium-high, and add the onion and garlic. Stirring occasionally, cook for 5 minutes, or until the vegetables are tender.

2. In a small bowl, combine the remaining ½ cup of stock and the catsup, chili sauce, vinegar, and liquid smoke, mixing until well blended. Stir the catsup mixture into the skillet mixture. Reduce the heat to medium, and cook for 5 minutes.

3. Place the water in a small bowl, and stir in the brown sugar until dissolved. Stir the sugar mixture into the skillet mixture. Increase the heat to medium-high, and bring to a boil. Continue to cook on high for 2 minutes, stirring constantly. Reduce the heat to medium, and cook at a slow simmer for 5 additional minutes, stirring occasionally.

4. Add the shredded turkey to the barbecue mixture, blending well. Cover and cook for 10 minutes, or until the turkey is heated through.

5. Spray the cut sides of the rolls lightly with the butter spray, and toast lightly in a toaster oven or under a preheated broiler.

6. Arrange the bottoms of the 4 rolls cut side up on a flat surface. Spoon about a quarter of the turkey mixture over each roll, and garnish with some of the onions and lettuce. Place the top of the roll over the lettuce, and cut the sandwich in half crosswise. Transfer each half to an individual serving plate, and serve hot.

NUTRITIONAL DATA (PER SERVING)

Fat: 4.5 grams   Calories: 265   % Calories from fat: 15%

Chicken Pita Tacos With Salsa

You will love these "tacos" for their spicy flavor and their ease of preparation!

1. Place the chicken stock in a medium-sized saucepan, and bring to a boil over high heat. Reduce the heat to medium, and add the onion and garlic, 1 teaspoon of the chili powder, and the cumin, oregano, onion salt, and pepper. Cook for 2 minutes, stirring occasionally.

2. Add the chicken breasts to the skillet mixture, cover, and simmer over medium heat for 10 to 15 minutes, or until the chicken is tender when pierced with a fork. Turn the breasts once or twice to insure even cooking and spice coverage.

3. While the chicken is simmering, place the Healthy Sour Cream in a small bowl, and stir in the remaining ½ teaspoon of chili powder until well blended. Cover and chill until needed.

4. Remove the chicken from the stock, and set aside to cool, allowing the stock to remain in the saucepan. When the chicken is cool, shred it with a fork.

5. Return the stock to a boil over medium-high heat, and boil, uncovered, for 3 minutes. Reduce the heat to medium, and stir in the chicken. Simmer the mixture until most of the stock has cooked away. Remove from the heat, and set aside.

6. Place 1 pita half on each of 4 individual serving plates, and line each with lettuce. Place the tomatoes, cheese, and chicken in a large bowl, and toss to mix. Spoon the mixture into the pitas. Top each with a tablespoon of the sour cream mixture and serve, accompanied by a bowl of the Terrific Tomato-Basil Salsa.

NUTRITIONAL DATA (PER SERVING)

Fat: 5.5 grams   Calories: 341   % Calories from fat: 14%

Yield: *4 servings*

1 cup Chicken Stock (page 92) or other fat-free chicken stock

1 small onion, finely chopped

1 large clove garlic, minced

1½ teaspoons chili powder, divided

½ teaspoon ground cumin

¼ teaspoon dried oregano

Onion salt to taste

Freshly ground black pepper to taste

2 boneless skinless chicken breast halves (6 ounces each)

¼ cup Healthy Sour Cream (page 106) or other nonfat sour cream

2 whole wheat pita pockets (8½-inch rounds), halved crosswise

2 cups romaine lettuce, torn into thin strips

1 large red tomato, diced

½ cup shredded fat-free Cheddar cheese

½ cup shredded reduced-fat sharp Cheddar cheese

1½ cups Terrific Tomato-Basil Salsa

Ham, Chicken, and Bacon Deli on Sourdough

Yield: *2 servings*

¼ cup Pickle and Onion Spread (page 55)

1½ tablespoons Oscar Mayer Real Bacon Bits

4 slices light sourdough bread, lightly toasted

4 romaine lettuce leaves

1 large Roma tomato, thinly sliced

4 slices sweet red onion

6 slices (½ ounce each) lean honey-glazed ham

4 slices (1 ounce each) Louis Rich Carving Board Grilled Chicken Breast

Although this sandwich has all the great flavor of a traditional deli-style sandwich, it's missing at least three-quarters of the fat found in most deli creations.

1. Place the sandwich spread and bacon bits in a small bowl, and mix until well blended.

2. Arrange the 4 bread slices on a flat surface, and spread each with the sandwich mixture. Set 2 of the slices aside.

3. Place 1 of the bread slices on each of 2 individual serving plates, and place 1 lettuce leaf on each of the slices. Follow with layers of tomato, onion, ham, chicken, and, finally, the remaining lettuce leaves. Top with the remaining slices of bread, pressing firmly to "meld" the sandwich together. Cut in half, and serve.

NUTRITIONAL DATA (PER SERVING)

Fat: 4 grams   Calories: 235   % Calories from fat: 15%

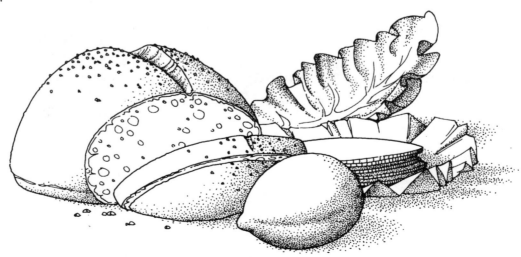

Tex-Mex Hot n' Spicy Sloppy Joes

Be sure you choose ground turkey with no more than 1.5 grams of fat per 4-ounce serving to make this saucy dish.

1. Lightly spray a large nonstick skillet with cooking spray, and preheat over medium heat. Add the turkey, and cook, stirring to crumble, until the juices begin to flow.

2. Add the onions to the skillet, and continue to cook and stir until the turkey browns.

3. Transfer the turkey mixture to paper towels, and drain thoroughly. Wipe the skillet with a paper towel, and return the turkey to the skillet.

4. Place the tomato sauce, salsa, peppers, cumin, brown sugar, salt, and pepper in a small bowl, and stir to mix. Stir the mixture into the skillet, and simmer over low heat for 15 to 20 minutes, stirring occasionally.

5. Place a split roll on each of 6 individual serving plates, and spoon the turkey mixture on the bottom half. Top with the second half, cut in half, and serve, accompanied by a bowl of Terrific Tomato-Basil Salsa (page 109), if desired.

NUTRITIONAL DATA (PER SERVING)

Fat: 2 grams   Calories: 255   % Calories from fat: 7%

Yield: *6 servings*

1¼ pounds lean ground turkey breast

½ cup chopped onions

1 can (8 ounces) tomato sauce

½ cup chunky salsa, mild or hot

1½ teaspoons chopped jalapeño peppers, seeds and veins removed*

½ teaspoon ground cumin

1 heaping tablespoon brown sugar

Salt to taste

Freshly ground black pepper to taste

6 whole wheat Kaiser rolls, halved and lightly toasted

*If you like a spicier dish, leave the pepper's seeds and veins intact.

Hot Peppers

Hot peppers—often referred to as chili peppers or, simply, chilies—lend a great deal of flavor and zip, as well as lots of vitamins A, C, and E, to a variety of foods. These peppers come in a wide range of colors, sizes, flavors, and degrees of heat. By gaining familiarity with the chilies most commonly found in supermarkets and specialty stores, and by learning how to handle them and use them in dishes, you will be able to add a distinct character not only to Tex-Mex dishes, but to many other foods, as well.

Knowing Your Hot Peppers

If you've never used hot peppers in your cooking, that first trip to the chili section of the produce aisle might be a little intimidating. The following discussion of some of the more common fresh and dried chilies should help you find just what you need for your dish—whether you're looking for the pepper specifically called for in your recipe, or you want to experiment with a different pepper that seems to be more to your taste.

Anaheim chilies. Also known as a New Mexico pepper, a Rio Grande pepper, a California green chili, a long green chili, or simply a green chili or mild green chili, this is one of the mildest of the hot peppers. Anaheim chilies are 5 to 7 inches long; bright, shiny green in color; and fairly flat. They are often dried and strung into colorful *ristras*, or wreaths.

Ancho chilies. This dried poblano chili (see below), is probably the most widely used pepper in Mexico. About 5 inches long, the ancho appears flat, almost cone shaped, and wrinkled like a prune. The heat of this dark brick red pepper varies from slightly hot to very hot.

Cayenne peppers. These peppers, which are small and thin, can be either red or green in color. While both types are quite hot, the red pepper is often the hotter of the two.

Chipotle chilies. These are jalapeño peppers that have been smoked and dried. Small and tapered, these chocolate-brown peppers vary in degrees of smoky heat.

Habañero chilies. The world's hottest chili pepper—more than seventy times hotter than the jalapeño!—the habañero is also called the Scotch bonnet. Small and fat, this pepper announces its flaming heat with its bright neon orange color.

Jalapeño peppers. Medium to dark green in color, jalapeños are about 2½ inches long and shaped somewhat like a bullet, tapering to a blunt point. These peppers can be extremely hot.

Pasilla chilies. About 6 inches long and narrow, pasillas vary in color from dark green to almost black when fresh, and have a deep, rich, moderately hot flavor. When dried, their color becomes a chocolate brown. Fresh pasillas should be roasted and skinned before they are added to dishes.

Poblano chilies. About 4 to 6 inches long and heart-shaped, the poblano ranges in color from dark green to almost black. The poblano has a mild fruity flavor, and can be slightly hot to hot. Usually, this pepper is roasted and skinned before being added to a dish. Dried, the poblano is known as the ancho chili.

Serrano chilies. Usually very hot, these green

chilies are about the same length as the jalapeños, but are slimmer and have a stronger taste.

Buying and Storing Chilies

When selecting fresh chilies, look for firm peppers with smooth, shiny skins and no visible dry cracks. Keep your chilies fresh by wrapping them in a paper bag or paper towels and placing them in the crisper of your refrigerator. Stored in this manner, they should keep for two to three weeks. Do not place the chilies in a plastic bag, as they will "sweat" and deteriorate quickly.

Place your dried chilies in an airtight container. Stored this way, they will last for several months in either the refrigerator or a cool, dry place.

Cooking With Hot Peppers

When cooking with either fresh or dried hot peppers, caution must be used. The capsaicin compound that gives chili peppers their heat need not be ingested to cause discomfort. Just touching the chili with your bare hands can irritate the skin, and extreme discomfort will result if you then touch your face and eyes while you're working. Be aware, however, that there may be a delay between the actual contact with this potent irritant and the feeling of pain.

The best approach is to be prepared. Always wear rubber gloves while cooking with hot chilies. If you *do* touch the peppers with your hands, immediately wash your hands and nails thoroughly with soapy water.

Most of the heat of a chili is found in its seeds and veins. So if you like the flavor of a particular chili but want to reduce some of its fiery impact, simply remove some or all of the seeds and/or veins until you get the level of heat you desire. Remember, though, that even when dealing with one type of chili, the level of heat can

vary. To test a pepper's heat, touch the flesh *lightly* with your tongue before using the chili in your recipe.

For a different flavor and texture, fresh chilies may be roasted before they are added to the dish. For information on this, see the inset "Roasting Peppers" on page 123.

When using dried chilies in your dishes, first wash them under cool running water. Then, still holding the chilies under running water, cut them open and discard the stems, seeds, and veins.

Once the seeds and veins have been removed, you may soften dried chilies in one of two ways. First, you may place the chilies in a saucepan or skillet along with a small amount of water, and bring them to a boil. Then remove them from the heat and allow them to sit in the water until they are softened. Drain and use. If you prefer, place the chilies in a heatproof bowl and cover them with boiling water. Allow the chilies to sit for 45 to 60 minutes, or until soft. Drain and use.

To purée dried chilies, place the softened chilies in a blender with a small amount of liquid, and process on mix or purée until a paste is formed. Press the puréed mixture through a fine mesh strainer to remove any leftover bits of peel.

Canned Hot Peppers

Chili peppers have become so popular that a wide variety is now available, both chopped and whole, in cans and jars. Although these chilies may be used directly from the can, I prefer to rinse them very thoroughly to rid them of the brine in which they were preserved. Then drain well before adding the chilies to your dish. You will be delighted to find the flavor of canned and jarred chilies comparable to that of fresh chilies. It couldn't be easier to add spark and interest to eggs, sandwiches, salads, and so many other dishes!

Pork Pita Pockets With Dill Sauce

Yield: *4 servings*

1 pound boneless pork tenderloin, partially frozen (freezing
makes slicing easier)

2 whole wheat pita pockets (6½-
inch rounds), halved crosswise

4 large red leaf lettuce leaves

Alfalfa sprouts

MARINADE

¼ cup plus 1 tablespoon apple
juice

¼ cup lemon juice

2 medium cloves garlic, minced

1 teaspoon dried oregano

1 teaspoon dry mustard

YOGURT SAUCE

8 ounces plain nonfat yogurt

1 medium cucumber, peeled
and chopped

½ teaspoon crushed garlic

½ teaspoon dill seeds

1 small sweet red onion, cut in
half and thinly sliced

You and your family will enjoy this delicious sandwich with its crunchy, chewy mixture of textures and its tantalizing blend of flavors.

1. Trim the pork of all visible fat. Cut the meat crosswise into ¼-inch slices. Then cut each slice into 1-inch strips. Allow the pork to thaw, and pat dry.

2. Place all of the marinade ingredients in a small bowl, and stir until well blended. Pour into a large resealable plastic bag. Add the pork strips, and shake the bag until the pork is well covered. Open the bag, expel as much air as possible, and reclose. Chill for at least 1 hour.

3. Place the all of the sauce ingredients except for the onion in a small bowl, and stir until mixed thoroughly. Do not beat or overstir. Gently stir in the red onion, cover, and chill until needed.

4. Lightly spray a medium-sized nonstick skillet with cooking spray, and preheat over medium-high heat. Remove the pork strips from the bag, discarding the marinade. Place the pork strips in the skillet, and stir-fry for 2 to 3 minutes, or until completely cooked.

5. Place 1 pita half on each of 4 individual serving plates, and line each half with lettuce. Fill with a quarter of the pork strips, and top with a dollop of yogurt sauce and a sprinkling of sprouts. Serve immediately.

NUTRITIONAL DATA (PER SERVING)

Fat: 4.5 grams   Calories: 234   % Calories from fat: 17%

Top Left: Light Egg Salad Sandwiches (page 46)
Top Right: Strawberry Coolers (page 214)
Center: Pork Pita Pockets With Dill Sauce (page 40)
Bottom: Barbecue Turkey Hoagies (page 34)

Top: Cabbage Slaw With Poppy Seed Dressing (page 70)
Center: Simple Four-Bean Salad (page 67)
Bottom: Basil Tomato Salad (page 72)

Smoky Bacon and Cheese Sandwich

These are quick, simple sandwiches to make for a light lunch or for breakfast. If you want to zip them up a little, add a splash of hot sauce to each slice of Canadian bacon as you stack the sandwich filling.

1. Brush each slice of Canadian bacon with liquid smoke. Preheat a medium-sized nonstick skillet over medium-high heat, and add the bacon. Cook for 1 to 2 minutes on each side, or until browned.

2. While the bacon is cooking, spray the cut surface of each muffin with the butter spray, and toast lightly in a toaster or toaster oven.

3. Arrange 2 hot muffin halves on each of 2 individual serving plates. For each sandwich, arrange a slice of bacon on 1 muffin half, followed by a slice of cheese. Follow with 2 more layers of bacon and cheese. Work quickly so that the heat of the muffin and bacon will slightly melt the cheese!

4. Top each sandwich with a muffin half, and serve immediately.

Quick Dish

Yield: *2 servings*

6 thin slices (½ ounce each) Canadian bacon

Liquid smoke

2 whole wheat or sourdough English muffins, split

I Can't Believe It's Not Butter spray

6 slices (¾ ounce each) fat-free sharp Cheddar cheese

NUTRITIONAL DATA (PER SERVING)

Fat : 2.5 grams   Calories: 280   % Calories from fat: 8%

Beef Teriyaki Steak Sandwiches

Yield: *8 servings*

2 pounds lean top round steak

8 slices pineapple canned in juice or water, drained (garnish)

8 sandwich-size onion rolls, split and lightly toasted

Lettuce leaves (garnish)

MARINADE

2 cups water

1 cup soy sauce

¼ cup red wine

½ cup brown sugar, packed

1 large onion, chopped

2 medium cloves garlic, minced

1 teaspoon ground ginger

Cabbage Slaw With Poppy Seed Dressing (page 70) is a delicious accompaniment to this sandwich, which makes a hearty entrée.

1. Place all of the marinade ingredients in a medium-sized bowl, and stir to mix well. Set aside.

2. Slice the steak into 8 equal servings. Pierce each piece several times with a fork, and place in a shallow dish. Pour the marinade over the steak, cover, and chill for several hours, preferably overnight. Turn the pieces only once.

3. Remove the steak from the marinade, and discard the marinade.

4. Line a broiling pan or shallow baking pan with aluminum foil. Arrange the steak pieces on the pan, and place in a preheated broiler, 2 to 3 inches below the heat source. Broil for 10 to 12 minutes on each side, or until the steak is done to your preference.

5. While the steaks are broiling, arrange the drained pineapple slices in a single layer on a shallow baking dish. When the steaks are done, remove from the oven and cover to keep warm. Place the pineapple under the broiler for 1 to 2 minutes, or just until the slices *begin* to brown; watch closely.

6. Place a split roll on each of 8 individual serving plates, and place a piece of steak on the bottom half. Top with the second half, garnish with a broiled pineapple slice and lettuce leaves, and serve hot.

NUTRITIONAL DATA (PER SERVING)

| Fat: 7 grams | Calories: 419 | % Calories from fat: 12% |

Tiny Cranberry-Beef Sandwiches

These tiny sandwiches may be chilled through and served cold. The sandwich spread itself may be served with a variety of low-fat or fat-free crackers or raw vegetable sticks.

1. Place the yogurt cheese, beef, sprouts, and cranberries in a medium-sized bowl, and stir until well blended.

2. Arrange 3 slices of the bread on a flat surface. (Trim the crusts if desired.) Spread the beef mixture on the slices, and top each with a lettuce leaf. Top with a second piece of bread, and cut in half diagonally to make 2 triangles. Cut each triangle in half.

3. Arrange 4 triangles on each of 3 individual serving plates. Garnish with 3 pickle slices, and serve.

NUTRITIONAL DATA (PER SERVING)

Fat: <1 gram   Calories: 203   % Calories from fat: 12%

Quick Dish

Yield: *3 servings*

1 cup So-Simple Yogurt Cheese (page 53)

1 package (2.5 ounces) thinly sliced dried beef, chopped

½ cup onion sprouts or other sprouts

⅓ cup chopped dried cranberries

6 thin slices honey-wheat bread

3 large red lettuce leaves

3 sweet midget pickles, cut into thirds lengthwise (garnish)

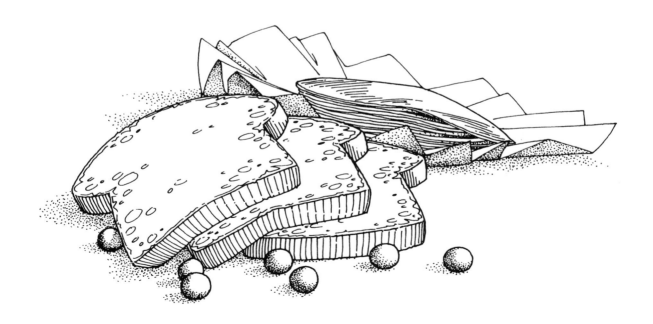

Hot and Zesty Sausage Sandwiches

Yield: *8 servings*

1 package (1 pound) Mr. Turkey Smoked Sausage, hot flavor

½ cup Dijon mustard

¼ cup diced jalapeño peppers or green or red chili peppers*

1 medium sweet red onion, sliced into thin strips

2 large tomatoes, chopped

8 sandwich-size sourdough French-style rolls, sliced partway through and lightly toasted

* If you want to reduce the spiciness, remove the pepper's seeds and veins.

This sandwich will set your mouth on fire, so be ready with a sip of something cool and sweet!

1. Cut the sausage into 8 equal pieces, and slice each piece in half lengthwise.

2. Line a broiling pan or shallow baking pan with aluminum foil. Arrange the sausage pieces on the pan, and place in a preheated broiler, 2 to 3 inches below the heat source. Broil for 2 to 3 minutes, or until the sausage begins to turn slightly brown. Turn, and broil for 2 to 3 additional minutes, or until slightly browned. Transfer the sausages to paper towels, and drain.

3. While the sausage is broiling, place the mustard and peppers in a small bowl, and mix until well blended. Set aside.

4. Place the onions and tomatoes in a medium-sized bowl, and stir to mix. Set aside.

5. Place a split roll on each of 8 individual serving plates, and spread both sides with the mustard mixture. For each sandwich, place 2 sausage pieces on the roll, side by side. Spoon some of the onion and tomato mixture down the center of the sausage pieces, and serve immediately.

NUTRITIONAL DATA (PER SERVING)

Fat: 7 grams	Calories: 227	% Calories from fat: 27%

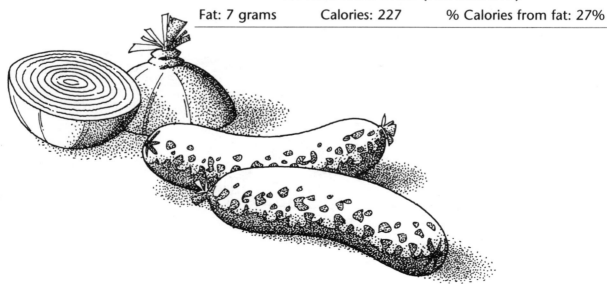

Feisty Franks

Years ago, when I discovered that most frankfurters contain between 16 and 18 grams of fat, I stopped serving them to my family. Since that time, however, several low-fat and fat-free hot dogs have appeared on the market, and once again, we can enjoy this easy-to-fix treat.

1. Place the catsup, water, liquid smoke, brown sugar, bacon, mustard, and pepper in a blender, and process on medium speed until well blended. Set aside.

2. Preheat a large nonstick skillet over medium-high heat. Slice each frank in half lengthwise, and place cut side down in the skillet. Cook for 2 minutes, turn, and cook for 2 additional minutes, or until browned.

3. Pour the catsup mixture over the franks, covering well. Reduce the heat to medium, and bring the mixture to a slow simmer. Cook for 4 minutes, and turn the franks. Spoon the sauce over the tops, and simmer for 4 additional minutes.

4. Place a split roll on each of 5 individual serving plates. Slice each frankfurter piece in half crosswise, and arrange 4 pieces on each bun. Garnish as desired, and serve hot.

Yield: *5 servings*

1 cup catsup

¼ cup water

2 teaspoons liquid smoke

3 tablespoons brown sugar

1 tablespoon Oscar Mayer Real Bacon Bits

½ teaspoon dry mustard

Freshly ground black pepper to taste

5 bun-size (2-ounce) low-fat frankfurters

5 whole wheat Kaiser rolls, halved and lightly toasted

NUTRITIONAL DATA (PER SERVING)

Fat: 4 grams   Calories: 305   % Calories from fat: 12%

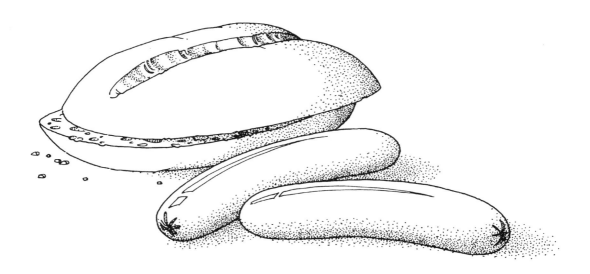

Light Egg Salad Sandwiches

Yield: 2 servings

6 hard-cooked eggs, cooled and peeled

4 slices light honey wheatberry bread, lightly toasted

Young curly endive (chicory) leaves

4 dill pickle spears (garnish)

DRESSING

3 tablespoons fat-free mayonnaise

2 teaspoons mustard

1½ tablespoons sweet pickle relish

½ teaspoon paprika

Salt to taste

Freshly ground black pepper to taste

Some people tell me that they feel guilty when they discard those high-fat egg yolks. But when you consider that each yolk contains 5 grams of fat and 210 milligrams of cholesterol, you're sure to feel better—especially after enjoying this deliciously light sandwich!

1. Cut each of the hard-cooked eggs in half, and discard 5 of the yolks. Chop the remaining yolk and egg whites as desired, and set aside.

2. Place all of the dressing ingredients in a medium-sized bowl, and mix until well blended. Add the chopped egg, and mix well. Cover and chill for at least 1 hour.

3. Arrange 2 slices of bread on each of 2 individual serving plates. For each sandwich, spread half of the chilled egg salad on 1 slice, and top with some endive. Top with the second piece of bread, and cut in half. Garnish with the 2 pickle spears, and serve.

NUTRITIONAL DATA (PER SERVING)

| Fat: 3.8 grams | Calories: 195 | % Calories from fat: 17% |

The Bread That Makes the Sandwich

As you scan the recipes in this chapter, you may notice that a variety of breads have been used, ranging from whole wheat Kaiser rolls—a healthy choice for hearty sandwiches—to flavorful onion rolls to pita pockets, and more. These days, even your local supermarket offers an amazing array of breads, each with its own texture, color, shape, size, density, and, of course, flavor. When devising your own sandwich recipes, you'll have the most appealing results when you choose a bread that complements the sandwich filling. Don't be afraid to experiment with new types of sandwich breads—including such nontraditional choices as fat-free tortillas. Even an ordinary filling becomes interesting when it is enclosed in a delicious, flavorful bread! Just keep an eye on the nutritional information on the bread package, as this can vary widely from brand to brand.

If you share my fondness for reading older cookbooks, you have probably seen directions to spread your sandwich bread with a layer of softened butter or mayonnaise before making your sandwich. This was done because it prevents a filling such as tomatoes from soaking through the bread. Now that we're all more fat-conscious, this extra helping of fat is not necessarily the best choice. However, you will have much the same results if you lightly toast the bread before adding the filling—a step that is included in many of my recipes. This will insure a delicious sandwich, and at the same time save fat and calories.

4

Delightful Dips,
Spreads, and Snacks

America first fell in love with the dip just after World War II, when the sour cream and onion dip enjoyed its heyday. While this creamy concoction still enjoys popularity, it now shares the spotlight with a growing ensemble of enticing dip and spread combinations. And fortunately for the low-fat cook, all of them can be made lower in fat than that original treat—without sacrificing the flavor and texture that we all love.

This chapter begins with a selection of dips and spreads, ranging from the piquant to the sweet. Healthy Refried Bean Dip is the perfect choice when you're in the mood for something spicy and robust. For a sophisticated treat, try Crab Pie Delight, a complex blend of flavors that will have everyone returning for more. Or top your cracker with sweetly tempting Zesty Orange Cream Cheese Spread.

In between meals, it's all too easy to keep hunger at bay by grabbing a handful of high-fat chips. If crisp and flavorful is what you're looking for, this chapter has several offerings that fill the bill with good taste *and* good nutrition. Snackin' Time boasts a not-to-be-believed crunchiness that will make it disappear before your eyes. Toasted Garlic Bagel Slices are good on their own or topped with low-fat dips and spreads. And if you're planning a Super Bowl Party, bake a batch of Mexitaly Nachos. Just be sure to make enough!

You'll notice that none of the recipes in this chapter has been marked as a Quick Dish. That's because virtually all of these treats are a snap to make! So invite the gang—or curl up with a good book—and enjoy some sensational snacks that are low in fat, but high in flavor.

Dips

Cranberry Horseradish Dip

Yield: 2 cups

1 cup strained canned whole
cranberry sauce

1 cup Healthy Sour Cream (page
106)

2 tablespoons prepared
horseradish

If you like horseradish, you will be delighted by this unusual blend of flavors.

1. Place all of the ingredients in a small bowl, and stir until blended.

2. Cover and chill for at least 1 hour before serving with raw cut vegetables or a selection of fat-free or reduced-fat crackers.

NUTRITIONAL FACTS (PER 1-TABLESPOON SERVING)

Fat: 0 gram   Calories: 18   % Calories from fat: 0%

Healthy Refried Bean Dip

Yield: 2½ cups

1 recipe Healthy Refried Beans
(page 159), or 1 can (1
pound) fat-free refried beans

½ teaspoon chili powder

2–3 dashes hot sauce or Tabasco
jalapeño hot sauce

¼ cup minced onion

¼ cup Healthy Sour Cream (page
106)

This dip is great served with low-fat or fat-free baked tortilla chips or Poppy Pita Pieces (page 58), or even spread across a tostata shell and topped with Terrific Tomato-Basil Salsa (page 109).

1. Place all of the ingredients in a medium-sized bowl, and stir until well blended.

2. Cover and chill for at least 1 hour before serving with baked tortilla chips, Poppy Pita Pieces, or cut raw vegetables.

NUTRITIONAL DATA (PER 1-TABLESPOON SERVING)

Fat: 0 gram   Calories: 15   % Calories from fat: 0%

Crab Pie Delight

This pie is a real party hit served with Poppy Pita Pieces (page 58), low-fat crackers, melba rounds, or raw vegetables for dipping. I love it!

1. Place the yogurt cheese, sour cream, mayonnaise, Worcestershire sauce, lemon juice, paprika, and garlic salt in a medium-sized mixing bowl, and stir until well blended. Add the Parmesan and Cheddar cheeses, and mix well. Add the crabmeat and scallions, and mix again.

2. Spread the crabmeat mixture evenly in a 9-inch pie pan. Set aside.

3. Tear the bread into pieces, and place in a blender or food processor. Process into fine crumbs.

4. Place the bread crumbs and parsley flakes in a plastic bag. Seal the bag, and shake until well blended. Sprinkle the mixture over the top of the dip.

5. Cover the pie with aluminum foil, and bake in a preheated 350°F oven for 20 to 25 minutes, or until the cheeses begin to bubble. Remove the foil, spray the top with the butter spray, and bake uncovered for 5 to 10 additional minutes, or until the bread crumbs are toasted.

6. Slice into 8 portions and serve immediately with the crackers and raw vegetables of your choice, or chill before serving.

Yield: 8 slices

½ cup So-Simple Yogurt Cheese (page 53)

¼ cup Healthy Sour Cream (page 106)

⅛ cup fat-free mayonnaise

⅛ cup light mayonnaise

½ teaspoon Worcestershire sauce

1 teaspoon lemon juice

¼ teaspoon paprika

Garlic salt to taste

¼ cup grated Parmesan cheese

¼ cup shredded fat-free Cheddar cheese

¼ cup shredded reduced-fat sharp Cheddar cheese

6 ounces flake-style imitation crabmeat, finely chopped

4 small scallions, finely chopped

1 slice whole wheat bread (made into fine crumbs)

1 tablespoon dried parsley, crushed fine

I Can't Believe It's Not Butter spray

NUTRITIONAL DATA (PER SLICE)

Fat: 1.5 grams   Calories: 80   % Calories from fat: 16%

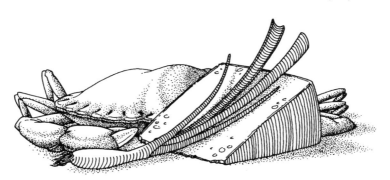

Five Alarm Dip

Yield: 1¼ cups

½ cup plus 1 tablespoon Healthy Sour Cream (page 106)

¼ cup plus 1 tablespoon fat-free mayonnaise

3 tablespoons light mayonnaise

2 teaspoons dried parsley, crushed

¼ cup Tabasco jalapeño hot sauce

Paprika

Serve this dip with Zesty Tortilla Chicken Strips (page 144) or cubed pieces of raw jicama and other raw vegetables. Reduce the amount of jalapeño hot sauce and use the dip as a tantalizing sandwich spread.

1. Place all of the ingredients except for the paprika in a small bowl, and stir until well blended.

2. Cover and chill for at least 1 hour. Sprinkle the paprika lightly over the top, and serve with your choice of raw vegetables.

NUTRITIONAL DATA (PER 1-TABLESPOON SERVING)

Fat: <1 gram   Calories: 10   % Calories from fat: 27%

Peanut Butter Dip

Yield: 1¼ cups

1 cup So-Simple Yogurt Cheese (page 53)

¼ cup reduced-fat peanut butter

1½ teaspoons Vanilla Butter & Nut extract

2 tablespoons granulated sugar

This dip is luscious with apple wedges or as a spread for graham crackers and toasted bagels.

1. Place all of the ingredients in a small bowl, and stir until well blended.

2. Cover and chill for at least 1 hour before serving with apple wedges and graham crackers.

NUTRITIONAL DATA (PER 1-TABLESPOON SERVING)

Fat: 1 gram   Calories: 32   % Calories from fat: 28%

Spreads

So-Simple Yogurt Cheese

The name of this recipe indicates just how simple it is to make this creamy, versatile spread. Use yogurt cheese as a nonfat substitute for cream cheese, mayonnaise, sour cream, sandwich spread, and much more. When making this tasty treat, be sure to choose yogurt that contains no gelatin or guar gum. These ingredients will keep the whey from separating from the "cheese."

Yield: 1 cup

16 ounces plain nonfat yogurt

1. Line a 4-inch strainer or funnel with a coffee filter or 2 layers of cheesecloth. Set the strainer or funnel over a 2-cup measuring cup or a jar. The strainer should fit over the cup without falling to the bottom.

2. Spoon the yogurt into the filter or cheesecloth, cover with plastic wrap, and place in the refrigerator for 4 hours, or overnight. The longer the yogurt sits, the more dense the cheese will become.

3. Place the yogurt cheese in a dish, cover, and chill until needed, or for up to a week. Discard the whey—the liquid that strains into the cup—or use it to replace the liquid in baked goods recipes and in soups.

NUTRITIONAL DATA (PER 1-TABLESPOON SERVING)

Fat: 0 gram   Calories: 11   % Calories from fat: 0%

Cheesy Apple Butter

Yield: 1½ cups

1 cup So-Simple Yogurt Cheese (page 53)

½ cup apple butter

1 tablespoon brown sugar (optional)

This spread may be used on bagels, cinnamon graham crackers, or Cinnamon Bagel Crisps (page 57), or as a delicious filling between 2 slices of whole wheat bread. It also makes a wonderful topping for baked apples or peaches, pancakes, oatmeal, French toast, and sweet potatoes.

1. Place the yogurt cheese, the apple butter, and, if desired, the brown sugar in a small bowl, and stir just until blended. Do not overstir, as the consistency will become too thin.

2. Cover and chill until needed, or store for up to 1 week.

NUTRITIONAL DATA (PER 1-TABLESPOON SERVING)
Fat: 0 gram   Calories: 20   % Calories from fat: 0%

Zesty Orange Cream Cheese Spread

Yield: about 3 cups

2 cups So-Simple Yogurt Cheese (page 53)

¾ cup sifted powdered sugar

1 teaspoon grated orange zest

3 tablespoons frozen orange juice concentrate, thawed

½ cup orange marmalade

Try this creamy spread on warmed slices of Orange Poppy Seed Loaf (page 189) or toasted Cranberry-Orange Twists (page 188). It also makes a delicious bagel topping!

1. Place the yogurt cheese, sugar, and orange zest in a medium-sized bowl, and stir just until blended.

2. While stirring, slowly add the juice concentrate to the cheese mixture. Stir just until creamy. Don't let the mixture get too thin.

3. Stir the marmalade into the cheese mixture only until blended. Cover and chill until needed, or store for up to 1 week.

NUTRITIONAL DATA (PER 1-TABLESPOON SERVING)
Fat: 0 gram   Calories: 30   % Calories from fat: 0%

Pickle and Onion Spread

This spread is wonderful on crackers, and adds great flavor to almost any type of savory sandwich.

Yield: 1⅓ cups

1. Place all of the ingredients in a small bowl, and stir until well blended.

2. Cover and chill until needed, or store for up to 2 weeks.

¾ cup plus 1 tablespoon fat-free mayonnaise

3 tablespoons light mayonnaise

⅛ cup catsup

⅛ cup chili sauce

⅛ cup sweet pickle relish

1 small onion, finely chopped

NUTRITIONAL DATA (PER 1-TABLESPOON SERVING)

Fat: .4 gram   Calories: 19   % Calories from fat: 16%

Snacks

Toasted Garlic Bagel Slices

Yield: *3 servings*

2 plain (3½-inch) bagels

I Can't Believe It's Not Butter spray

½ teaspoon garlic salt, or to taste

Simple, quick, tasty, satisfying, versatile, and low-fat is the bagel. Add some crunch, and you have the perfect snack!

1. Cut each bagel lengthwise into 3 equal slices, and arrange in a single layer on a large baking sheet.

2. Lightly spray the top of each slice with the butter spray, and sprinkle the garlic salt over each of the sprayed surfaces.

3. Place the bagel slices on the center rack of a preheated 400°F oven, and bake for 3 to 5 minutes, or until the tops begin to turn a light golden brown. Watch closely to avoid burning!

4. Serve hot from the oven, or, for more crunch, allow to cool before serving. Do not store, as this will cause the slices to lose their crunchiness.

NUTRITIONAL DATA (PER 2-SLICE SERVING)
Fat: .6 gram   Calories: 133   % Calories from fat: 4%

Cinnamon Bagel Crisps

A favorite of mine as I was growing up was leftover pie dough rolled out, cut in pieces, sprinkled with cinnamon and sugar, and baked. Later, I wanted to recreate the crispy, cinnamon sweetness of my childhood treat without the fat found in pie crust dough. This is a very satisfying substitute. By the way, if you slice a lot of bagels, as I do, consider investing in a bagel slicer. I wouldn't want to be without mine!

1. Cut each bagel lengthwise into 4 equal slices, and arrange in a single layer on a large baking sheet. Set aside.

2. Place the sugar and cinnamon in a small dish, and stir to blend well.

3. Lightly spray the top of each slice with the butter spray, and sprinkle the sugar and cinnamon mixture over each of the sprayed surfaces.

4. Place the bagel slices on the center rack of a preheated 400°F oven, and bake for 3 to 5 minutes, or until the tops begin to turn a light golden brown. Watch closely to avoid burning!

5. Serve hot from the oven, or, for more crunch, allow to cool before serving. Do not store, as this will cause the slices to lose their crunchiness.

Yield: *4 servings*

2 plain (3½-inch) bagels

2 tablespoons granulated sugar

½ teaspoon ground cinnamon, or to taste

I Can't Believe It's Not Butter spray

NUTRITIONAL DATA (PER 2-SLICE SERVING)

Fat: .5 gram	Calories: 122	% Calories from fat: 3%

Poppy Pita Pieces

Yield: *8 servings*

4 whole wheat pita pockets (8½-inch rounds)

2 tablespoons poppy seeds

½ teaspoon garlic salt

1 teaspoon onion powder

1 teaspoon dried oregano

I Can't Believe It's Not Butter spray

These spicy tidbits are delicious served all by themselves as a snack, or as an accompaniment to soups and salads.

1. Split each pita pocket in half lengthwise by cutting around the edge. Cut each of the resulting rounds into 8 wedges, and arrange the wedges, inside facing up, in a single layer on 2 large baking sheets. Set aside.

2. Place the poppy seeds, garlic salt, onion powder, and oregano in a small dish, and stir until well mixed.

3. Lightly spray the wedges with the butter spray, and sprinkle the sprayed surfaces with the poppy seed mixture. Lightly spray each piece once more, making sure not to dislodge the spices.

4. Place the baking sheets on the center rack of a preheated 400°F oven, and bake for 8 to 10 minutes, or until the wedges are crisp and begin to turn light brown. Remove the wedges from the baking sheets, and cool completely before serving. Or, for crisper wedges, allow the pita pieces to cool on the sheets. Store in an airtight container.

NUTRITIONAL DATA (PER 8-PIECE SERVING)

Fat: 1 gram   Calories: 96   % Calories from fat: 9%

Snackin' Time

This treat has a crunchy sweetness similar to that of honey-roasted nuts. It also makes a great topping for frozen yogurt!

1. Place the cereal and pretzel sticks in a large bowl, and mix well. Set aside.

2. Place all of the remaining ingredients in a small bowl, and whisk together until the egg whites are slightly frothy.

3. Pour the egg mixture over the pretzel mixture. Then, using your hands, gently toss until well coated.

4. Spread the pretzel mixture evenly on 2 nonstick 13-x-9-inch jelly roll or cookie sheets with sides. Place on the center rack of a preheated 325°F oven, and bake for 12 to 15 minutes, or until lightly browned. Stir every 5 minutes, and do not let the mixture get too brown.

5. Remove the pan from the oven, and allow to cool for 10 minutes before removing the mixture from the pan. Cool completely, break apart, and serve immediately or store in an airtight container for up to 1 week.

Yield: *10 servings*

7 cups bite-size plain Shredded Wheat cereal

1 package (9 ounces) fat-free pretzel sticks, broken into halves or thirds

2 egg whites, slightly beaten

2 tablespoons lemon juice

¼ cup granulated sugar

¼ teaspoon ground ginger

½ teaspoon ground nutmeg

2 teaspoons ground cinnamon

NUTRITIONAL DATA (PER 1-CUP SERVING)

Fat: <1 gram   Calories: 194   % Calories from fat: 3%

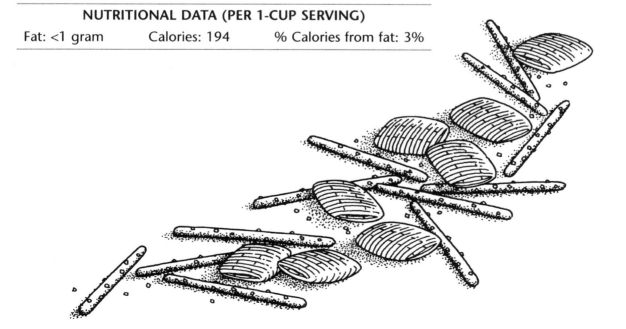

Chili-Cheese Snacks

Yield: *7 servings*

4 cups Corn Chex or Crispix Cereal

3 cups fat-free pretzel sticks, broken into thirds

2 egg whites

2½ tablespoons cheese-flavored sprinkles

1 tablespoon chili powder

1 teaspoon ground cumin

1 teaspoon onion powder

½ teaspoon garlic salt

These snacks just tingle with crunchy flavor!

1. Place the cereal and pretzel sticks in a large bowl, and mix well. Set aside.

2. Place all of the remaining ingredients in a small bowl, and whisk together until the egg whites are slightly frothy.

3. Pour the egg mixture over the cereal mixture. Then, using your hands, gently toss until well coated.

4. Spread the pretzel mixture evenly on 2 nonstick 13-x-9-inch jelly roll or cookie sheets with sides. Place on the center rack of a preheated 325°F oven, and bake for 12 to 15 minutes, or until lightly browned. Stir every 5 minutes, and do not let the mixture get too brown.

5. Remove the pans from the oven, and allow to cool for 10 minutes before removing the mixture from the pan. Cool completely, break apart, and serve immediately or store in an airtight container for up to 1 week.

NUTRITIONAL DATA (PER 1-CUP SERVING)

Fat: 0 gram   Calories: 160   % Calories from fat: 0%

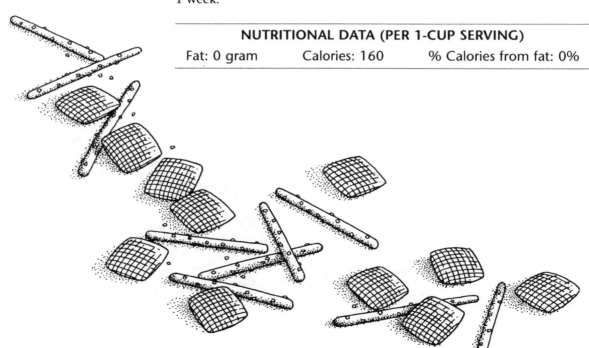

Mexitaly Nachos

This dish marries the flavors of Mexico and Italy to make a party-perfect crowd pleaser.

1. Preheat a large nonstick skillet over medium-high heat. Add the sausage, and cook, stirring often, until heated through and beginning to brown. Transfer the sausage to paper towels, and drain. Transfer to a covered dish to keep warm.

2. Place the refried beans and picante sauce in a small saucepan, stir to mix, and heat over low heat until warmed through.

3. Place the cheeses in a small bowl, and stir to mix. Set aside.

4. Arrange the corn chips in a single layer on a large nonstick cookie sheet with sides. Spoon the warmed bean mixture evenly over the tops of the tortilla chips. Follow with layers of the sausage, tomato, scallions, and, if desired, peppers. Top with the cheese.

5. Bake in a preheated 400°F oven for 10 to 12 minutes, or until the cheese is melted. Serve hot, accompanying the chips with a bowl of Healthy Sour Cream (page 106), if desired. (To reheat any leftovers, place in a 400°F oven for 10 minutes, or until the chips are crisp and the topping is heated through.)

Yield: *8 servings*

8 ounces Mr. Turkey Low-Fat Italian-Style smoked sausage, diced

1 recipe Healthy Refried Beans (page 159), or 1 can (1 pound) fat-free refried beans

1 cup mild or hot picante sauce

1 cup shredded fat-free Cheddar cheese

½ cup shredded reduced-fat Cheddar cheese

10 ounces Baked Tostitos Corn Chips

1 medium tomato, diced

2 medium scallions, chopped

2 medium jalapeño peppers, sliced and seeds removed (optional)

NUTRITIONAL DATA (PER SERVING)

| Fat: 5 grams | Calories: 319 | % Calories from fat: 14% |

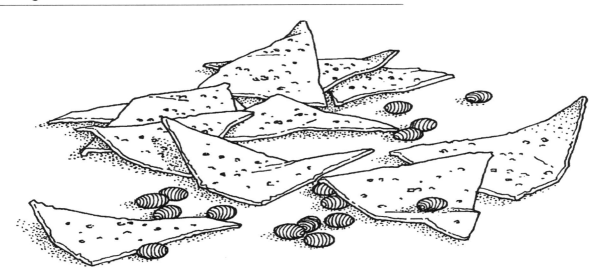

5

Sensational Salads and Dressings

My children laugh whenever I describe the salad my mother served when I was a child. Her salad consisted of just three ingredients: iceberg lettuce, tomatoes, and mayonnaise.

Fortunately, we've come a long way since then. Now, the availability of a wide variety of greens, as well as greater culinary interest in the salad, has led to the creation of an endless number of tempting, healthful, truly delicious dishes. In this chapter, I've tried to show you just a few of the tantalizing combinations you can enjoy—and still keep your dishes low in fat. For instance, if you're looking for a classic green salad, try Italian Mixed Green Salad, a dish that tosses together a medley of greens with garden fresh vegetables for a delightfully refreshing combination. Searching for an enticing first course? Try Multi-Colored Pea Salad—a great favorite in my house. Savory crunch and appealing presentation make Belgian Endive With Chicken Salad not only a wonderful salad, but also an excellent pick-up appetizer. And versatile Aloha Fruit Salad can start your meal with a burst of tropical flavor, or serve as a light dessert.

Playing an important supporting role, the salad dressing you choose enhances your dish and brings the different flavors together. This chapter offers an enticing array of choices, from sweet and fruity Orange Cream Dressing, to savory Red Wine Vinaigrette, to creamy Thousand Island. There are dressings for green salads, fruit salads, slaws, and more. And they are all made deliciously low-fat or completely fat-free by replacing the usual oil, sour cream, or full-fat mayonnaise with vinegar, lemon juice, nonfat yogurt, or other low-fat or fat-free ingredients. Add just a sprinkling of herbs and spices, and I guarantee that you'll never miss the fat!

Salads

Creamy Cucumbers

Yield: *5 servings*

2 medium cucumbers, scrubbed
and thinly sliced

1 small sweet red onion, thinly
sliced and separated into rings

CREAMY DRESSING

8 ounces plain nonfat yogurt

½ cup Red Wine Vinaigrette
(page 87)

½ teaspoon crushed dried sweet
basil

1 teaspoon sugar

Garlic salt and freshly ground
black pepper to taste

This salad makes a refreshing accompaniment to a wide variety of sandwiches. Drained, it makes a tasty sandwich garnish.

1. Place the cucumbers and onions in a medium-sized bowl, and gently toss to mix. Set aside.

2. Place all of the dressing ingredients in a small bowl, and blend gently with a wire whisk just until the mixture is smooth. Do not over-blend, as this may cause the yogurt to separate.

3. Pour the dressing over the cucumber mixture, and toss gently to coat.

4. Cover and chill for at least 2 hours, gently tossing once or twice. Toss once more just before serving cold.

NUTRITIONAL DATA (PER SERVING)

Fat: 0 gram	Calories: 42	% Calories from fat: 0%

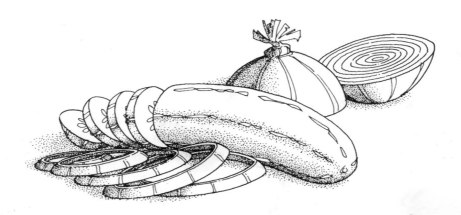

Top: Rojo Verde Salad (page 68)

Center: Poppy Pita Pieces (page 58)

Bottom Left: Chicken Salad in Tomato Cups (page 73)

Bottom Right: Trim Thousand Island Dressing (page 82) and Tomato-Bacon Dressing (page 86)

Top: Potato Cheese Soup (page 101)
Center: Chicken Pasta Soup (page 100)
Bottom: Creole Crab Soup (page 104)

Bacon, Leaf Lettuce, and Tomato Salad

Every once in a while, I get a yen for a bacon, lettuce, and tomato sandwich. I have found that this salad satisfies that yen with a fraction of the calories and fat! For even more bacon flavor, serve this salad with Tomato-Bacon Dressing (page 86).

1. Wash and dry the lettuce, and tear it into bite-sized pieces. Place the lettuce in a large salad bowl.

2. Add the onion, tomatoes, and bacon to the bowl, and gently toss to mix.

3. Pour the dressing of your choice over the salad, and gently toss to coat. Top with the croutons, and serve immediately.

NUTRITIONAL DATA (PER SERVING)

Fat: 1 gram   Calories: 70   % Calories from fat: 12%

Quick Dish

Yield: *4 servings*

1 small head red leaf lettuce

1 small head green leaf lettuce

1 small sweet red onion, thinly sliced and separated into rings

2 medium tomatoes, coarsely chopped

3 tablespoons Oscar Mayer Real Bacon Bits

1 cup fat-free garden herb Tostettes or other fat-free croutons

Bean Sprout Salad

This is a great Asian-style dish to serve with Beef Teriyaki Steak Sandwiches (page 42), Grilled Teriyaki Halibut Steaks (page 153), or Teriyaki Steak in Wine Sauce (page 138).

1. Place the sprouts, zucchini, bell pepper, and onion in a medium-sized salad bowl, and toss to mix. Set aside.

2. Place all of the dressing ingredients in a small bowl, and stir to mix well.

3. Pour the dressing over the bean sprout mixture, and gently toss until well coated. Cover and chill for at least 1 hour before serving.

NUTRITIONAL DATA (PER SERVING)

Fat: 0 gram   Calories: 65   % Calories from fat: 0%

Yield: *8 servings*

5 cups fresh bean sprouts

1 medium unpeeled zucchini, cut into thin 3-inch strips

1 cup thin strips red bell pepper

1 small onion, finely chopped

SWEET AND SOUR DRESSING

¾ cup La Choy sweet and sour sauce

2 teaspoons soy sauce

Dash ground ginger

¼ teaspoon garlic powder

Italian Mixed Green Salad

Yield: *6 servings*

1 clove garlic, peeled and halved

2 cups bite-sized pieces romaine lettuce

1 cup thin strips radicchio lettuce

1 cup bite-sized pieces escarole

1 cup bite-sized pieces curly endive (chicory)

1 cup bite-sized pieces arugula

1 medium yellow bell pepper, sliced into thin strips

1 medium sweet red onion, thinly sliced and separated into rings

10 cherry tomatoes, sliced

1 recipe Red Wine Vinaigrette (page 87)

A crisp burst of flavor is created by bringing together five different salad greens.

1. Completely rub the inside of a large salad bowl with the cut garlic, and discard the garlic.

2. Add the salad greens and the bell pepper to the bowl, and gently toss to mix. Add the onion and tomatoes, and toss to mix. For added crispness, cover and chill for at least 1 hour.

3. Pour the dressing over the salad, and toss gently to coat. Serve immediately.

NUTRITIONAL DATA (PER SERVING)

Fat: 0 gram   Calories: 30   % Calories from fat: 0%

Simple Four-Bean Salad

This salad may be served as a hearty side dish or as a light entrée on a bed of spinach leaves.

1. Place all of the beans and vegetables in a medium-sized bowl, and toss well to mix.

2. Pour the dressing over the salad, add salt to taste, and toss gently to coat.

3. Cover and chill for at least 1 hour before serving.

NUTRITIONAL DATA (PER SERVING)

Fat: 1 gram   Calories: 196   % Calories from fat: 5%

Quick Dish

Yield: *4 servings*

1 cup canned red kidney beans, drained

1 cup canned black beans, drained

1 cup canned French-cut green beans, drained, or 1 cup frozen French-cut green beans, thawed and drained

1 cup canned pinto beans, drained

1 medium onion, diced

¼ cup diced pimentos

⅓ cup Red Wine Vinaigrette (page 87)

Salt to taste

Rojo Verde Salad

Yield: 6 servings

1 large bunch romaine lettuce

1 small head red leaf lettuce

1 package (10 ounces) fresh spinach

1 cup shredded red cabbage

1 can (4 ounces) chopped or diced red chilies

½ cup chopped green bell pepper

½ cup chopped red bell pepper

½ cup finely chopped celery (optional)

2 large scallions, finely chopped (include tops)

1 large tomato, chopped

10 small radishes, sliced

1 can (8 ounces) sweet peas, drained

1 medium sweet red onion, thinly sliced and separated into rings

This red and green salad is a treat to the eye at any time of the year, but is especially festive at Christmas! If you are not going to serve this salad the same day it is prepared, be sure to tear the lettuce and spinach, instead of chopping the greens with a knife. This will prevent the edges from browning.

1. Wash and dry the romaine and red leaf lettuce. Chop the lettuce and spinach into bite-sized pieces, and place in a large salad bowl.

2. Add all of the remaining vegetables except for the peas and onions to the bowl, and mix. Add the peas, and gently toss to mix.

3. Arrange the onion rings over the top of the salad. To enhance crispness, cover and chill until ready to serve. Accompany with the dressing of your choice.

NUTRITIONAL DATA (PER SERVING)

Fat: 0 gram   Calories: 73   % Calories from fat: 0%

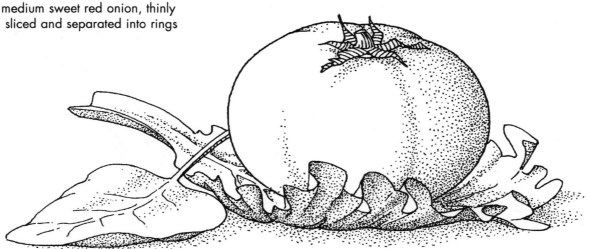

Multi-Colored Pea Salad

This colorful salad is also delicious served with a creamy dressing such as Mayonnaise-Style Salad Dressing (page 86) or Fat-Free Thousand Island Dressing (page 82).

1. Place all of the vegetables, except for the peas and onion, in a large salad bowl. Add the cheeses, and toss to mix well. Add the peas, and gently toss to mix. Set aside.

2. Place all of the dressing ingredients in a blender, and process on medium-high speed until well blended.

3. Pour the dressing over the salad, and gently toss to coat. Arrange the onion rings over the top, cover, and chill for 2 to 3 hours before serving.

NUTRITIONAL DATA (PER SERVING)

Fat: 1.7 grams	Calories: 97	% Calories from fat: 16%

Yield: *8 servings*

1 cup assorted shredded lettuce greens

1 cup shredded red cabbage

1 cup cauliflower florets

1 large stalk celery, finely chopped

1 medium carrot, shredded

1 medium tomato, chopped

1 small unpeeled cucumber, chopped

1 cup chopped yellow bell pepper

½ cup diced red pimento

½ cup shredded fat-free Cheddar cheese

½ cup shredded reduced-fat Cheddar cheese

1 can (15 ounces) sweet peas, drained

1 small sweet red onion, thinly sliced and separated into rings

DRESSING

⅔ cup water

¼ cup red wine vinegar

3 tablespoons tarragon vinegar

1 tablespoon sugar

¼ teaspoon freshly ground black pepper

½ teaspoon onion salt

Cabbage Slaw
With Poppy Seed Dressing

Yield: *10 servings*

1 small head green cabbage, shredded (about 4 cups)

1 small head red cabbage, shredded (about 2 cups)

1 large carrot, shredded

4 medium scallions, finely chopped (include tops)

1 recipe Honey-Poppy Seed Dressing (page 84)

This slaw has a sweet crunchiness that makes it an ideal accompaniment for sandwiches. As a bonus, the cabbage provides plenty of vitamins A, B complex, C, and K, as well as potassium, calcium, and magnesium, making this salad healthy as well as tasty.

1. Place all of the vegetables in a large salad bowl, and toss to mix.

2. Pour the dressing over the salad mixture, and gently toss until well mixed. Cover and chill for 1 to 3 hours before serving.

NUTRITIONAL DATA (PER SERVING)

Fat: .2 gram	Calories: 70	% Calories from fat: 3%

Making the Most of Your Tossed Green Salad

Long gone are the days when iceberg lettuce was the only green you'd find in your salad bowl. While still widely available, iceberg has been joined by crunchy romaine, crisp Belgian endive, red and green leaf lettuce, curly escarole, tender Boston, deep green spinach, colorful radicchio, and many more varieties of lettuce and greens, each with its own unique flavor, texture, and appearance. Experiment with all of them to find those that make the most satisfying combinations and best suit your particular tastes and needs.

The success of any green salad depends not only on using varied greens, but also on keeping those greens crisp and appealing until serving time. Upon returning from your trip to the market, take the time to clean all of your salad greens. This will keep them fresh for a longer period of time, and will ready them for whatever dish you have in mind. Discard the wilted, discolored, or bitter outer leaves, and wash the remaining greens gently but thoroughly under cold running water. Drain and thoroughly dry your greens in a salad spinner or in loosely rolled paper toweling. Then store them in an airtight container in the crisper of your refrigerator until you're ready to prepare your salad. Stored in this way, they should remain fresh for a week or more.

When making your salad, unless you plan to serve the dish immediately, tear the greens rather than cutting them. This will prevent the edges from browning. To keep the greens from wilting, either serve the dressing on the side or dress the salad lightly just before serving. Then enjoy a delightfully crisp salad that looks as good as it tastes!

Crispy Oriental Salad With Chicken

The delicate flavor of the chicken, combined with a delightful crunch-iness, makes this dish perfect as a light luncheon entrée. Tantalizing Orange-Coconut Yogurt Dressing (page 85) would add a lovely touch to this salad.

1. Wash and dry the lettuce, and chop it into bite-sized pieces. Place the lettuce in a large salad bowl.

2. Add all of the remaining vegetables to the bowl, and toss until well mixed. Gently toss in the chicken, cover, and chill for at least 1 hour.

3. Just before serving, toss in the rice noodles. Serve, with your choice of dressing on the side.

NUTRITIONAL DATA (PER SERVING)

Fat: 3.5 grams   Calories: 195   % Calories from fat: 16%

Yield: 6 servings

1 large bunch romaine lettuce

1½ cups shredded red cabbage

1 large carrot, shredded

1 cup small snow peas (cut in half if large)

1 cup fresh bean sprouts

1 medium red bell pepper, chopped

4 medium scallions, chopped (include tops)

3 cups diced cooked chicken breast (about 3 skinless, bone-less breast halves)

1 can (3 ounces) La Choy rice noodles

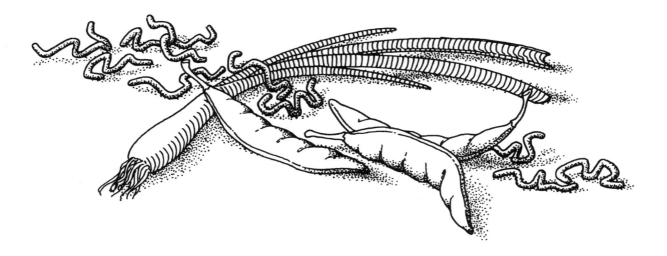

Basil Tomato Salad

Quick Dish

Yield: *6 servings*

2 cups chopped red plum
  tomatoes or halved red
  cherry tomatoes

2 cups chopped yellow plum
  tomatoes or halved yellow
  cherry tomatoes

½ cup shredded fat-free
  mozzarella cheese

½ cup shredded reduced-fat
  mozzarella cheese

1 cup slivered fresh basil leaves

1 recipe Red Wine Vinaigrette
  (page 87)

Freshly ground black pepper
  to taste

This deliciously colorful salad is bursting with flavor! Do try to use fresh basil leaves in this salad for best results. Either red and yellow plum tomatoes or red and yellow cherry tomatoes may be used, as both types have the intense flavors that complement the basil and cheese.

1. Place the tomatoes and the cheese in a medium-sized salad bowl, and toss to mix.

2. Sprinkle the basil leaves and dressing over the salad. Add pepper to taste, and toss gently until well blended. Serve immediately or, for best flavor, cover and chill for at least 30 minutes before serving.

NUTRITIONAL DATA (PER SERVING)

Fat: 1 gram   Calories: 80   % Calories from fat: 11%

Chicken Salad in Tomato Cups

Try to get really red tomatoes bursting with glorious garden-fresh flavor for your tomato cups.

1. Cut a thin slice from the top of each tomato, and reserve the slices. Cut around the inside edge of each tomato, leaving a ¼-inch-thick shell. Scoop out and reserve the pulp, leaving the tomato cup intact. Arrange the cups in a shallow oblong container, and set aside.

2. Dice the reserved tomato slices and pulp, and place in a large bowl. Add the egg whites and chicken, and stir to mix. Set aside.

3. Place the onion, celery, bell pepper, relish, basil, mayonnaise, and 1 teaspoon of the paprika in a medium-sized bowl. Add salt and pepper to taste, and mix thoroughly. Spoon the vegetable mixture over the chicken mixture, and stir until well blended.

4. Using a spoon, divide the chicken mixture among the tomato cups. Sprinkle the top of each cup with the remaining paprika.

5. Cover the tomatoes and chill for at least 1 hour. Line 6 individual serving plates with the lettuce leaves, and place 1 stuffed tomato on each plate. Serve.

Yield: *6 servings*

6 medium to large firm red tomatoes

6 hard boiled whole egg whites, chopped

4 cups diced or shredded cooked chicken breasts (about 4 skinless, boneless breast halves)

1 medium onion, chopped

2 medium stalks celery, chopped (include tops)

1 small green bell pepper, chopped

½ cup sweet pickle relish

2 teaspoons crushed dried basil

⅓ cup fat-free mayonnaise

¼ cup light mayonnaise

1½ teaspoons paprika, divided

Salt and freshly ground black pepper to taste

Crisp leaf lettuce (garnish)

NUTRITIONAL DATA (PER SERVING)

Fat: 5 grams   Calories: 255   % Calories from fat: 18%

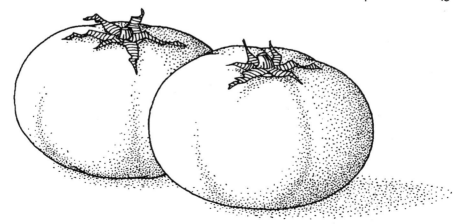

Carrot, Jicama, and Raisin Salad

Yield: *8 servings*

2 cups shredded carrots
(about 3 medium)

2 cups shredded jicama (about 1
large)

¾ cup dark raisins

Dark green spinach leaves
(garnish)

DRESSING

½ cup fat-free mayonnaise

½ cup 1% small curd cottage
cheese

½ cup plus 2 tablespoons frozen
orange juice concentrate,
thawed

1 teaspoon lemon juice

⅛ teaspoon dry mustard

The jicama (pronounced hi-kah-mah) is a Mexican root vegetable sometimes called the Mexican potato. However, it actually belongs to the legume family, and is also known as the yam bean. Whatever you choose to call it, the jicama is as sweet and crunchy as an apple. Just be sure to remove the fibrous white layer beneath the skin as you peel it. Then toss together this pretty, crunchy salad.

1. Place the carrots, jicama, and raisins in a large salad bowl, and toss to mix. Set aside.

2. Place all of the dressing ingredients in a blender, and process on medium-high speed until well blended, occasionally stopping the blender to scrape the sides.

3. Pour the dressing over the salad, and toss gently until well coated. Cover and chill for at least 1 to 2 hours.

4. To serve, toss the salad once again. Line a large serving dish with the spinach leaves, and spoon the salad over the leaves. (If preferred, line 8 individual salad plates with the spinach, and divide the salad among the plates.) Serve immediately.

NUTRITIONAL DATA (PER SERVING)

Fat: 0 gram   Calories: 118   % Calories from fat: 0%

Belgian Endive With Chicken Salad

Belgian endive, also known as French endive, is perfect in this savory chicken salad. Do try to get Desert Glory cocktail tomatoes for this recipe. These tomatoes are packaged and delivered to the market while still on a section of vine, and have an absolutely wonderful flavor even in the late winter months!

1. Cut away the core from each head of endive. Separate the leaves, rinse with cold running water, and pat dry. Set aside.

2. Place the chicken and onion in a medium-sized bowl. Add salt and pepper to taste, and stir to mix. Pour the dressing over the mixture, and stir until well-blended.

3. Slice the tomatoes in half crosswise. Then cut into quarters, and add to the chicken mixture. Gently toss to mix.

4. Divide the chicken mixture by spooning equal amounts into the broader end of each individual endive leaf. Arrange the stuffed leaves in circles on a serving platter, with the broader ends inward so that the leaves form a sort of flower. Cover and chill for at least 1 hour before garnishing with the parsley and serving.

Yield: *6 servings*

3 heads Belgian endive

3 cups shredded cooked chicken breasts (about 3 skinless, boneless breast halves)

½ cup finely chopped sweet red onion

Salt and freshly ground black pepper to taste

1 cup Mayonnaise-Style Salad Dressing (page 86)

10 Desert Glory cocktail tomatoes or other cherry tomatoes

Fresh parsley sprigs (garnish)

NUTRITIONAL DATA (PER SERVING)

Fat: 2 grams   Calories: 155   % Calories from fat: 12%

Crunchy Chicken and Sprouts Salad

Yield: 6 servings

4 cups bite-sized pieces romaine lettuce

2 cups bite-sized pieces curly endive (chicory)

3 cups shredded cooked chicken breasts (about 3 skinless, boneless breast halves)

2 medium red tomatoes, chopped

4 large scallions, finely chopped (include tops)

1 package (8 ounces) Crunchy Sprouts (pea and bean sprout mixture) or lentil sprouts

DRESSING

½ cup fat-free mayonnaise

2 tablespoons light mayonnaise

¼ cup nonfat buttermilk

¼ cup catsup

⅛ cup bottled chili sauce

3 tablespoons sweet pickle relish

1 teaspoon sugar (optional)

5 hard boiled whole egg whites, diced

This salad is a veritable powerhouse of protein and fiber. The fiber—and some of the protein—comes in part from the pea and bean sprouts, whose peppery flavor helps make this a delicious way to get a high dose of vitamins. Chicken and egg whites lend added protein to this tantalizing dish.

1. Place all of the dressing ingredients, except for the egg whites, in a small bowl, and stir until well mixed. Stir in the egg whites, cover, and chill until needed.

2. Place the lettuce, endive, chicken, tomatoes, and scallions in a large salad bowl, and toss until well mixed.

3. Pour the dressing over the salad, and toss to coat. Add the sprouts, toss lightly, and serve immediately.

NUTRITIONAL DATA (PER SERVING)

Fat: 2.7 grams   Calories: 223   % Calories from fat: 11%

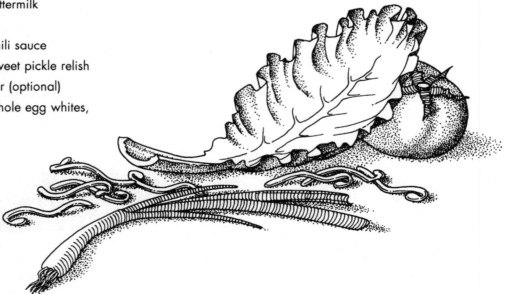

Sweet Potato Slaw

The combination of crunchy raw sweet potatoes, jicama, and turnips is an unusual one, but is oh so delicious when tossed with Caramel-Honey Dressing (page 87).

Yield: *10 servings*

1. Place the unpeeled whole sweet potato in boiling water for approximately 1 minute. Drain and pat dry. Peel and shred the potato.

2. Place the sweet potato, jicama, and turnip in a large salad bowl, and toss to mix. Pour the dressing over the salad, and toss until well coated. Cover and chill for at least 1 hour, tossing once or twice during chilling.

3. Line 10 individual serving dishes with the romaine leaves. Toss the salad once more, and divide it among the serving plates, spooning the salad over the lettuce. Sprinkle with the almonds, and serve immediately.

1 large sweet potato (about 1 pound)

1 cup shredded jicama (about 1 medium)

1 cup shredded turnip (about 1 large)

Romaine lettuce leaves (garnish)

1 recipe Caramel-Honey Dressing (page 87)

2 ounces slivered almonds, toasted (below) and chopped

NUTRITIONAL DATA (PER SERVING)

Fat: 2.8 grams   Calories: 120   % Calories from fat: 21%

Toasting and Roasting Nuts and Seeds

Although you may think that you have to avoid nuts and seeds when following a low-fat diet, keep in mind that although high in fat, these foods contain a wealth of nutrients. And, of course, they add great flavor and crunch to a wide range of dishes, from cookies and cakes to casseroles and stir-fries.

The key to using nuts and seeds in a healthful diet is moderation. But how do you cut down on these ingredients without cutting down on taste? By toasting or roasting your seeds and nuts before adding them to your dish! These techniques enhance flavor so much that you'll find that you can use less without losing out on flavor.

To toast nuts or seeds in a hot, dry skillet, preheat a heavy skillet over low to medium heat. Then add the nuts or seeds and cook, stirring constantly, until they become light golden-brown in color. Watch carefully to prevent burning! The rule is that the smaller the nut or seed, the more quickly it will toast.

To roast nuts or seeds in the oven, spread them in a single layer on a rimmed baking sheet, and place the sheet in a preheated 375°F to 400°F oven. Bake, stirring occasionally, for 3 to 10 minutes, or until a light golden-brown. Again, be vigilant! Small seeds, especially, can burn quickly.

After your seeds or nuts have reached the proper color, quickly remove them from the skillet or pan to cool. Use immediately, or store in an airtight container in the refrigerator for several months, or in the freezer for up to a year.

Orange-on-Orange Salad With Chicken Tenderloins

Yield: *4 servings*

1 cup Chicken Stock (page 92) or other fat-free chicken stock, divided

1 medium onion, cut in half crosswise and thinly sliced

1 large clove garlic, minced

1½ pounds boneless skinless chicken breast tenderloins, or 1½ pounds chicken breast cut into 1-inch strips

½ teaspoon grated orange zest

1 orange bell pepper, cut into julienne strips

Salt and freshly ground black pepper to taste

3½ medium sweet navel oranges

6 cups bite-sized pieces romaine lettuce, red leaf lettuce, and curly endive (chicory)

1 large carrot, shredded

1 medium unpeeled cucumber, cut in half lengthwise and thinly sliced

1 recipe Orange Cream Dressing (page 83)

½ cup canned La Choy rice noodles

Sweet orange bell pepper strips add intrigue to this pretty, deliciously textured one-dish meal!

1. Place ⅔ cup of the chicken stock in a large nonstick skillet, and bring to a boil over medium-high heat. Toss in the onion and garlic, and cook until tender.

2. Add the chicken to the skillet. Sprinkle in the orange zest and toss until well blended. Continue to cook uncovered, turning occasionally, for 5 to 10 minutes, or until the chicken begins to brown.

3. Reduce the heat to medium, and add the remaining ⅓ cup of stock and the bell pepper strips to the skillet. Add salt and pepper to taste, and stir to mix. Tossing occasionally, cook until the chicken is cooked through and tender. Remove the skillet from the heat and set aside for approximately 10 minutes, or until the chicken has cooled slightly.

4. While the chicken cools, peel the oranges and cut into bite-sized pieces, removing and discarding the membranes. Place the orange pieces, salad greens, carrot, and cucumber in a large salad bowl, and toss to mix.

5. To serve, divide the salad mixture among 4 individual serving plates, mounding the salad on the plates. Arrange the chicken over the greens, and drizzle each salad with some of the dressing. Sprinkle with the rice noodles, and serve immediately.

NUTRITIONAL DATA (PER SERVING)

Fat: 5.7 grams	Calories: 430	% Calories from fat: 12%

Chilled Tuna With Beans

An unusual blend of ingredients makes this delicious salad both refreshing and robust.

1. Place the beans, onions, and dressing in a medium-sized salad bowl, and toss until well mixed. Cover and chill for 1 hour.

2. Break the tuna into large chunks. Add it to the chilled bean mixture, and toss well, adding salt and pepper to taste.

3. Garnish with the chopped parsley, and serve immediately.

NUTRITIONAL DATA (PER SERVING)

Fat: 1.5 grams   Calories: 174   % Calories from fat: 8%

Quick Dish

Yield: *6 servings*

2 cans (15½ ounces each) Great Northern beans, rinsed and drained

1 sweet red onion, thinly sliced

¾ cup Red Wine Vinaigrette (page 87)

1 can (9 ounces) chunk light tuna packed in water, drained and chilled

Salt and freshly ground pepper to taste

Chopped fresh parsley (garnish)

Italian Pasta Salad

Yield: *8 servings*

1 package (12 ounces) tri-color pasta spirals

8 ounces Mr. Turkey Italian Style Smoked Sausage, chopped

3 Roma tomatoes, chopped

½ cup shredded carrots

½ red bell pepper, chopped

½ green bell pepper, chopped

2 medium scallions, chopped

⅓ cup grated Parmesan cheese

1½ cups Red Wine Vinaigrette (page 87)

This dish is as colorful as it is tasty!

1. Cook the pasta according to package directions. Rinse under cool running water, and drain well. Set aside.

2. Preheat a large skillet over medium heat. Add the sausage, and cook, stirring occasionally, for 5 minutes, or until heated through. Transfer the sausage to paper towels to drain, and set aside to cool.

3. Place the pasta, cooled sausage, vegetables, and cheese in a large bowl, and toss to mix thoroughly. Pour the salad dressing over the mixture, and toss until well blended. Cover and chill for at least 1 hour before serving.

NUTRITIONAL DATA (PER SERVING)

Fat: 4 grams   Calories: 245   % Calories from fat: 15%

Aloha Fruit Salad

Yield: *4 servings*

1 cup sliced fresh strawberries

4 medium kiwi, peeled, halved lengthwise, and cut crosswise into ¼-inch slices

1 cup fresh pineapple chunks or drained canned pineapple chunks

2 teaspoons lemon juice

3 tablespoons sugar, divided

Fresh mint leaves (garnish)

You will love this refreshing salad on a hot summer day. It's a versatile dish that can be served before a meal, with a meal, or as a light desert. For a real treat, accompany it with a bowl of Orange-Coconut Yogurt Dressing (page 85).

1. Place all of the fruits in a medium-sized bowl, and toss gently to mix.

2. Sprinkle the lemon juice and 2 tablespoons of the sugar over the fruit mixture. Toss gently, cover, and chill for 2 to 3 hours.

3. To serve, divide the fruit among 4 individual dessert or salad dishes. Sprinkle the remaining sugar over the top, and garnish with the mint leaves. Serve immediately, accompanying the salad with a bowl of Orange-Coconut Yogurt Dressing, if desired.

NUTRITIONAL DATA (PER SERVING)

Fat: <1 gram   Calories: 111   % Calories from fat: 4%

Tropical Ambrosia Supreme

The expression "to die for" pretty well describes this sensuous dish! To speed preparation, consider using jarred mango, which can now be found in some produce departments. Just be sure to drain it before adding it to the salad.

1. Place the banana slices in a large bowl. Add the lemon juice, and toss to mix.

2. Add all of the remaining fruits, and gently toss until well blended. Set aside.

3. Place the yogurt, juice concentrate, extract, and, if desired, the mint leaves in a small bowl, and stir until well blended. Pour the yogurt mixture over the fruit, and toss gently until well mixed. Cover and chill for at least 1 hour.

4. To serve, toss the salad gently to mix. Top with a sprinkling of the almonds, and serve immediately.

Yield: *8 servings*

2 medium bananas, halved lengthwise, then cut crosswise into ¼-inch slices

2 teaspoons lemon juice

2 cups fresh strawberry halves

2 cups chopped fresh mango

1 cup fresh pineapple tidbits or drained canned pineapple tidbits

4 medium kiwi, peeled, halved lengthwise, and cut crosswise into ¼-inch slices

8 ounces nonfat vanilla yogurt

2 tablespoons frozen orange juice concentrate, thawed

2 teaspoons coconut-flavored extract

2 teaspoons dried mint leaves (optional)

2 ounces slivered almonds, toasted (page 77)

NUTRITIONAL DATA (PER SERVING)

Fat: 4 grams	Calories: 166	% Calories from fat: 21%

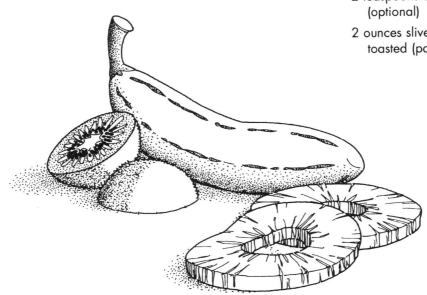

Dressings

Trim Thousand Island Dressing

Yield: *2½ cups*

¾ cup fat-free mayonnaise

3 tablespoons light mayonnaise

½ cup nonfat buttermilk

⅓ cup catsup

¼ cup bottled chili sauce

¼ cup sweet pickle relish

½ cup finely chopped sweet red onion

1 teaspoon sugar (optional)

Freshly ground black pepper to taste

6 hard boiled whole egg whites, diced

This dressing is one of my favorites because it's not only wonderful on any type of salad, but also can be used in all kinds of recipes, such as Bacon, Lettuce, and Tomato Pizza (page 127). If you prefer a thinner mixture, just add a little more buttermilk.

1. Place all of the ingredients, except for the egg whites, in a covered container, and stir until well blended. Stir in the egg whites.

2. Cover the dressing and chill until ready to serve.

NUTRITIONAL DATA (PER TABLESPOON)

Fat: <1 gram   Calories: 15   % Calories from fat: 12%

Variation

To make Fat-Free Thousand Island Dressing, simply eliminate the light mayonnaise and use a full cup of fat-free mayonnaise.

NUTRITIONAL DATA (PER TABLESPOON)

Fat: 0 gram   Calories: 13   % Calories from fat: 0%

Orange Cream Dressing

This creamy dressing is full of flavor and packed with vitamin C!

Yield: *2 cups*

1. Peel the orange. Remove and discard the membranes, and chop the remaining pulp.

2. Place the orange bits and all of the remaining ingredients in a blender, and process on Chop until smooth and creamy, occasionally stopping the blender to scrape the sides.

3. Transfer the dressing to a covered container, and chill until ready to serve.

1 medium sweet navel orange

1 cup 1% small curd cottage cheese

½ cup sweetened orange juice

¼ cup white wine vinegar

1 teaspoon sugar

½ teaspoon grated orange zest

NUTRITIONAL DATA (PER TABLESPOON)
Fat: 0 gram   Calories: 10   % Calories from fat: 0%

Southwestern Sour Cream Dressing

This is a very versatile dressing. If you desire a thicker mixture to use on dishes such as Quick Fiesta Baked Potatoes (page 134), just omit the buttermilk.

Yield: *2 cups*

1. Place all of the ingredients in a blender, and process on medium-high speed until well blended and creamy, occasionally stopping the blender to scrape the sides.

2. Transfer the dressing to a covered container, and chill for at least 1 hour before serving.

2 cups Healthy Sour Cream (page 106)

½ cup nonfat buttermilk

1 teaspoon chili powder

½ teaspoon dry mustard

2 teaspoons sugar

2 tablespoons bottled chili sauce

Dash hot pepper sauce (optional)

Onion salt to taste

NUTRITIONAL DATA (PER TABLESPOON)
Fat: 0 gram   Calories: 15   % Calories from fat: 0%

Hot Southwestern Fat-Free Dressing

Yield: 1½ cups

1 cup water

⅓ cup white wine vinegar

1 can (4 ounces) diced green
  chilies, drained

1 small clove garlic, minced

1 small jalapeño pepper, seeded
  and finely chopped

1 teaspoon chili powder

½ teaspoon ground cumin

1 teaspoon crushed dried cilantro

Dash hot pepper sauce (optional)

This dressing is hot, so if you have extra-sensitive taste buds, try omitting the jalapeño pepper and the pepper sauce.

1. Place all of the ingredients in a blender, and process on medium-high speed until well mixed.

2. Transfer the dressing to a covered container, and chill for at least 1 hour before serving.

NUTRITIONAL DATA (PER TABLESPOON)

Fat: 0 gram   Calories: 2   % Calories from fat: 0%

Honey-Poppy Seed Dressing

Yield: 1½ cups

1 cup fat-free Miracle Whip
  Dressing or other fat-free mayonnaise

⅓ cup white wine vinegar

¼ cup honey

½ teaspoon dry mustard

2 teaspoons poppy seeds,
  toasted (page 77)

½ cup finely chopped red onion
  (optional)

This sweet dressing is wonderful on any green salad, fruit salad, or slaw.

1. Place all of the ingredients, except for the poppy seeds and onion, in a small bowl. Using a whisk, mix until well blended. Stir in the toasted poppy seeds and, if desired, the onion.

2. Transfer the dressing to a covered container, and chill until ready to serve.

NUTRITIONAL DATA (PER TABLESPOON)

Fat: 0 gram   Calories: 17   % Calories from fat: 0%

Tomato-Garlic Vinaigrette

*T*his dressing is excellent over Bacon, Leaf Lettuce, and Tomato Salad *(page 65) or over any mixed green salad.*

1. Place all of the ingredients, except for the salt and pepper, in a blender, and process on medium-high speed until well mixed.

2. Add salt and pepper to taste, and process for 1 additional minute.

3. Transfer the dressing to a covered container, and chill for at least 1 hour before serving.

Yield: *2½ cups*

1 cup water

⅓ cup red wine vinegar

1 can (8 ounces) tomato sauce

1 teaspoon Dijon mustard

1 large clove garlic, minced

1 tablespoon crushed dried
cilantro leaves

½ teaspoon sugar

Salt and freshly ground black
pepper to taste

NUTRITIONAL DATA (PER TABLESPOON)

Fat: 0 gram   Calories: 6   % Calories from fat: 0%

Orange-Coconut Yogurt Dressing

*T*his dressing is tantalizing over fruit salad, and is also a delight over *angel food cake.*

1. Place all of the ingredients in a covered container, and stir until well blended.

2. Cover the dressing and chill for at least 1 hour before serving.

Yield: *1½ cups*

8 ounces nonfat vanilla yogurt

½ cup frozen orange juice
concentrate, thawed

2 tablespoons honey

2 teaspoons grated orange zest

2 teaspoons coconut-flavored
extract

NUTRITIONAL DATA (PER TABLESPOON)

Fat: 0 gram   Calories: 11   % Calories from fat: 0%

Tomato-Bacon Dressing

Yield: *2 cups*

1 cup water

⅓ cup red wine vinegar or cider vinegar

1 can (11⅛ ounces) Campbell's Italian Tomato Soup, undiluted

1 large clove garlic, finely minced

2 tablespoons Oscar Mayer Real Bacon Bits

1 teaspoon sugar

Freshly ground black pepper to taste

The savory combination of tomato and bacon make this intensely flavored dressing a favorite around my house.

1. Place all of the ingredients in a blender, and process on medium-high speed until well mixed.

2. Transfer the dressing to a covered container, and chill for at least 1 hour before serving.

NUTRITIONAL DATA (PER TABLESPOON)

| Fat: 0 gram | Calories: 10 | % Calories from fat: 0% |

Mayonnaise-Style Salad Dressing

Yield: *1 cup*

8 ounces plain nonfat yogurt

2 tablespoons Dijon mustard

1 medium clove garlic, minced

1 tablespoon lemon juice

1 teaspoon dill seed

½ teaspoon paprika

2 teaspoons sugar

Freshly ground black pepper to taste

This recipe makes an all-purpose mayonnaise-type dressing that's delicious on a variety of salads, and makes a great spread for sandwiches, too.

1. Place all of the ingredients in a covered container, and stir until creamy and well blended.

2. Cover the dressing and chill until ready to serve.

NUTRITIONAL DATA (PER TABLESPOON)

| Fat: 0 gram | Calories: 9 | % Calories from fat: 0% |

Red Wine Vinaigrette

This fresh-tasting vinaigrette adds a light, flavorful touch to almost any salad greens, and is absolutely wonderful splashed on luscious vine-ripened summer tomatoes.

1. Place all of the dressing ingredients in a blender, and process on medium-high speed until well blended.

2. Transfer the dressing to a covered container, and chill for at least 1 hour before serving.

Yield: *1 cup*

¾ cup water

¼ cup red wine vinegar

1 teaspoon sugar

1 clove garlic, finely minced

1 teaspoon dried basil

1 tablespoon dried sweet bell pepper flakes

Onion salt to taste (optional)

NUTRITIONAL DATA (PER TABLESPOON)

Fat: 0 gram   Calories: 1   % Calories from fat: 0%

Caramel-Honey Dressing

Caramel and honey always make a tasty combination, and this dressing is no exception! Be sure to try it over fresh or frozen fruit.

1. Place all of the ingredients in a covered container, and stir until well blended.

2. Cover the dressing and chill until ready to serve.

Yield: *2¼ cups*

16 ounces light nonfat Creme Caramel or Caramel Apple yogurt

¼ cup frozen apple juice concentrate, thawed

1 tablespoon plus 1 teaspoon lemon juice

2 tablespoons honey

1 tablespoon plus 1 teaspoon crushed dried parsley flakes

2 teaspoons dried sweet bell pepper flakes

½ cup minced sweet red onion

NUTRITIONAL DATA (PER TABLESPOON)

Fat: 0 gram   Calories: 13   % Calories from fat: 0%

6

Soup's On!

Everybody loves soup, and no store-bought brew, however good, can capture the glorious taste of a soup that's been lovingly prepared in your own kitchen. As an added bonus, homemade soups are unrivaled for their bounty of vitamins, minerals, and fiber. And when properly prepared, they are surprisingly low in fat.

In my family, homemade soup is everybody's favorite comfort food, for I most often cook up an aromatic pot on cloudy and rainy days. As the family's meal planner, I value the versatility of soups, too, as they can be used to tease the appetite at the start of a meal, to stave off hunger between meals, or as a warming, satisfying one-dish meal.

Most good soups begin with a slowly simmered stock, and this chapter shows you how to make several foolproof, intensely flavored soup bases, including ones made from beef, chicken, turkey, fish, and vegetables, as well as an intriguing Oriental stock. Following this, you will discover recipes for such old-time favorites as Potato Cheese Soup, Country Split Pea Soup With Ham, and Chicken Pasta Soup. For a change of pace, try sizzling Onion Soup Suprema, which will delight you with its vivid colors and distinctive Southwestern flair. And don't miss Creole Crab Soup, a richly flavored dish made outrageously delicious with fresh crabmeat.

If it's been a while since you experienced the embracing warmth of a bowl of homemade soup, it's time to take out your soup pot and choose from among the many tantalizing recipes that this chapter has to offer. Low-fat and luscious, each one is guaranteed to dispel the chill of a cold day, to lift the spirits, and to satisfy both the appetite and the soul.

Stocks

Brown Beef Stock

Yield: *8 cups*

4–5 pounds beef bones, cut into chunks

¼ cup cold water

1 large yellow onion, coarsely chopped

2 large cloves garlic, minced

2 medium carrots, coarsely chopped

2 large stalks celery, coarsely chopped (include tops)

16 cups cold water

1 teaspoon dried thyme

1 tablespoon crushed dried parsley

2 bay leaves

6 black peppercorns

Salt to taste

This is a richly flavored, deep brown stock that you will find an invaluable ingredient in many gravies, sauces, and soups. If you want your stock to have a less intense color, simply use unroasted bones.

1. Arrange the bones in a single layer in a shallow roasting pan, and place uncovered in a preheated 450°F oven for 45 minutes, or until brown on all sides. Turn the bones once or twice during roasting.

2. While the bones are roasting, place the ¼ cup water in a large, heavy soup pot, and place over medium heat. When the water is hot, add the onions, garlic, carrots, and celery, and sauté, stirring often, for about 8 minutes, or until the vegetables are tender.

3. Drain the roasted bones of all fat, and add them to the pot, along with the 16 cups of water. Increase the heat to medium to medium-high, and bring the water to a slow boil.

4. Reduce the heat just to the point of a gentle simmer. Skim any residue that may rise to the surface, and stir in the seasoning.

5. Partially cover the pot, and continue to simmer for 4 hours, stirring the soup occasionally and adding cold water as necessary.

6. Remove the bones, and cool the stock until lukewarm. Strain through a double layer of cheesecloth or a fine-mesh sieve, and chill until the fat rises to the top. Skim off and discard the fat, and, if desired, clarify the stock. Use immediately, or store in the refrigerator or freezer until needed. (For details on cooling, straining, defatting, clarifying, and storing, see the inset on page 91.)

NUTRITIONAL DATA (PER 1-CUP SERVING)

| Fat: 0 gram | Calories: 20 | % Calories from fat: 0% |

Making the Perfect Stock

Stock—also referred to as broth or bouillon—is the savory, rich liquid made by simmering poultry, meat, fish, bones, or vegetables, along with herbs and spices, in water. The flavorful result can be used as a base for soups, stews, sauces, and gravies, or can replace butter and oil when sautéing vegetables and other ingredients. Although bouillon cubes and canned broths allow you the same versatility—and can be used with good results in any of the recipes in this chapter—absolutely nothing compares to homemade stock. I try to always have some in my freezer for ready use.

Fortunately, it's easy to make a good stock—one that's both rich in flavor and low in fat. Just start with the freshest ingredients available, and follow these simple guidelines:

☐ When beginning your preparation, always use cold water to cover your ingredients. Then bring the water to a boil *slowly* over medium to medium-high heat.

☐ As the stock simmers, residue—foam or scum—will rise to the top. Carefully skim off and discard all such residue *before* adding any seasoning.

☐ Once the seasoning has been added, slowly simmer the stock—with the cover partially ajar—for the remainder of the cooking time. This will prevent the liquid from evaporating too quickly, while still allowing the steam to escape.

☐ Do not cool your stock too slowly, as it can spoil easily. Instead, fill the sink with cold water that comes two to three inches below the top of your uncovered pot. Place the soup pot in the water, adding ice cubes until the water reaches just below the rim of the pot. Keep the pot in the water until the stock is lukewarm.

☐ To strain your stock, slowly pour the lukewarm stock through a colander that has been lined with a double thickness of dampened cheesecloth or a fine-mesh sieve. This will trap any remaining particles of vegetables or meat.

☐ To defat your stock, place the lukewarm liquid in the refrigerator until the fat has hardened and risen to the surface. Then simply spoon off and discard the congealed fat. To remove any remaining fat, lay a paper towel over the surface of the stock and lift it off, taking the fat with it.

☐ If you wish to clarify your stock for use in clear soups or gravies, simply stir together ¼ cup water, 1 crushed egg shell, and 1 egg white for every 4 cups of defatted stock. (Your stock *must* be defatted before it's clarified.) Stir the mixture into the stock, and reheat to a slow simmer. Cook uncovered for 10 minutes. Then remove the pot from the heat and, using a large spoon, skim the egg white and other residue from the surface of the liquid. Strain once more through a cheesecloth-lined colander, and refrigerate or freeze for future use.

Your homemade stock will keep in your refrigerator for up to four days. To store your stock for up to six months, pour it into freezer containers and freeze until needed. If you find that you often need small amounts of stock, freeze it in ice cube trays and then transfer the frozen cubes to freezer bags. For optimum flavor, always be sure to bring the frozen stock to a boil before using it in your recipes.

Chicken Stock

Yield: *6 cups*

3–4 pounds skinless chicken pieces (I prefer skinless chicken breasts with ribs attached)

8 cups cold water

1 large yellow onion, coarsely chopped

1 large stalk celery, coarsely chopped (include tops)

1 large carrot, coarsely chopped

1 large clove garlic, sliced (optional)

1 teaspoon crushed dried basil leaves

1 teaspoon poultry seasoning

1 tablespoon crushed dried parsley

2 small bay leaves

5 black peppercorns

Salt to taste

This stock is exactly what you need to poach those chicken breasts that are used in so many culinary masterpieces! In addition, the cooked meat that you remove from the pot may be used in a variety of dishes, including Belgian Endive With Chicken Salad (page 75) and Chicken Salad in Tomato Cups (page 73). If you desire a darker stock, use chicken bones as well as chicken meat.

1. Place all of the ingredients except for the seasoning in a large, heavy soup pot, and bring to a slow boil over medium to medium-high heat.

2. Skim any residue that may rise to the surface. Reduce the heat just to the point of a gentle simmer, and stir in the seasoning.

3. Partially cover the pot, and simmer for 2 to 2½ hours, or until the chicken meat is tender. Remove the chicken pieces from the pot, and refrigerate for use in other recipes.

4. Cool the stock until lukewarm, strain through a double layer of cheesecloth or a fine-mesh sieve, and chill until the fat rises to the top. Skim off and discard the fat, and, if desired, clarify the stock. Use immediately, or store in the refrigerator or freezer until needed. (For details on cooling, straining, defatting, clarifying, and storing, see the inset on page 91.)

NUTRITIONAL DATA (PER 1-CUP SERVING)

Fat: 0 gram   Calories: 20   % Calories from fat: 0%

NUTRITIONAL DATA (PER 3 OUNCES CHICKEN MEAT)

Fat: 3 grams   Calories: 144   % Calories from fat: 18%

Turkey Stock

This stock recipe is similar to the recipe for Chicken Stock found on page 92. The main difference is that this one uses the carcass of the bird instead of the meat. Of course, turkey meat also makes a flavorful broth, but turkey bones make a more richly colored stock.

1. Break up the carcass, and place it in a large, heavy soup pot. Add all of the remaining ingredients except for the seasoning and bring to a slow boil over medium to medium-high heat.

2. Skim any residue that may rise to the surface. Reduce the heat just to the point of a gentle simmer, and stir in the seasoning.

3. Partially cover the pot, and simmer for 2 to 2½ hours. Remove and discard the carcass.

4. Cool the stock until lukewarm, strain through a double layer of cheesecloth or a fine-mesh sieve, and chill until the fat rises to the top. Skim off and discard the fat, and, if desired, clarify the stock. Use immediately, or store in the refrigerator or freezer until needed. (For details on cooling, straining, defatting, clarifying, and storing, see the inset on page 91.)

Yield: *8 cups*

1 turkey carcass

10 cups cold water

2 large carrots, coarsely chopped

2 medium stalks celery, coarsely chopped (include tops)

1 large onion, chopped

1 large clove garlic, minced

1 large bay leaf

1 teaspoon poultry seasoning

1 tablespoon crushed dried parsley

5 black peppercorns

Salt to taste

NUTRITIONAL DATA (PER 1-CUP SERVING)

Fat: 0 gram   Calories: 20   % Calories from fat: 0%

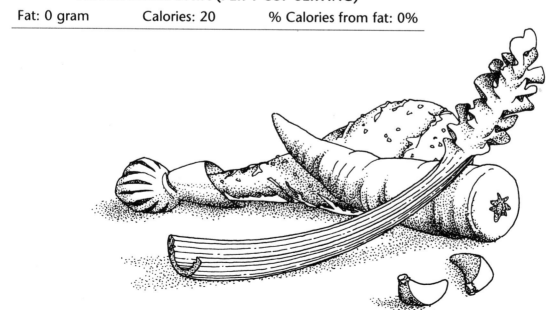

Oriental Stock

Yield: *9 cups*

2–3 pounds chicken bones

10 cups cold water

2 cups shredded Chinese cabbage

2 slices (¼ inch each) ginger root

1 large clove garlic, minced

1 teaspoon poultry seasoning

Salt to taste

This stock is perfect to use in place of oil when you sauté ingredients for stir-fries.

1. Place all of the ingredients except for the poultry seasoning and salt in a large, heavy soup pot, and bring to a slow boil over medium to medium-high heat.

2. Skim any residue that may rise to the surface. Reduce the heat just to the point of a gentle simmer, and stir in the seasoning.

3. Partially cover the pot, and simmer for 1½ hours. Remove and discard the chicken bones.

4. Cool the stock until lukewarm, strain through a double layer of cheesecloth or a fine-mesh sieve, and chill until the fat rises to the top. Skim off and discard the fat, and, if desired, clarify the stock. Use immediately, or store in the refrigerator or freezer until needed. (For details on cooling, straining, defatting, clarifying, and storing, see the inset on page 91.)

NUTRITIONAL DATA (PER 1-CUP SERVING)

Fat: 0 gram	Calories: 3	% Calories from fat: 0%

Fish Stock

This stock is excellent for poaching all types of fish, and makes a great base for seafood sauces, as well.

1. Place all of the ingredients except for the seasonings in a large, heavy soup pot, and bring to a slow boil over medium to medium-high heat.

2. Skim any residue that may rise to the surface. Reduce the heat just to the point of a gentle simmer, and stir in the seasoning.

3. Partially cover the pot, and simmer for 45 minutes to an hour. Remove and discard the fish parts.

4. Cool the stock until lukewarm, strain through a double layer of cheesecloth or a fine-mesh sieve, and cool. While straining, do not press the fish parts, as this will cloud the stock. (For details, see the inset on page 91.) As fish has very little fat, rather than chilling the stock to defat it, simply pull paper towel strips through the surface of the stock to absorb and remove what little fat there may be. Use immediately, or store in the refrigerator or freezer until needed.

Yield: *8 cups*

8 cups cold water

2 pounds fish bones, heads, and tails (halibut or haddock are my favorite)

1 medium onion, thinly sliced

1 clove garlic, minced

Juice of 1 medium lemon (optional)

1 teaspoon dried thyme

1 bay leaf

4 black peppercorns

Salt to taste

NUTRITIONAL DATA (PER 1-CUP SERVING)

Fat: 0 gram   Calories: 7   % Calories from fat: 0%

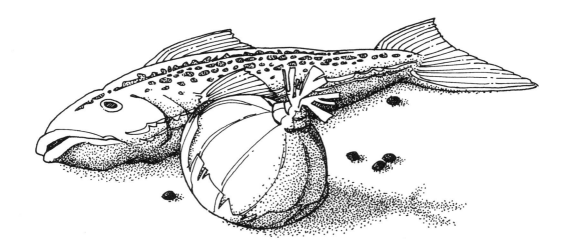

Vegetable Stock

Yield: *8 cups*

8 cups cold water

2 large yellow onions, thinly sliced

2 large cloves garlic, minced

2 cups coarsely chopped carrots (about 3 medium)

2 large stalks celery, coarsely chopped (include tops)

2 cups coarsely chopped cabbage (optional)

4 medium tomatoes, coarsely chopped

1 teaspoon dried thyme

2 bay leaves

5 black peppercorns

1 tablespoon crushed dried parsley

Salt to taste

This is the perfect stock to use as a base for vegetable soups and sauces, or when sautéing vegetables for use in recipes.

1. Place all of the ingredients except for the seasonings in a large, heavy soup pot, and bring to a slow boil over medium to medium-high heat.

2. Skim any residue that may rise to the surface. Reduce the heat just to the point of a gentle simmer, and stir in the seasoning.

3. Partially cover the pot, and simmer for 1 hour. During cooking, check the water level occasionally, and add more cold water if necessary to maintain the original level throughout the cooking time.

4. Cool the stock until lukewarm, and strain through a double layer of cheesecloth or a fine-mesh strainer. (Defatting isn't necessary.) For a thicker stock, leave the cooled stock unstrained, pour it into a blender, and process into a purée, adding additional water, if necessary. Use immediately, or store in the refrigerator or freezer until needed. (For details on cooling, straining, and storing, see the inset on page 91.)

NUTRITIONAL DATA (PER 1-CUP SERVING)

Fat: 0 gram   Calories: 35   % Calories from fat: 0%

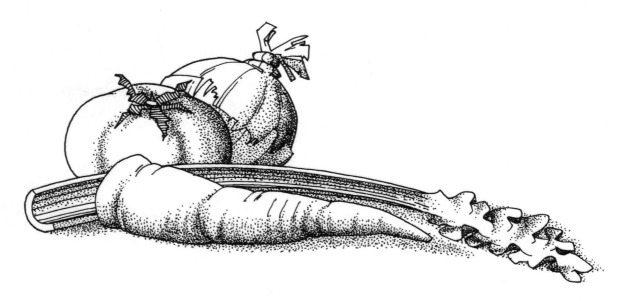

Soups

Turkey-Tomato Vegetable Soup

My children—who are now grown—tell me that whenever they smell this soup cooking, warm "fuzzy" memories of their childhood come flooding back. Brew up a pot and start a few memories of your own!

1. Place the stock in a large soup pot, and bring to a boil over medium-high heat. Boil for 1 minute, and reduce the heat to medium.

2. Add the turkey, onions, garlic, and celery to the pot, and stir to mix. Cover and simmer over medium heat for 15 minutes.

3. Stir in the potatoes, carrots, and seasonings. Cover and simmer for 30 additional minutes.

4. Stir in the tomatoes and peas, cover, and simmer for 15 to 30 additional minutes, or until the vegetables are tender and the flavors are well blended. Taste, adding additional onion salt, if desired. Remove and discard the bay leaf, and serve hot.

NUTRITIONAL DATA (PER SERVING)

Fat: 1.5 grams   Calories: 184   % Calories from fat: 7%

Yield: *12 servings*

8 cups Turkey Stock (page 93), Chicken Stock (page 92), or other fat-free stock

1 pound cooked turkey breast, cut into bite-sized chunks (about 2 cups)

1 large onion, coarsely chopped

1 large clove garlic, minced

2 medium stalks celery, coarsely chopped (include tops)

4 medium baking potatoes, peeled and cut into ¾-inch cubes

2 large carrots, sliced

1 teaspoon poultry seasoning

1 teaspoon crushed dried thyme

2 teaspoons crushed dried basil

1 large bay leaf

8 black peppercorns

Onion salt to taste

1 can (28 ounces) diced tomatoes in juice, undrained

1⅔ cups drained canned or frozen green peas

Chilled Tomato Soup

Yield: *4 servings*

1½ cups nonfat buttermilk

1 can (14½ ounces) diced
   tomatoes flavored with garlic,
   oregano, and basil

1 can (6 ounces) tomato paste

¾ cup water

2 teaspoons lemon juice

2 teaspoons sugar

1 small onion, coarsely chopped

2 teaspoons dried crushed basil

Garlic salt and freshly ground
   black pepper to taste

¼ cup freshly grated Parmesan
   cheese (optional)

*As delicious as this soup is chilled, it is also wonderful when heated
and served hot. For a special treat, accompany the soup with Basil-
Garlic Cheese Bread (page 99).*

1. Place all of the ingredients except for the Parmesan cheese in a
blender, and process on medium-high speed for 1 to 2 minutes, or
until smooth and well blended.

2. Detach the covered blender container from the blender's base, and
place it in the refrigerator. Chill for at least 1 hour, or until the soup is
cold.

3. Serve cold, topping each bowlful with a tablespoon of cheese, if
desired. If you wish to serve the soup hot, just pour the mixture into
a medium-sized saucepan, and cook over medium heat just until heated through. Take care not to let the soup come to a boil. Serve hot,
topped with the cheese.

NUTRITIONAL DATA (PER SERVING)

Fat: 1.6 grams   Calories: 130   % Calories from fat: 11%

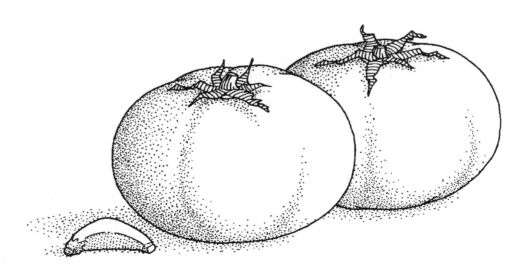

Soup and Bread—The Perfect Companions

Although most often served as an appetizer, soups make light but satisfying entrées when accompanied by a crisp salad or a loaf of crusty bread.

The following bread is an especially delightful companion for your favorite soup. Hot and savory, this is a loaf you'll serve time and time again.

Basil-Garlic Cheese Bread

1. Slice the bread in half lengthwise and place the halves, cut sides up, on a small pan.

2. Spray the cut surfaces of each loaf half twice with the butter spray. Rub the garlic halves over the sprayed surfaces, and sprinkle with the basil. Lightly spray the surfaces once more, making sure to spray at a distance from the bread to avoid blowing the basil off the bread.

3. Sprinkle the Parmesan cheese over the basil, and place the bread under a preheated broiler for 2 to 3 minutes, or until the top is lightly browned. Watch closely, as it can burn quickly! Slice each half into 8 pieces, and serve hot.

Quick Dish

Yield: *16 servings*

1 large (1 pound) loaf French bread

I Can't Believe It's Not Butter spray

1 large clove garlic, halved

1 tablespoon crumbled dried basil

2 tablespoons freshly grated Parmesan cheese

NUTRITIONAL FACTS (PER PIECE)

Fat: 1 gram   Calories: 73   % Calories from fat: 12%

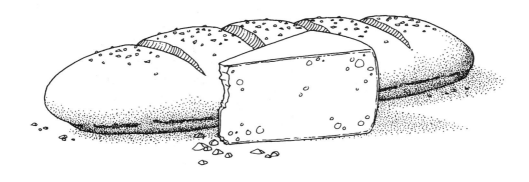

Chicken Pasta Soup

Yield: *10 servings*

12 cups Chicken Stock (page 92) or other fat-free stock

4 cups diced or shredded cooked chicken breast (about 2½ pounds)

1 large onion, chopped

1 large clove garlic, minced

2 medium stalks celery, chopped (include tops)

1 teaspoon poultry seasoning

1 teaspoon dried thyme

2 teaspoons dried basil

1 teaspoon dried oregano

½ teaspoon dried sage

1 bay leaf

8 black peppercorns

2 medium carrots, shredded

7 ounces tiny pasta shells

Garlic salt and freshly ground black pepper to taste

This is a great soup to make when you have leftover cooked chicken on hand. If you also have homemade stock in your freezer, your soup will be ready in no time flat!

1. Place the stock in a large soup pot, and bring to a slow boil over medium-high heat.

2. Reduce the heat just to the point of a gentle simmer, and add the chicken, onion, garlic, celery, and seasonings. Cover and simmer for 30 minutes.

3. Increase the heat to medium-high, and bring the soup to a low boil. Stir in the carrots and pasta, and continue to cook uncovered for 15 to 20 minutes, or until the pasta is tender but not soft.

4. Remove the soup from the heat, and remove and discard the bay leaf. Add the garlic salt and pepper to taste, and allow the soup to sit, covered, for 10 minutes so that the pasta absorbs the flavors of the other ingredients. Serve hot.

NUTRITIONAL DATA (PER SERVING)

Fat: 2 grams	Calories: 197	% Calories from fat: 9%

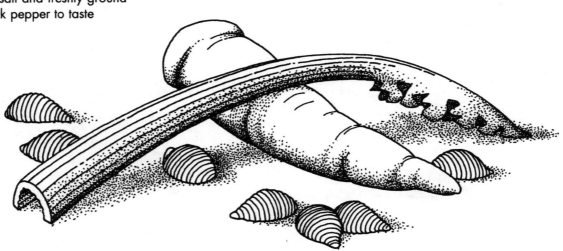

Potato Cheese Soup

This recipe makes a lovely soup—thick and of a soft golden color, with the orange of the carrots and the freckles of parsley and bacon peeking through. It's an all-time favorite around my house!

1. Place the stock in a large pot, and bring to a boil over medium-high heat.

2. Reduce the heat to just the point of a simmer, and add the potatoes, carrots, onion, celery, and parsley. Cover and cook for 15 minutes, or until the potatoes are tender. Then mash the potatoes slightly by pressing them against the pan with a large spoon or fork.

3. While the vegetables are cooking, place 3 tablespoons of the bacon and all of the cheese in a small bowl, and stir to combine. Set aside. In another small bowl, combine the remaining tablespoon of bacon with the scallions. Set aside.

4. Place the cornstarch and skim milk in a small bowl, and mix with a whisk until smooth. Stir the mixture into the soup.

5. Stir the evaporated skim milk into the soup. Add salt and pepper to taste, and stir to blend well. Continue to stir and cook over medium to medium-low heat until the soup becomes thick and bubbly.

6. After the soup has been bubbling for 1 minute, gradually stir in the cheese and bacon mixture. Continue to cook, stirring constantly, until the cheese has melted.

7. Serve hot, topping each bowlful with a sprinkling of the scallion and bacon mixture.

NUTRITIONAL DATA (PER SERVING)

Fat: 2.5 grams   Calories: 200   % Calories from fat: 11%

Quick Dish

Yield: 8 servings

5 cups Chicken Stock (page 92) or other fat-free stock

5 medium all purpose potatoes, peeled and diced

2 medium carrots, finely shredded

1 large onion, finely chopped

2 medium stalks celery, finely chopped

1 tablespoon crushed dried parsley

¼ cup Oscar Mayer Real Bacon Bits, divided

¾ cup shredded reduced-fat sharp Cheddar cheese

¾ cup shredded fat-free Cheddar cheese

4 small scallions, finely chopped (include tops)

¼ cup cornstarch

½ cup skim milk

1 can (12 ounces) evaporated skim milk

Salt and freshly ground black pepper to taste

Country Split Pea Soup With Ham

Quick Dish

Yield: *8 servings*

10 cups Vegetable Stock (page 96), Chicken Stock (page 92), or other fat-free stock, divided

2 medium yellow onions, finely chopped

1 large clove garlic, minced

½ cup diced red bell pepper

2 large carrots, shredded

1 large stalk celery, thinly sliced (include tops)

1 pound dried green split peas, sorted, rinsed, and drained

3 medium potatoes, peeled and diced

1 pound lean thick-sliced smoked ham, cut into ½-inch pieces

1 large bay leaf

1 teaspoon dried thyme

⅛ teaspoon ground cloves

Salt and freshly ground black pepper to taste

1 cup chopped scallions (include tops) (about 4 medium)

This is a deliciously full-flavored, hearty soup that makes a wonderful meal accompanied by a crisp green salad and a warm crusty loaf of bread. Although I prefer using smoked ham for this soup, you may substitute honey-baked ham instead. Just be aware that this will give you a sweeter soup.

1. Place 1 cup of the stock in a large soup pot, and bring to a boil over medium-high heat.

2. Reduce the heat to medium, and add the onions, garlic, bell pepper, carrots, and celery. Cook uncovered for about 15 minutes, or until the vegetables become tender, stirring occasionally.

3. Gradually stir in the remaining 9 cups of stock. Increase the heat to medium-high, and bring the soup to a boil. Reduce the heat just to the point of a gentle simmer, and add the split peas, potatoes, ham, and seasonings, stirring to mix.

4. Partially cover the pot, and continue to simmer for 1 hour to an hour and 15 minutes, or until the peas are very soft and the soup is quite thick. Stir often to prevent the soup from sticking to the pot.

5. Remove the pot from the heat. Remove and discard the bay leaf, and stir the soup thoroughly. Serve hot, garnishing each bowlful with a sprinkling of scallions.

NUTRITIONAL DATA (PER SERVING)

Fat: 2 grams	Calories: 295	% Calories from fat: 6%

Onion Soup Suprema

The Mexican flair of this tantalizing soup teases the taste buds and provides a refreshing change of pace from the usual onion soup. For added South-of-the-Border flavor, replace the fat-free croutons with fat-free tortilla chips.

1. Place 2 cups of the stock in a large soup pot, and bring to a boil over medium-high heat.

2. Reduce the heat to medium, and add the onions and garlic to the pot. Cook uncovered for 15 to 20 minutes, or until the onions are tender, stirring frequently.

3. Remove the soup from the heat and gradually stir in the remaining 4 cups of stock and the tomato juice, picante sauce, and chilies. Add pepper to taste.

4. Return the soup to the stove, and bring to a boil over high heat. Reduce the heat just to the point of a gentle simmer, and cook uncovered for 30 to 40 minutes.

5. Serve the soup hot, topping each bowlful with 6 croutons and a sprinkling of shredded cheese.

Yield: *6 servings*

6 cups Vegetable Stock (page 96), Beef Stock (page 90), or other fat-free stock, divided

6 medium yellow onions, cut into thin slivers

2 large cloves garlic, minced

4 cups tomato juice

1 cup chunky picante sauce

2 cans (4 ounces each) peeled diced green chilies

Freshly ground black pepper to taste

36 garlic-onion fat-free croutons

1 cup finely shredded reduced-fat Monterey Jack or Cheddar cheese

---

NUTRITIONAL DATA (PER SERVING)

Fat: 4 grams   Calories: 206   % Calories from fat: 17%

Creole Crab Soup

Yield: 6 servings

7 cups Fish Stock (page 95), Vegetable Stock (page 96), Chicken Stock (page 92), or other fat-free stock, divided

1 medium yellow onion, chopped

1 large clove garlic, minced

1 large carrot, shredded

1 large stalk celery, chopped (include the tops)

½ cup chopped green bell pepper

2 cans (14½ ounces each) cut or chopped peeled tomatoes, undrained

1 large bay leaf

1 teaspoon crushed dried oregano

¼ teaspoon freshly ground black pepper

1 pound fresh lump crabmeat, picked over

This is a richly flavored, colorful soup with a mellow seafood taste. If you prefer to use cooked crabmeat rather than fresh, simmer the soup for only 5 minutes after adding the crabmeat.

1. Place 1 cup of the stock in a large soup pot, and bring to a boil over medium-high heat.

2. Reduce the heat to medium, and add the onion, garlic, carrot, celery, and bell pepper to the pot. Cook uncovered for 10 to 15 minutes, or until the vegetables are tender, stirring occasionally.

3. Add the remaining 6 cups of stock and the tomatoes and seasoning to the pot. Increase the heat to high, and bring to a low boil, stirring to blend thoroughly.

4. Reduce the heat just to the point of a gentle simmer, and cook uncovered for 30 minutes, stirring occasionally.

5. Gently stir in the crabmeat, and simmer gently for 10 additional minutes, or until heated through. Do not stir during cooking, as the crabmeat may break into pieces. Serve hot.

NUTRITIONAL DATA (PER SERVING)

Fat: 1 gram   Calories: 160   % Calories from fat: 6%

7
Finishing Touches—
Sauces, Toppings, and Relishes

What's a fast way to turn a ho-hum dish into an instant hit? The answer is simple. Just add a flavorful sauce, topping, or relish. These culinary marvels can turn the simplest, blandest entrée, side dish, or dessert into a delectable creation.

This chapter presents a galaxy of low-fat, absolutely luscious sauces, toppings, and relishes, each of which is designed to add spark and visual appeal to a wide variety of dishes. The collection begins with savory sauces and toppings. Looking for a topping for baked potatoes? Yogurt-Dill Sauce is the perfect choice—creamy and full of flavor. Smoky Honey Barbecue Sauce is delicious on any grilled meat, or as an ingredient in baked beans. And Terrific Tomato-Basil Salsa adds color and spice to just about anything, from salads to casseroles.

If your favorite low-fat dessert needs just a little something to make it truly special, you'll be delighted by a bonanza of sweetly tempting toppings. And from Creamy Vanilla Cheese Topping to Mint Chocolate Creme Sauce, all are so deliciously decadent that nobody would guess they're virtually fat-free.

Relishes have long been valued for their ability to add a splash of color and a tang of flavor to so many dishes. In this tradition, I present colorful Piquant Mango-Pineapple-Orange Relish, Pickled Carrots, and Mint Onion Relish—condiments that can turn any dish into a main event.

So the next time you want to add zip to an otherwise boring dish—or to make a good meal even better—just flip through the following pages and pick a sauce that's sure to please. No meal need ever be dull again!

Savory Sauces & Toppings

Healthy Sour Cream

Yield: *2 cups*

2 cups 1% small curd cottage cheese

2 tablespoons lemon juice

2 tablespoons plain nonfat yogurt (optional)

Sour cream-flavored sprinkles to taste

This is a delicious no-fat topping for baked potatoes and other vegetables, as well as an endlessly versatile ingredient for sauces, dressings, and many other dishes.

1. Place all of the ingredients in a blender, and process on medium-high speed until smooth.

2. Transfer the mixture to a small container, cover tightly, and chill until ready to serve. Store in the refrigerator for up to 1 week.

NUTRITIONAL DATA (PER 1-TABLESPOON SERVING)
Fat: 0 gram   Calories: 12   % Calories from fat: 0%

Parmesan Cheese Topping

Yield: *1¼ cups*

1 cup 1% creamed or small curd cottage cheese

¼ cup plain nonfat yogurt

½ teaspoon crushed dried basil

2 tablespoons grated Parmesan cheese

A wonderful topping for soups, baked potatoes, and salad greens, this flavorful sauce may also be stirred into hot pasta directly before serving. If you prefer, you may substitute dill leaves or seeds for the basil.

1. Place all of the ingredients except for the Parmesan cheese in a blender, and process on medium-high speed until smooth and creamy.

2. Transfer the mixture to a small serving dish, and stir in the Parmesan, blending thoroughly. Serve immediately, or cover tightly and chill until ready to serve. Store in the refrigerator for up to 1 week.

NUTRITIONAL DATA (PER 1-TABLESPOON SERVING)
Fat: <1 gram   Calories: 13   % Calories from fat: 18%

Yogurt-Dill Sauce

Dill is a delicious seasoning for seafood, broiled meats and poultry, sandwich spreads, salads, slaws, stuffings, any vegetable dish, and, of course the supreme pickle, making this creamy dill sauce the perfect accompaniment for a variety of dishes.

1. Place all of the ingredients in a small container, and gently stir until well blended.

2. Cover the sauce and chill for at least 1 hour before serving. Store in the refrigerator for up to 1 week.

Yield: *1½ cups*

12 ounces plain nonfat yogurt

2 teaspoons Dijon mustard

2 tablespoons chopped fresh dill, or 2 teaspoons dried dill

1 teaspoon sugar (optional)

NUTRITIONAL DATA (PER 1-TABLESPOON SERVING)
Fat: 0 gram   Calories: 6   % Calories from fat: 0%

My All-Purpose Italian Tomato Sauce

Whenever I use this sauce in a dish, my friends ask for the recipe. With a cooked-all-day taste, this is fabulous in casseroles, as well as on rice and pasta dishes. Finally, I'm divulging my recipe—and my secret that it's fast and easy to make. Of course, you should feel free to keep the secret from your own friends, if you want to.

1. Place the pasta sauce in a large pot with a lid. Add all of the remaining ingredients, and stir to blend.

2. Place the pot over medium heat, and bring to a slow simmer. Reduce the heat to medium-low or low, cover, and gently simmer for 20 to 30 minutes, stirring occasionally.

3. Remove the pot from the heat, and stir the sauce thoroughly. Cover and let sit for 5 to 10 minutes before serving over pasta or rice. If using the sauce in a casserole, allow it to cool before adding it to other casserole ingredients.

Yield: *7½ cups*

2 jars (30 ounces each) Ragu Chunky Tomatoes, Garlic, and Onions Pasta Sauce

½ cup chopped green bell pepper

1 large clove garlic, finely minced

1 tablespoon crushed dried basil

2 teaspoons crushed dried oregano

2 teaspoons fennel seed (optional)

2 teaspoons sugar

2 heaping tablespoons dehydrated onion flakes

NUTRITIONAL DATA (PER ½-CUP SERVING)
Fat: 3.7 grams   Calories: 125   % Calories from fat: 27%

Smoky Honey Barbecue Sauce

Yield: *2½ cups*

½ cup white vinegar

1 can (6 ounces) tomato paste

1 cup catsup

¼ cup water

½ cup honey

2 tablespoons liquid smoke

2 tablespoons Worcestershire sauce

⅓ cup brown sugar, packed

¼ cup dehydrated onion flakes

1 large clove garlic, finely minced

2 teaspoons dry mustard

1 tablespoon paprika

½ teaspoon freshly ground black pepper

Salt to taste

*T*his recipe makes a thick sweet and savory sauce that is excellent with any meat, with chicken, or as an ingredient in recipes such as *Savory Pinto Bean Bake (page 158).*

1. Place all of the ingredients in a blender, and process on high speed until smooth and well mixed, scraping the sides occasionally.

2. Pour the mixture into a medium-sized saucepan, and bring to a slow boil over medium heat. Reduce the heat to low, just to the point of a slow simmer; cover; and cook for 10 to 15 minutes, stirring occasionally.

3. Use immediately, or transfer to a covered container and chill until ready to use. Store in the refrigerator for up to 2 to 3 weeks.

NUTRITIONAL DATA (PER 1-TABLESPOON SERVING)

Fat: 0 gram   Calories: 33   % Calories from fat: 0%

Terrific Tomato-Basil Salsa

These days, salsas are popular all over the United States, as are so many dishes of Mexican origin. This salsa is both wonderfully flavorful and a snap to make. And, like most salsas, it is highly versatile, and can be used not only as a delicious, colorful condiment, but also as an ingredient in chilies, soups, and casseroles, as well as any sauce that needs a little zip.

1. Place all of the ingredients except for the salt and pepper in a medium bowl, and stir gently until blended. Season to taste with the salt and pepper.

2. Cover tightly, and let stand at room temperature for at least 30 minutes, or until the flavors are well blended. Serve immediately, or store in the refrigerator for up to 2 weeks.

Yield: *3 cups*

2 large unpeeled red tomatoes, chopped or diced

1 can (4 ounces) diced green chilies, rinsed and drained

1 large onion, finely chopped

1 medium clove garlic, minced

2 tablespoons finely minced fresh sweet basil

2 tablespoons finely minced fresh cilantro

Juice of 1 medium lemon or lime (about 3 tablespoons)

2 teaspoons sugar (optional)

1–2 teaspoons chili powder (optional)

Salt and freshly ground black pepper to taste

NUTRITIONAL DATA (PER ¼-CUP SERVING)

Fat: 0 gram   Calories: 14   % Calories from fat: 0

Meat and Poultry Orange Glaze Sauce

Yield: 1½ cups

1 cup brown sugar, not packed

½ teaspoon grated orange zest

½ teaspoon ground cinnamon

½ teaspoon dry mustard

⅛ teaspoon ground cloves (optional)

1 cup water

¼ cup frozen orange juice concentrate, thawed

1 tablespoon plus 1 teaspoon cornstarch

This savory glazing sauce may be used to top any meat or poultry, which can then be baked in the oven or cooked on the stovetop. I use it in my Ham and Yam Bake (page 139) with such tasty results that there are never any leftovers!

1. Place the brown sugar, orange zest, cinnamon, mustard, and cloves in a small bowl, and stir until well blended. Set aside.

2. Place the water, juice concentrate, and cornstarch in a small bowl, and whisk until well blended. Pour the mixture into a small saucepan, and place over medium to medium-high heat. Add the brown sugar mixture and, stirring, bring to a slow simmer.

3. Reduce the heat to medium-low and cook, stirring constantly, for 5 to 10 minutes, or until the sauce begins to thicken. Use immediately, or store in a covered container in the refrigerator for up to 1 week.

NUTRITIONAL DATA (PER 1-TABLESPOON SERVING)

Fat: 0 gram   Calories: 34   % Calories from fat: 0%

Presto Pizza Sauce

Yield: 2 cups

1 can (8 ounces) tomato sauce

1 can (6 ounces) tomato paste

6 ounces water

1 medium clove garlic, minced

2 teaspoons crushed dried sweet basil

1 teaspoon crushed dried oregano

¼ teaspoon crushed dried marjoram

1 teaspoon sugar

This is a delicious yet quick-to-make sauce. Just keep the ingredients on hand, and you'll be able to bake savory homemade pizza at a moment's notice.

1. Place all of the ingredients in a small saucepan, and stir to mix. Bring to a simmer over medium heat, cover, and cook for 5 to 10 minutes, stirring occasionally.

2. Remove the pot from the heat, and allow the sauce to cool to room temperature before using.

NUTRITIONAL DATA (PER ½-CUP SERVING)

Fat: 0 gram   Calories: 50   % Calories from fat: 0%

Sweet Sauces & Toppings

Strawberry Sauce

Here is a quick, simple, and delicious sauce to drizzle over frozen yogurt, angel food cake, fruit, pancakes, or any number of other dishes.

1. Trim, rinse, and quarter the strawberries, and place them in a medium-sized pot. Stir in the sugar and lemon zest, and bring to a boil over medium to medium-high heat, stirring occasionally.

2. Reduce the heat to medium-low, just to the point of a gentle simmer, and cook uncovered for about 5 minutes, or until slightly thickened. Remove the pot from the heat, and allow to cool to room temperature.

3. Transfer the sauce to a covered container, and chill for several hours before serving. Store in the refrigerator for up to 1 week.

Yield: 1½ cups

1 quart fresh strawberries

½ cup sugar

1 teaspoon grated lemon zest

NUTRITIONAL DATA (PER 1-TABLESPOON SERVING)

Fat: 0 gram	Calories: 24	% Calories from fat: 0%

Mixed Berry Sauce

Yield: 1½ cups

1 package (12 ounces) frozen mixed berries (any combination), partially thawed

⅓ cup sugar

1 teaspoon grated orange zest

Absolutely delicious and simple to prepare, this sauce is wonderful on frozen yogurt, ice cream, pancakes, French toast, angel food cake— on just about anything. For a summertime treat, place it in a blender with ½ cup of ice cubes, and mix into a delightfully refreshing drink.

1. Place all of the ingredients in a medium-sized saucepan. Mix thoroughly, and bring to a boil over medium to medium-high heat, stirring occasionally.

2. Reduce the heat to medium-low, just to the point of a gentle simmer, and cook uncovered for 5 to 10 minutes, or until slightly thickened, stirring 2 or 3 times during cooking. Remove the pot from the heat, and allow to cool to room temperature.

3. Transfer the sauce to a covered container, and chill for several hours before serving. Store in the refrigerator for up to 1 week.

NUTRITIONAL DATA (PER 1-TABLESPOON SERVING)

Fat: 0 gram   Calories: 19   % Calories from fat: 0%

Cinnamon Sauce

Yield: 1¼ cups

2½ tablespoons brown sugar

1½ tablespoons all purpose flour

1¼ cups unsweetened apple juice

2 teaspoons fat-free margarine

¼ teaspoon ground cinnamon

1 teaspoon butter-flavored extract

Dash butter-flavored salt or plain salt

This is a delicious topping for pancakes, waffles, French toast, or frozen vanilla yogurt.

1. Place the brown sugar and flour in a small saucepan, and stir until well blended. Place the saucepan over low heat, and slowly stir in the apple juice until well blended.

2. Turn the heat to medium, and bring the mixture to a boil, stirring constantly. Add all of the remaining ingredients, stirring to blend thoroughly.

3. Stirring occasionally, cook for 3 minutes, or until the sauce reaches the desired consistency. Serve warm.

NUTRITIONAL DATA (PER 1-TABLESPOON SERVING)

Fat: 0 gram   Calories: 15   % Calories from fat: 0%

Maple-Cinnamon Syrup

Pour this cinnamony syrup over pancakes, waffles, or French toast. You may substitute pure maple syrup for the light maple syrup used in this recipe, but remember that the calorie count will double!

Yield: *1 cup*

1 cup light maple-flavored syrup

½ teaspoon ground cinnamon

1. Place the maple syrup and cinnamon in a small saucepan, and whisk together until well blended. Place the saucepan over medium-high heat and, stirring constantly, bring to a boil.

2. Continue to cook for 1 minute, stirring. Reduce the heat to low, and keep warm until needed.

NUTRITIONAL DATA (PER 2-TABLESPOON SERVING)
Fat: 0 gram   Calories: 50   % Calories from fat: 0%

Brandied Apricot Sauce

This is absolutely luscious served with or over just about anything, from cake or fruit to pancakes, vegetables, and meat!

Yield: *1 cup*

½ cup apricot preserves

½ cup water

¼ cup apricot brandy

1 tablespoon reduced-fat margarine

1 teaspoon butter-flavored sprinkles

1 teaspoon vanilla extract

1. Place all of the ingredients except for the vanilla extract in a small saucepan, and stir to mix. Whisking constantly, bring to a slow boil over medium to medium-high heat.

2. Cook the mixture at a gentle boil for 2 to 3 minutes or until slightly thickened, continuing to whisk. Remove the pot from the heat, and whisk in the vanilla.

3. Serve immediately, or transfer the mixture to a covered container and chill for at least 1 hour before serving. Store in the refrigerator for up to 2 weeks.

NUTRITIONAL DATA (PER 1-TABLESPOON SERVING)
Fat: .4 gram   Calories: 39   % Calories from fat: 9%

Chocolate Syrup

Yield: 1⅓ cups

½ cup plus 1 tablespoon cocoa
  powder

½ cup plus 2 tablespoons sugar

Dash salt (optional)

¾ cup warm water

½ cup plus 1 tablespoon light
  corn syrup

1 teaspoon vanilla extract

I try to keep some of this syrup on hand at all times, as its versatility makes it a real lifesaver. Spoon it over ice cream or cake for a quick but special dessert, or stir a couple of teaspoons into hot skim milk for a soothing cup of hot chocolate on a sleepless night.

1. Place the cocoa powder, sugar, and salt in a medium-sized saucepan, and stir until well blended. Set aside.

2. Place the warm water and corn syrup in a small bowl, and stir to mix. Add the corn syrup mixture to the cocoa mixture, and stir until well blended.

3. Bring the cocoa mixture to a slow boil over medium to medium-high heat, whisking constantly. Continue to boil for 2 minutes, continuing to whisk.

4. Remove the pot from the heat and whisk in the vanilla extract. Allow the syrup to cool to room temperature, transfer to a covered container, and refrigerate until needed. (The sauce will thicken as it cools.) Store in the refrigerator for up to 2 weeks.

NUTRITIONAL DATA (PER 1-TABLESPOON SERVING)

Fat: .2 gram   Calories: 50   % Calories from fat: 3%

Mint Chocolate Cream Sauce

This recipe makes a sinfully delicious topping for frozen yogurt, ice cream, or cake. And I haven't found a fruit that wasn't even more delicious when crowned with a spoonful of this sauce!

1. Place the cocoa, sugar, and salt, if desired, in a medium-sized saucepan, and stir to blend well. Set aside.

2. Place the milk and flour in a small bowl, and whisk until well blended. Set aside.

3. Place the cocoa mixture over medium-high heat, and slowly pour in the milk mixture, whisking constantly. Reduce the heat to medium, and simmer, continuing to whisk, for 5 minutes. If necessary, reduce the heat slightly to keep the mixture from boiling over.

4. Remove the pot from the heat, and whisk in the extracts. Allow the sauce to cool to room temperature. (The sauce will thicken as it cools.) Transfer the sauce to a covered container, and store in the refrigerator for up to 1 week.

Yield: *2 cups*

½ cup plus 1 tablespoon cocoa powder

½ cup plus 2½ tablespoons sugar

Dash salt (optional)

1½ cups skim milk

1 tablespoon plus 1 teaspoon all purpose flour

½ teaspoon mint extract

1 teaspoon vanilla extract

1 teaspoon butter-flavored extract

NUTRITIONAL DATA (PER 1-TABLESPOON SERVING)

Fat: .2 gram	Calories: 26	% Calories from fat: 6%

Variation

For a more intense flavor, substitute ½ teaspoon of peppermint extract for the mint extract.

Caramel Creme Cheese Sauce

Yield: 1⅓ cups

½ cup So-Simple Yogurt Cheese
(page 53)

8 ounces light nonfat Creme
Caramel yogurt

3 tablespoons brown sugar,
packed

1 teaspoon caramel or vanilla
extract

½ teaspoon cinnamon

This thick, tantalizing sauce is great spooned over hot or cold cereal, baked sweet potatoes, frozen yogurt, ice cream, or plain cake, and also makes a wonderful dip for fresh fruit or Cinnamon Bagel Crisps (page 57). I am always finding new ways to serve this versatile sauce!

1. Place all of the ingredients in a small bowl, and stir until well blended, smooth, and creamy.

2. Transfer the mixture to a covered container, and chill for 1 to 2 hours before serving. Store in the refrigerator for up to 1 week.

NUTRITIONAL DATA (PER 1-TABLESPOON SERVING)

Fat: 0 gram   Calories: 32   % Calories from fat: 0%

Creamy Vanilla Cheese Topping

Yield: 1 cup

1 cup So-Simple Yogurt Cheese
(page 53)

1½ tablespoons honey

½ teaspoon vanilla extract

Made with So-Simple Yogurt Cheese (page 53), this delicious topping is excellent on virtually any chilled fruit.

1. Place all of the ingredients in a blender, cover, and process on low speed until creamy.

2. Transfer to a serving dish and serve immediately, or cover tightly and chill until ready to serve. Store in the refrigerator for up to 1 week.

NUTRITIONAL DATA (PER TABLESPOON)

Fat: 0 gram   Calories: 17   % Calories from fat: 0%

Fat-Free Whipped Cream

The secret to making this whipped cream—or any whipped cream—is to begin with ice cold ingredients and beaters. Then even this fat-free topping whips up light and fluffy!

1. Pour the milk into a medium-sized bowl. Place this bowl and the beaters from your electric mixer in a larger bowl, and place in the freezer for 30 to 45 minutes, or until the smaller bowl's surface becomes frosty.

2. Remove the bowls from the freezer, and take the small bowl out of the larger bowl. Immediately, using the chilled beaters in an electric mixer, beat the milk on high for about 1 minute, or until very frothy. Still beating, gradually add the powdered sugar and the extract. Continue to beat for 2 to 3 minutes, or until the mixture is very stiff.

3. Serve immediately, or cover tightly and refrigerate for up to 30 minutes. If the whipped cream deflates, beat once more with chilled beaters until the mixture again becomes stiff.

Yield: *3 cups*

1 cup evaporated skim milk

½ cup powdered sugar

1 teaspoon vanilla extract or the extract of your choice

NUTRITIONAL DATA (PER 1-TABLESPOON SERVING)

Fat: 0 gram   Calories: 10   % Calories from fat: 0%

Creamy Chocolate Cheese Topping

Yield: *1 cup*

1 cup So-Simple Yogurt Cheese
(page 53)

2 tablespoons chocolate syrup

1 tablespoon plus 1 teaspoon
powdered sugar

Here is the perfect topping for any dessert, including fresh fruit.

1. Place all of the ingredients in a small dish, and stir until smooth and creamy.

2. Serve immediately, or cover tightly and chill until ready to serve. Store in the refrigerator for up to 1 week.

NUTRITIONAL DATA (PER 1-TABLESPOON SERVING)

Fat: 0 gram   Calories: 19   % Calories from fat: 0%

Variation

For a creamy topping with a chocolate malt flavor, stir in 3 tablespoons of instant chocolate malted milk powder. Delicious!

NUTRITIONAL DATA (PER 1-TABLESPOON SERVING)

Fat: 0 gram   Calories: 24   % Calories from fat: 0%

Old-Fashioned Butterscotch Sauce

This lighter version of an old favorite is a lovely sauce that can dress up even the plainest of cakes, or turn a scoop of frozen yogurt or low-fat ice cream into a festive event.

1. Place the margarine in a heavy medium-sized saucepan, and melt over medium heat.

2. Stir the brown sugar and milk into the margarine. Continue to stir over medium heat until the mixture comes to a boil; then allow the mixture to remain at a boil for 1 minute, stirring constantly. Remove from the heat, and allow to sit at room temperature for about 5 minutes, or until slightly thickened.

3. Stir the extracts into the sauce. Cool slightly and serve, or cover tightly and store in the refrigerator for up to 1 week.

Yield: 1 cup

2 tablespoons reduced-fat margarine

1 cup brown sugar, packed

½ cup evaporated skim milk

½ teaspoon vanilla extract

½ teaspoon butter-flavored extract

NUTRITIONAL DATA (PER 1-TABLESPOON SERVING)

Fat: <1 gram   Calories: 60   % Calories from fat: 10%

Relishes

Pickled Carrots

Yield: *6 cups*

6 cups thinly sliced carrots (6 to 8 medium)

1 medium green bell pepper, cut into thin strips

1 can (11⅛ ounces) Campbell's Italian Tomato Soup, undiluted

¾ cup white wine vinegar

⅓ cup sugar

1 medium onion, quartered

The vibrant colors of this tangy relish give it great visual impact. While it dresses up almost any type of sandwich, it will also help turn many main dishes into special events.

1. Place the carrots and bell pepper in a large bowl. Toss to mix, and set aside.

2. Place the soup, vinegar, and sugar in a blender, and process on medium-high speed until well mixed. Add the onion, and process on Chop until the onion is finely chopped and blended into the sauce.

3. Pour the tomato mixture over the carrot mixture, and toss gently to cover well. Cover and chill for several hours before serving. Store in the refrigerator for up to 2 weeks.

NUTRITIONAL DATA (PER ¼-CUP SERVING)

Fat: 0 gram   Calories: 45   % Calories from fat: 0%

Mint Onion Relish

In large quantities, mint is said to be an aphrodisiac. So be sure to make this dish, accented by the red of the pimento, part of your next Valentine's Day table!

1. Place the mint, vinegar, and sugar in a small saucepan, and stir to mix. Place over low heat, and simmer gently for 25 minutes, stirring occasionally.

2. Remove the pan from the heat, and stir in the onions and pimentos, tossing gently until well mixed.

3. Transfer the relish to a serving dish, cover, and chill for several hours, or until the onions are crisp, before serving. (You may wish to add more vinegar if needed to completely cover the onions.) Store in the refrigerator for up to 2 weeks.

Yield: 1½ cups

⅔ cup chopped fresh mint, or 2 teaspoons dried mint

⅔ cup white vinegar

1½ tablespoons sugar

1½ cups thinly sliced small onions

1 jar (2 ounces) chopped red pimento

NUTRITIONAL DATA (PER 1-TABLESPOON SERVING)

Fat: 0 gram   Calories: 46   % Fat from calories: 0%

Piquant Mango-Pineapple-Orange Relish

Yield: *2½ cups*

1 cup diced canned mango in light syrup, rinsed and drained, or 1 cup diced peeled fresh mango

1 cup diced fresh or canned pineapple

1 can (11 ounces) mandarin oranges in juice, drained and cut in half

¼ cup chopped roasted red bell pepper (page 123)

2 teaspoons crushed dried sweet basil, or 2 tablespoons chopped fresh basil

2 small scallions, minced (include tops) (optional)

2 teaspoons crushed dried cilantro (optional)

1 tablespoon lime or lemon juice

2 tablespoon mango- or orange-flavored liqueur

2 tablespoons honey

This relish is so full of vivid colors and lively flavors that it will dress up any meat, fish, or poultry dish. It is also wonderful served alongside a sandwich, and makes a deliciously pretty gift spooned into a clear-glass jar and capped with a decorative lid.

1. Place the fruits, red pepper, and basil in a medium-sized bowl. Add the scallions and cilantro if desired, and toss lightly to mix.

2. Place the lime juice, liqueur, and honey in a small bowl, and whisk until well blended. Pour the lime juice mixture over the fruit mixture, and stir gently to coat.

3. Cover the relish, and chill for several hours before serving. Store in the refrigerator for up to 4 days.

NUTRITIONAL DATA (PER ½-CUP SERVING)

| Fat: 0 gram | Calories: 60 | % Calories from fat: 0% |

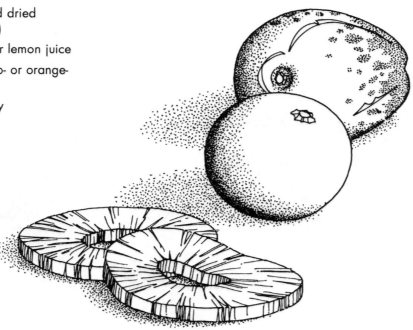

Roasting Peppers

Although roasted peppers are available in jars, nothing compares with the taste of a freshly roasted pepper. Roasting a pepper truly enhances its flavor, adding new depth and a meatier texture. And by roasting the peppers yourself, you can enjoy not only red bell peppers—the type most often found in jars—but also green bell peppers, yellow bell peppers, and any of the hot peppers.

Fortunately, it's easy to roast peppers in the broiler of your oven. Just follow these simple steps:

1. Rinse the peppers and dry them well, leaving them whole.

2. Arrange the peppers on the broiler pan of the oven or on a baking sheet, and place in a pre-heated broiler, 2 to 3 inches from the heat. Leaving the door of the broiler open so that you can watch the peppers closely, broil until all sides of the peppers are blistered and charred, turning the peppers often with tongs to get even blistering.

3. Transfer the peppers to a paper or plastic bag, twist to close, and tie tightly. Allow the peppers to steam in the bag for 10 to 15 minutes, or until they are cool enough to handle.

4. Using a small knife—and wearing rubber gloves if you are handling hot peppers—gently scrape the charred skins from the peppers. Cut the peppers open and remove the veins and seeds, washing out any remaining seeds under running water.

5. Use the peppers immediately; store in the refrigerator for up to 1 week; or wrap each pepper individually in plastic wrap, place in a sealed plastic bag, and store in the freezer for up to a year.

8

~

The
Main Event

The main dish is the star of the meal—the dish around which all others are planned. For many years, this "star" was usually meat. We now, know, of course, that many meatless dishes can also make satisfying main events. But you'll be delighted to hear that even traditional beef and pork dishes have their place in a healthy diet. In fact, leaner cuts of meat—as well as simple but innovative cooking techniques—will make it possible for you to enjoy virtually all of your favorite entrées without guilt. This chapter will show you how it's done.

The chapter begins with a classic beef dish, Company Steaks. Made with a savory marinade, this is perfect special-occasion fare. Following this you'll find an exciting collection of recipes for a wide range of dishes. Pork Tenderloin With Plum Sauce is so delicious that my family enjoys it both hot and cold. Beef and Dumpling Goulash is full of old-fashioned flavor. Crispy Lemon-Lime Sesame Chicken shows just how scrumptious the ever-popular chicken breast can be. And if you're interested in vegetarian fare, you'll find that this, too, is well represented by such varied and tantalizing creations as Honey-Wheat Pizza, Pronto Vegetarian Chili, and Red Beans With Long Grain and Wild Rice. These dishes have so much pizzazz that you'll never miss the meat!

For anyone who feels that they just don't have time to cook a nourishing dinner for their family, this chapter presents a number of Quick Dishes—entrées that can be made in well under an hour. And from Bacon, Lettuce, and Tomato Pizza to Ham and Yam Bake, all are as delicious as they are easy to prepare.

Company Steaks

Yield: *8 servings*

2 pounds lean eye of round steak, 2 inches thick

Unseasoned meat tenderizer

MARINADE

1½ cups water

¼ cup dry red wine

½ cup plus 2 tablespoons soy sauce

1 tablespoon lemon juice

1 teaspoon Worcestershire sauce

¼ cup brown sugar, packed

A sweet and savory marinade tenderizes these quickly cooked steaks into wonderful company fare. Serve with either Oven-Baked Spiced Potato Slices (page 172) or Roasted Parmesan Potato Wedges (page 173) for an unforgettable meal.

1. To make the marinade, place all of the marinade ingredients in a small bowl and stir well to mix. Set aside.

2. Trim the steak of all visible fat, and cut into 8 equal pieces. Pierce the steaks several times with a fork, and lightly sprinkle the meat tenderizer over the surface of the steaks. Using your fingers, rub the tenderizer into the meat.

3. Place the steaks in a shallow dish or a resealable plastic storage bag. Pour the marinade over the steaks, and either cover with plastic wrap or seal the storage bag. Place in the refrigerator for several hours or, preferably, overnight, turning each steak only once while marinating.

4. Line a broiler pan with aluminum foil, and remove the steaks from the marinade, reserving the marinade. Place the steaks on a rack in the broiler pan. Set aside.

5. Pour the marinade into a small saucepan, and bring to a fast boil over high heat. Reduce the heat to medium-high, and continue to boil for 2 to 3 minutes. Remove from the heat.

6. Place the steaks in a preheated broiler, 3 inches below the heat source. Broil for 2 to 5 minutes, or until the tops are lightly browned. Baste with the marinade, turn over, and broil for 2 to 5 additional minutes, or until lightly browned. Baste the steaks again, turn, and broil for about 2 minutes. Continue to cook, basting and turning, until the steaks reach the desired degree of doneness. Serve immediately.

NUTRITIONAL DATA (PER SERVING)

Fat: 5 grams   Calories: 197   % Calories from fat: 23%

Bacon, Lettuce, and Tomato Pizza

When counting fat grams and calories, all the toppings together on this pizza don't even begin to come close to a pizza with one topping of pepperoni! And it's delicious, to boot!

1. Place the cheeses in a small bowl, and toss to mix well. Set aside.

2. Place the pizza crust on a pizza pan or large baking sheet, and spread the sauce to within 1 inch of the edge of the crust. Arrange the tomatoes over the sauce, and sprinkle with the shredded cheese.

3. Bake in a preheated 400°F oven for 8 to 10 minutes, or until the crust is crisp and the cheese has melted.

4. While the pizza is in the oven, place the lettuce, onion, and bacon in a large bowl. Add the dressing, and toss until well blended.

5. When the pizza has finished baking, spread the lettuce mixture over the top. Slice and serve hot.

Yield: *8 slices*

½ cup shredded fat-free mozzarella cheese

½ cup shredded fat-free Cheddar cheese

1 large (10 ounce) thin Boboli pizza shell, or another prepared pizza crust

1 cup Presto Pizza Sauce (page 110)

3 large Roma tomatoes, thinly sliced

3 cups shredded romaine lettuce

½ cup finely chopped sweet red onion

3 tablespoons Oscar Mayer Real Bacon Bits

½ cup Fat-Free Thousand Island Dressing (page 82)

NUTRITIONAL DATA (PER SLICE)

Fat: 2.75 grams   Calories: 162   % Calories from fat: 15%

Making the Most of Your Daily Bread

Sometimes the simple addition of a savory loaf of bread can make even an ordinary meal special. Serve the same loaf with an already-special entrée, and you have a truly memorable meal! Try the following crusty, flavorful breads with any of the main dishes in this chapter—or with your favorite soup or salad—and you'll see what I mean.

Crusty Onion-Dill Mini Loaves

Yield: *4 servings*

½ cup warm water

1 package active dry yeast

1 cup 2% small curd or creamed cottage cheese

2 egg whites

2⅓ cups sifted all purpose flour, divided

1 tablespoon dehydrated onion flakes

2 tablespoons sugar

½ teaspoon dill seed

1 teaspoon butter-flavored salt or plain salt

¼ teaspoon baking soda

I Can't Believe It's Not Butter spray

You will be amazed by these loaves, which bake up beautifully with no kneading. Serve this bread with Company Steaks (page 126).

1. Place the warm water in a large bowl, and sprinkle with the yeast. Stir until the yeast dissolves, and set aside until needed.

2. If using a microwave oven, place the cottage cheese in a micro-wave-safe dish, and microwave on high just until warm. If using a conventional stove, place the cottage cheese in a small saucepan, and cook over medium heat just until warm. Add the cottage cheese to the yeast mixture, stirring to mix.

3. Place the egg whites in a small bowl, and whisk slightly. Stir into the yeast mixture, and set aside.

4. Place 1 cup plus about 2 tablespoons of the flour and all of the onion flakes, sugar, dill seed, butter-flavored salt, and baking soda in a medium-sized bowl, and stir to mix well.

5. Add the flour mixture to the yeast mixture, and, using an electric mixer, blend on medium speed until well mixed.

6. Using a spoon, stir enough of the remaining flour into the dough to make a soft dough. Cover the bowl with a clean kitchen towel or with plastic wrap, and let rise in a warm draft-free place for 1 to 1½ hours, or until the dough has doubled in size.

7. Lightly spray 4 nonstick mini loaf pans, each 5½ by 3 inches, with cooking spray. Using a large spoon, stir the dough down. With your hands, divide the dough into 4 parts. Shape each portion into 1 loaf, and place each loaf in a pan. Cover the pans and let rise in a warm draft-free place for an hour to 90 minutes, or until the dough has doubled in size.

8. Bake on the center rack of a preheated 350°F oven for 25 minutes. Cover the tops of the bread with aluminum foil, and bake for 15 additional minutes, or until the bread is golden brown.

9. Remove the bread from the oven, and remove the loaves from the pans. Arrange the loaves on wire racks, top side up, and spray the tops lightly with the butter spray while still warm. Allow to cool for at least 10 minutes before slicing and serving.

NUTRITIONAL DATA (PER LOAF)

Fat: 1.5 grams   Calories: 300   % Calories from fat: 5%

Mo-Hotta Pepper Bread

This is a nice companion for a hot bowl of Sirloin Chili (page 131).

Quick Dish

Yield: *16 servings*

1. Slice the bread in half lengthwise and place the halves, cut sides up, on a small pan. Set aside.

2. In a small bowl, stir together the cilantro, red pepper flakes, and cayenne pepper.

3. Spray the cut surfaces of each loaf half twice with the butter spray. Sprinkle the cilantro mixture over the sprayed surfaces as evenly as possible, and lightly spray the surfaces once more. Be sure to spray a distance from the bread to avoid blowing the mixture off the bread.

4. Place the bread under a preheated broiler for 2 to 3 minutes, or until lightly browned. Watch the loaf closely to prevent burning. Slice each half into 8 pieces, and serve hot.

1 large (1 pound) loaf French bread

1 tablespoon crushed dried cilantro or parsley

½ teaspoon crushed red pepper flakes

¼ teaspoon cayenne pepper

I Can't Believe It's Not Butter spray

NUTRITIONAL DATA (PER PIECE)

Fat: 1 gram   Calories: 70   % Calories from fat: 13%

Pronto Vegetarian Chili

Quick Dish

Yield: 6 servings

½ cup Vegetable Stock (page 96), Brown Beef Stock (page 90), or other fat-free stock

1 large onion, chopped

1 large clove garlic, minced

1 medium green bell pepper, chopped

2 small jalapeño peppers, seeded, deveined, and finely chopped

1 tablespoon chili powder

½ teaspoon ground cumin

⅛ teaspoon ground cinnamon

1 tablespoon crushed dried cilantro

1 can (14½ ounces) diced tomatoes, undrained

2 cans (8 ounces each) tomato sauce

1 tablespoon white or yellow cornmeal

1 can (1 pound) dark red kidney beans, rinsed and drained

1 can (1 pound) light red kidney beans, rinsed and drained

1 can (1 pound) whole kernel corn, drained

Salt to taste

6 scallions, chopped (garnish)

This recipe makes a deliciously thick and colorful chili with a full-bodied flavor—and it's done in only about 30 minutes! I love to serve this over split baked potatoes.

1. Place the stock in a large heavy skillet or pot, and bring to a boil over medium-high heat. Reduce the heat just to the point of a simmer, and stir in the onions and garlic. Sauté, stirring often, for 5 minutes, or until the onions are soft.

2. Stir the bell pepper, jalapeño peppers, and seasonings into the beef stock, and cook uncovered for 5 minutes, stirring often.

3. Add the tomatoes, tomato sauce, cornmeal, and beans to the pot, and stir to blend thoroughly. Cover and continue to simmer for 15 minutes, stirring often to keep the beans from sticking to the pot.

4. Stir the corn into the chili, and add salt to taste. Cover, and continue to simmer for about 10 minutes, or just until the corn is heated through. Serve hot, garnishing each bowlful with a sprinkling of scallions.

NUTRITIONAL DATA (PER 1-CUP SERVING)

Fat: .8 gram	Calories: 205	% Calories from fat: 3%

Sirloin Chili

Chili originated in Mexico, dating back to the Aztec civilization. However, this dish—in its many, many versions—is now enjoyed throughout the United States. If you prefer, you may make this savory entrée with ground sirloin instead of sirloin strips.

1. Place the stock in a large soup pot and heat over medium-high heat. Add the sirloin, onion, and garlic, and cook, stirring frequently, until the meat is browned.

2. Add the water to the pot, and bring to a low simmer, adjusting the heat if necessary. Cook for 20 minutes, stirring occasionally.

3. Reduce the heat to medium-low, and stir in the tomato sauce, tomato paste, chilies, and seasonings, blending thoroughly.

4. Stir the chili beans into the mixture, and add salt to taste. Return to a slow simmer over medium heat, cover, and cook for 30 minutes, or until the meat is tender and the flavors are well blended. Stir occasionally to keep from sticking. Serve hot.

NUTRITIONAL DATA (PER 1-CUP SERVING)

Fat: 3 grams	Calories: 270	% Calories from fat: 10%

Yield: 10 servings

¼ cup Brown Beef Stock (page 90) or other fat-free beef stock

1¼ pound lean boneless top sirloin steak, trimmed and cut into ½-inch strips

1 large onion, chopped

2 large cloves garlic, minced

3½ cups water

1 can (15 ounces) Hunt's Just for Chili tomato sauce or plain tomato sauce

1 can (12 ounces) tomato paste

2 cans (4 ounces each) diced green chilies

1 teaspoon dried thyme

½ teaspoon ground black pepper (optional)

1 tablespoon sugar

1–2 tablespoons chili powder

1 teaspoon ground cumin

1 teaspoon dried oregano

3 cans (15¾ ounces each) mild or hot chili beans in chili sauce, undrained

Salt to taste

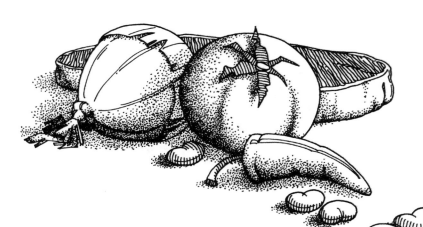

Fat-Free Chili Toppings

While my husband, David, loves to stir a tablespoon of peanut butter into his chili, there are plenty of healthy chili toppings that will enhance your dish without adding any extra fat. Try one—or all!—of these the next time you have a bowl of chili, and enjoy a low-fat taste of the Southwest.

☐ Shredded lettuce
☐ Shredded fat-free Cheddar or mozzarella cheese
☐ Chopped scallions or onions
☐ Sliced mushrooms
☐ Chopped green, red, or yellow bell pepper
☐ Diced or shredded raw jicama

☐ Healthy Sour Cream (page 106)
☐ Diced tomatoes
☐ Plain nonfat yogurt
☐ Crushed fat-free tortilla chips
☐ Fat-free croutons
☐ Chopped fresh cilantro
☐ Diced red pimentos

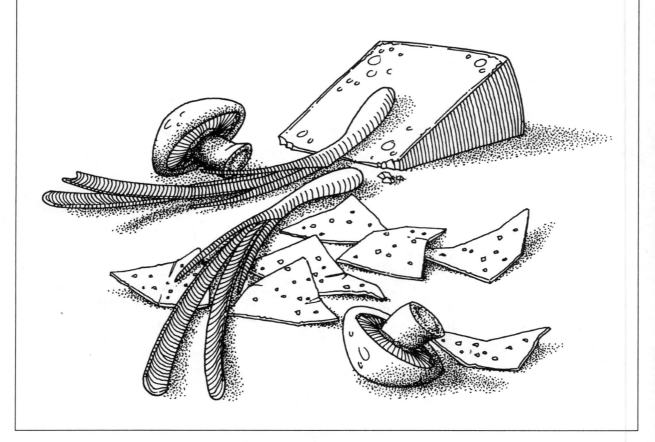

Honey-Wheat Pizza

The honey-wheat crust makes this pizza an instant favorite with everyone who tastes it.

1. Spray a 15-inch pizza pan with cooking spray, and sprinkle the cornmeal over the entire pan. Set aside.

2. Knead the dough and allow to rise as directed on the package. Once the dough has doubled in size, place it on a lightly floured surface, and roll it into a ball. Cover the dough with a clean kitchen towel, and let it sit for 15 to 20 minutes.

3. Transfer the ball of dough to the pizza pan and, using the palm of your hand, stretch and pat it out to cover the surface of the pan, forming a slight rim at the edge. If the dough is too sticky to spread easily, spray it lightly with cooking spray. Be sure to distribute the dough as evenly as possible, and to avoid causing tears.

4. Spread the sauce evenly over the crust, leaving ½ inch of the edge without sauce.

5. Place the cheeses in a small bowl, and toss to mix. Sprinkle the cheeses over the sauce. Arrange the onion and green pepper over the cheese.

6. Bake in a preheated 400°F oven for 15 to 20 minutes, or until the crust is golden brown. Slice and serve hot.

NUTRITIONAL DATA (PER SLICE)

Fat: 3 grams	Calories: 240	% Fat from calories: 11%

Quick Dish

Yield: *8 servings*

CRUST

2 tablespoons yellow or white cornmeal

1 loaf (1 pound) frozen honey-wheat bread dough, thawed

Cooking spray (optional)

1½ cups Presto Pizza Sauce (page 110)

TOPPING

¾ cup shredded reduced-fat mozzarella cheese

¾ cup shredded fat-free mozzarella cheese

1 small sweet red onion, thinly sliced and separated into rings

1 small green bell pepper, cut into thin strips

Quick Fiesta Baked Potato

Quick Dish

Yield: *4 servings*

4 medium baking potatoes

2 cups Sirloin Chili (page 131)

1 cup drained canned whole
   kernel corn

4 medium scallions, chopped

½ red bell pepper, chopped

½ green bell pepper, chopped

Salt and pepper to taste

¼ cup Southwestern Sour Cream
   Dressing (page 83)

*M*ake this dish the next time you have leftover Sirloin Chili, and *you'll have a deliciously satisfying meal in minutes!*

1. Using a fork, pierce each potato 4 times. If using a conventional oven, place the potatoes directly on the oven rack and bake in a preheated 400°F oven for 45 minutes, or until soft. If using a microwave oven, microwave each potato on high for 7 to 8 minutes, or until soft. Remove the potatoes from the microwave, and allow to sit for 2 minutes before using.

2. While the potatoes are cooking, place the chili and corn in a small saucepan, and stir to mix. Cover and cook over medium heat until hot, stirring occasionally.

3. Place the scallions and bell peppers in a bowl, and stir to mix. Set aside.

4. Cut each potato in half lengthwise, and place 2 halves on each of 4 individual serving plates. Using a fork, slightly mash each potato, adding salt and pepper to taste.

5. Spoon a fourth of the hot chili mixture over each potato. Follow with a sprinkling of the scallion mixture and a tablespoon of the dressing, and serve hot.

NUTRITIONAL DATA (PER SERVING)

Fat: 1.5 grams   Calories: 400   % Calories from fat: 3%

Baked Potato Italiano

If you haven't tried the combination of potato and tomato sauce, you are in for a real treat!

1. Using a fork, pierce each potato 4 times. If using a conventional oven, place the potatoes directly on an oven rack, and bake in a pre-heated 400°F oven for 45 minutes, or until soft. If using a microwave oven, microwave each potato on high for 7 to 8 minutes, or until soft. Remove the potatoes from the microwave, and allow to sit for 2 minutes.

2. While the potatoes are cooking, place the tomato sauce in a small saucepan. Cover and cook over medium-low heat until hot, stirring occasionally.

3. Place the cheeses and scallions in a small bowl, and stir to mix. Set aside.

4. Cut each potato in half lengthwise, and place 2 halves on each of 4 individual serving plates. Spoon ¼ cup of the hot sauce over each potato. Follow with a sprinkling of the cheese mixture, and serve hot.

Quick Dish

Yield: *4 servings*

4 medium baking potatoes

1 cup My All-Purpose Italian Tomato Sauce (page 107)

½ cup shredded fat-free mozzarella cheese

½ cup shredded reduced-fat mozzarella cheese

2 medium scallions, finely chopped (include tops)

NUTRITIONAL DATA (PER SERVING)

Fat: 3.8 grams   Calories: 353   % Calories from fat: 10%

Spanish Pot Roast With Potatoes

Yield: *10 servings*

3-pound top round roast, trimmed of all visible fat

Unseasoned meat tenderizer

2 cups Brown Beef Stock (page 90) or other fat-free beef stock, divided

1 large onion, sliced

1 large clove garlic, minced

2 cups Tomato-Bacon Dressing (page 86)

6 large red potatoes, peeled and quartered lengthwise

1 tablespoon cornstarch

Salt and freshly ground black pepper to taste

The combination of flavors in the Tomato-Bacon Dressing and the beef stock blends with those of the meat and potatoes, making this an all-time favorite in my house.

1. Using a fork, pierce the roast in several places. Lightly sprinkle the meat tenderizer over the entire surface of the meat, and set aside.

2. Place ¼ cup of the stock in a large pot or roasting pan, and bring to a boil over medium-high heat. Add the roast, and brown on all sides. Transfer the roast to a large plate, and set aside.

3. Add the onion and garlic to the pot, and cook, stirring occasionally, until tender. Reduce the heat to medium, add the dressing, and mix well. Cook uncovered for 5 minutes.

4. Stir 1½ cups of the remaining stock into the pot, and mix thoroughly. Return the roast to the pot, spooning the sauce over it until well covered. Cover and simmer over medium heat for 1 hour, turning the roast occasionally to keep it from sticking to the pot.

5. Add the potato wedges to the pot, making sure that all is covered by the liquid. Continue to simmer for an additional 45 minutes, or until the meat and potatoes are tender, occasionally spooning the sauce over the potatoes and roast.

6. Transfer the roast and potatoes to a large serving platter, and cover to keep warm.

7. To defat the liquid that remains in the pot, first allow it to sit for a minute or 2. Then spoon the fat from the top with a fat-skimming ladle or a large serving spoon. You may also pour the liquid into a fat separator cup, allow it to sit for a few minutes, and then pour the defatted sauce back into the pot.

8. Place the remaining ¼ cup of stock and the cornstarch in a small dish, and stir until the cornstarch is dissolved. Stir the cornstarch mixture into the liquid in the pot, and bring the mixture to a boil over medium-high heat. Immediately reduce the heat to medium-low, just to the point of a simmer, and cook for about 10 minutes, or until the sauce reaches the desired consistency. Add salt and pepper to taste.

9. Slice the roast, and arrange the beef and potatoes on a large serving platter. Pour the sauce over the beef and potatoes, and serve hot.

NUTRITIONAL DATA (PER SERVING)

Fat: 5.8 grams	Calories: 367	% Calories from fat: 14%

Top: Quick Fiesta Baked Potato (*page 134*)
Center: Honey-Wheat Pizza (*page 133*)
Bottom: Sirloin Chili (*page 131*)

Top Left: Minted Glazed Carrots (page 162)

Top Right: Roasted Rosemary and
Garlic Potatoes (page 169)

Center Left: Pork Medallions in Apricot Sauce (page 137)

Center Right: Crispy Lemon-Lime Sesame Chicken (page 143)
with Piquant Mango-Pineapple-Orange Relish (page 122)

Pork Medallions in Apricot Sauce

The glisten of apricot sauce over pork medallions makes this succulent entrée as visually appealing as it is delicious.

1. Arrange the pork medallions on a cutting board, and pound each one to ½-inch thickness. Sprinkle both sides of each with the lemon pepper seasoning.

2. Place the stock in a large nonstick skillet, and bring to a boil over medium-high heat. Reduce the heat to medium, add the medallions, and cook for 5 to 10 minutes on each side, or until the center is no longer pink when cut with a knife. Transfer the medallions to a large plate, and cover to keep warm.

3. Place the preserves, lemon juice, and mustard in a small bowl, and stir to mix well. Increase the heat under the skillet to medium-high, and bring the stock to a boil. Add the preserve mixture, and cook for 2 minutes, stirring constantly. Reduce the heat to medium, and, still stirring, simmer for 3 to 5 additional minutes, or until the sauce is well blended and thickened.

4. Return the medallions to the skillet, covering them well with the sauce. Cover and cook for 5 minutes, or until heated through.

5. Arrange the medallions on a serving platter, and spoon the sauce over them. Garnish with the parsley, and serve hot.

Yield: 4 servings

1¼-pound pork tenderloin, trimmed of visible fat and cut crosswise into 8 medallions

2 teaspoons lemon pepper seasoning

½ cup Chicken Stock (page 92) or other fat-free chicken stock

½ cup apricot preserves

1 tablespoon lemon juice

2 teaspoons Grey Poupon mustard or other Dijon mustard

Fresh parsley sprigs (garnish)

NUTRITIONAL DATA (PER SERVING)

Fat: 5.6 grams   Calories: 300   % Calories from fat: 17%

Teriyaki Steak in Wine Sauce

Yield: *4 servings*

1¼-pound lean boneless top sirloin steak, trimmed of all visible fat

⅓ cup Brown Beef Stock (page 90) or other fat-free beef stock

1 tablespoon cornstarch

1 cup sliced fresh mushrooms (optional)

MARINADE

1 cup water

½ cup dry red wine

¼ cup soy sauce

2 tablespoons dehydrated onion flakes

1 large clove garlic, minced

2 tablespoons brown sugar

This dish has a rich and flavorful brown sauce. For a real treat, spoon the sliced beef over beds of fluffy rice or Cheesy Garlic Mashed Potatoes (page 175).

1. To make the marinade, place all of the marinade ingredients in a small bowl, and stir to mix well.

2. Place a large resealable plastic bag in a bowl, with the bag's edges over the sides of the bowl. Pour in the marinade, and set aside.

3. Pierce both sides of the steak in several places with a fork. Place the steak in the plastic bag and close the bag, expelling as much air as possible. Gently shake the bag to make sure that the steak is well covered, and lay in a flat container for 2 hours at room temperature, or overnight in the refrigerator. Turn the bag 2 or 3 times while marinating.

4. Line a broiler pan with aluminum foil, and remove the steak from the marinade, placing it on a rack in the broiler pan. Set aside.

5. Pour the marinade into a small saucepan, and bring to a fast boil over high heat. Reduce the heat to medium or medium-high, and continue to boil the marinade for 2 to 3 minutes. Remove from the heat.

6. Place the steaks in a preheated broiler 3 to 4 inches below the heat source. Broil for 2 to 5 minutes, or until lightly browned. Baste with a little of the marinade, turn over, and broil for 2 to 5 additional minutes, or until lightly browned. Baste again, turn, and broil for about 5 minutes. Continue to cook, basting and turning, until done.

7. Place the beef stock and cornstarch in a small saucepan, and stir well to dissolve the cornstarch. Bring the mixture to a boil over medium-high heat, stirring constantly. Reduce the heat just to the point of a simmer, and slowly stir in the remaining marinade and, if desired, the mushrooms. Simmer, stirring occasionally, for 5 additional minutes, or until the sauce thickens to the desired consistency.

8. Thinly slice the steak, and arrange the slices on a large serving platter. Spoon the sauce over the steak, and serve hot.

NUTRITIONAL DATA (PER SERVING)

| Fat: 6 grams | Calories: 268 | % Calories from fat: 20% |

Variation

To broil Teriyaki Steak on a grill, place the steak 4 to 6 inches above the coals or other heating element. Cook for 4 to 5 minutes on each side, basting each side as you turn the steak. Grill until cooked to your preference.

Ham and Yam Bake

Wait until you see how easy it is to put this dish together, how little cooking time it needs, and, best of all, how really delicious it is! Toss together a green side salad, and you have a complete meal.

1. Spoon enough of the sauce over the bottom of a 9¾-x-9¾-x-2-inch covered casserole dish to cover the bottom of the dish.

2. Layer the ham slices over half of the dish, spooning the glaze over each layer. Arrange the yams over the other half of the dish. Pour the remaining sauce over both the ham and the yams, covering well.

3. Cover and bake in a preheated 375°F oven for 30 minutes, or until the ham and yams are heated through and the glaze has thickened and become bubbly. Serve hot.

Quick Dish

Yield: *8 servings*

1 recipe Meat and Poultry Orange Glaze Sauce (page 110)

1½ pounds 97% fat-free smoked ham, cut into thick slices

2 cans (24 ounces each) whole yams or sweet potatoes in light syrup, rinsed and drained

NUTRITIONAL DATA (PER SERVING)

Fat: 3 grams   Calories: 330   % Calories from fat: 8%

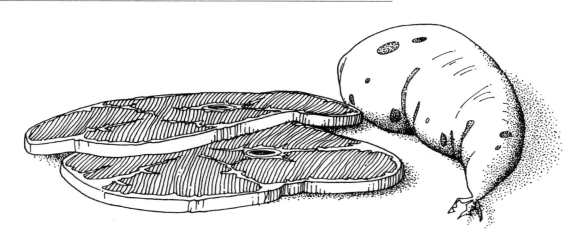

Pork Tenderloin With Plum Sauce

Yield: 4 servings

1¼-pound pork tenderloin, trimmed of all visible fat

¾ cup bottled Kikkoman Teriyaki Marinade and Sauce or other bottled marinade, divided

1 can (1 pound) whole purple plums in heavy syrup, undrained

2 tablespoons sugar

1 tablespoon cornstarch

½ cup thin strips red bell pepper

The combination of pork and plum sauce make this dish succulent whether served hot or cold.

1. Pierce both sides of the tenderloin in several places with a fork, and set aside.

2. Place a large resealable plastic bag in a bowl, with the edges over the sides of the bowl so that the bag remains open. Pour in ½ cup of the teriyaki sauce. Add the tenderloin and close the bag, expelling as much air as possible. Gently shake the bag to make sure that the tenderloin is well covered, and lay the bag in a flat container for at least 2 hours or, preferably, overnight, in the refrigerator. Turn the bag 2 or 3 times while marinating to evenly distribute the liquid.

3. About 15 minutes before removing the tenderloin from the refrigerator, drain the syrup from the plums, and set the plums aside. Place the syrup, sugar, and cornstarch in a small bowl, and whisk until well blended.

4. Pour the plum syrup mixture into a small saucepan, and bring to a boil over medium-high heat. Reduce the heat to medium-low, just to the point of a simmer, and continue to cook, stirring constantly, until the syrup begins to thicken and darken in color. Remove the pan from the heat.

5. Slowly stir the drained plums into the syrup mixture, blending well. Place the pot over medium heat, and cook, stirring constantly, for 3 to 5 minutes, or until of the desired consistency. Set aside.

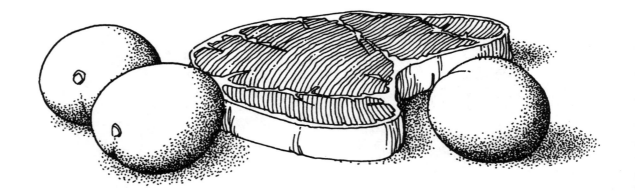

6. Place the remaining ¼ cup of teriyaki sauce in a small saucepan, and place over medium-high heat. Add the bell pepper, and simmer for 3 to 5 minutes, or just until the peppers are crisp-tender. Reduce the heat to medium, and stir in the plum sauce. Cook for 2 to 3 additional minutes, or until the flavors are well blended. Remove from the heat, and cover to keep warm.

7. Line a broiler pan with aluminum foil. Remove the tenderloin from the marinade, placing it on a rack in the broiler pan. Set aside.

8. Pour the marinade into a small saucepan, and bring to a fast boil over high heat. Reduce heat to medium or medium-high, and continue to boil the marinade for 2 to 3 minutes. Remove the heat and allow to cool to room temperature.

9. Place the tenderloin in a preheated broiler, 6 to 7 inches under the heat source. Broil for 7 to 10 minutes on each side, or until the meat is no longer pink when cut with a knife. (Watch closely to prevent burning!) During cooking, baste the meat every 5 minutes with the cooled marinade.

10. Slice the tenderloin, and arrange the pieces on a serving platter. Spoon the plum sauce over the meat, and serve hot.

NUTRITIONAL DATA (PER SERVING)

| Fat: 5 grams | Calories: 310 | % Calories from fat: 14% |

Beef and Dumpling Goulash

Yield: *10 servings*

8 cups Brown Beef Stock (page 90) or other fat-free beef stock, divided

1½ pounds lean top sirloin beef, trimmed of all visible fat and cut into ½-inch strips

1 large onion, chopped

1 large clove garlic, minced

1 medium stalk celery, chopped

1 medium carrot, shredded

2 cans (8 ounces each) tomato sauce

2 teaspoons chili powder

2 teaspoons paprika

2 teaspoons dried thyme

2 teaspoons crushed dried basil

1 bay leaf

1 teaspoon garlic salt

1 teaspoon freshly ground black pepper

2 teaspoons sugar

1 package (10 ounces) frozen cut green beans

1 package (12 ounces) yolk-free dumpling ribbons

The paprika used in this dish makes it Hungarian in spirit and delicious in taste!

1. Place ½ cup of the stock in a large nonstick pot, and bring to a boil over medium-high heat. Add the beef, onions, garlic, and celery, and cook for 5 to 10 minutes, or until the meat is browned and the vegetables are tender.

2. Stir the remaining 7½ cups of stock and the carrot, tomato sauce, seasonings, and sugar into the beef mixture. Reduce the heat just to the point of a simmer, and cook partially covered for 30 minutes, or until the beef is tender, stirring occasionally.

3. Increase the heat to medium-high, and bring the goulash to a slow boil. Stir in the green beans and dumpling ribbons, and simmer uncovered for 8 to 10 minutes, or until the noodles are tender. If the goulash seems dry, stir in ¼ cup or so of water during cooking. Serve hot.

NUTRITIONAL DATA (PER SERVING)

Fat: 4.4 grams   Calories: 315   % Calories from fat: 12%

Crispy Lemon-Lime Sesame Chicken

You are going to love this crispy chicken! For best results, use chicken fillets of even size. Piquant Mango-Pineapple-Orange Relish (page 122) complements this dish beautifully!

1. To make the marinade, place all of the marinade ingredients in a large bowl, and stir to mix well. Set aside.

2. Rinse the chicken under cold water, and pat dry with paper towels. Add the chicken pieces to the marinade mixture, and toss until all the pieces are well coated.

3. Place a large resealable plastic bag in a bowl, with the edges over the sides of the bowl so that the bag remains open. Place the chicken pieces and the marinade in the bag, expelling as much air as possible. Seal the bag, and lay it in a flat container for at least 1 hour in the refrigerator, turning the bag occasionally to evenly distribute the liquid.

4. While the chicken is marinating, place the corn flakes in a large resealable plastic bag. Cover with a kitchen towel, and use a rolling pin to crush the flakes into fine crumbs.

5. Add the remaining coating ingredients to the corn flake crumbs, seal the bag, and shake to mix thoroughly. Pour the mixture into a pie pan or other shallow dish, and set aside.

6. Spray two large nonstick baking sheets with 2 coats of cooking spray. Remove the chicken pieces from the marinade, and roll each piece in the corn flake mixture, coating well. Arrange the pieces in a single layer on the baking sheets, and spray the tops lightly with the cooking spray.

7. Bake on the center rack of a preheated 400°F oven for 40 to 45 minutes, or until easily pierced with a fork and no longer pink when cut with a knife. During baking, turn each piece every 10 to 15 minutes to insure even browning. Serve hot.

Yield: *10 servings*

2½ pounds skinless boneless chicken breast, cut into 10 equal pieces

Cooking spray

MARINADE

8 ounces light nonfat lemon yogurt

1 small onion, minced

2 medium cloves garlic, minced

2 tablespoons lime juice

1 teaspoon grated lemon peel

1 teaspoon lemon pepper seasoning

1 teaspoon paprika

COATING

6 cups corn flakes

1 teaspoon dried thyme

1 teaspoon poultry seasoning

1 teaspoon garlic salt

1 teaspoon paprika

2 tablespoons sesame seeds

NUTRITIONAL DATA (PER SERVING)

Fat: 4.8 grams   Calories: 277   % Calories from fat: 15%

Zesty Tortilla Chicken Strips

Yield: *4 servings*

2 egg whites

1 tablespoon water

18 ounces skinless boneless chicken breast, cut into 1- to 1½-inch strips

Butter-flavored cooking spray

COATING

1 cup finely crushed Baked Tostitos corn chips or other baked corn chips

½ teaspoon onion powder

½ teaspoon poultry seasoning

½ teaspoon garlic salt

½ teaspoon crushed red pepper flakes

1 tablespoon brown sugar

Dash freshly ground black pepper

These are great served with a fresh green salad and a cool, sweet dessert to calm the delicious fire in your mouth!

1. To make the coating, place all of the coating ingredients in a large resealable plastic bag, close the bag, and shake to mix thoroughly. Set aside.

2. Place the egg whites and water in a medium-sized bowl, and whisk until well blended.

3. Rinse the chicken under cold water, and pat dry with paper towels. Place the chicken in the egg mixture, and turn to coat well. Then place the chicken in the bag of coating, close the bag, and shake until all of the strips are thoroughly coated.

4. Lightly spray a large baking sheet with butter-flavored cooking spray. Take 1 chicken strip out of the bag at a time, and arrange on the baking sheet, making sure that the strips do not touch one another.

5. Lightly spray the tops of the strips with the cooking spray, and bake on the center rack of a preheated 400°F oven for 15 to 20 minutes, or until light golden brown, easily pierced with a fork, and no longer pink when cut with a knife. Turn once during baking. Serve hot.

NUTRITIONAL DATA (PER SERVING)

Fat: 5 grams   Calories: 245   % Calories from fat: 18%

Spicy Chicken With Bow Ties

This Italian-style casserole is sure to please everyone!

1. Rinse the chicken under cold water, and pat dry with paper towels. Sprinkle garlic salt and pepper over the chicken pieces to taste.

2. Pour the chicken broth into a large Dutch oven, and preheat over medium-high heat. Add the chicken, and cook, stirring occasionally, until all sides are white.

3. Remove the chicken from the heat, and stir in the pasta sauce, buttermilk, and basil. Place over medium-high heat, bring to a simmer, cover, and cook for 15 minutes.

4. While the chicken mixture is cooking, prepare the bow ties according to package directions. Drain.

5. Remove the chicken from the heat, and stir in the prepared bow ties and Parmesan cheese. Lightly spray a 13-x-9-inch baking dish with cooking spray, and transfer the chicken mixture to the dish.

6. Cover the dish with aluminum foil, and bake in a preheated 350°F oven for 30 to 35 minutes. Allow to sit for 5 to 10 minutes before serving.

Yield: *12 servings*

20 ounces skinless boneless chicken breast, cut into bite-sized pieces

Garlic salt to taste

Freshly ground black pepper to taste

½ cup Chicken Stock (page 92) or other fat-free chicken broth

2 jars (30 ounces each) Ragu Chunky Tomatoes, Garlic, and Onion Pasta Sauce

1 cup nonfat buttermilk

1 tablespoon crushed dried basil

1 pound bow tie pasta

½ cup grated Parmesan cheese

NUTRITIONAL DATA (PER SERVING)

Fat: 8 grams   Calories: 348   % Calories from fat: 21%

Kraut, Apple, and Sausage Bake

Yield: *8 servings*

1½ cups Chicken Stock (page 92), Vegetable Stock (page 96), or other fat-free stock, divided

1 pound Healthy Choice low-fat smoked sausage, or other low-fat smoked sausage, cut into ½-inch slices

1 large onion, finely chopped

½ cup brown sugar, packed

3 medium unpeeled golden Delicious apples, cored and cut into ½-inch slices

2 cans (1 pound each) Bavarian-style sauerkraut with caraway seeds, drained

The famous French scientist Louis Pasteur praised sauerkraut as "one of the most useful and healthful vegetable dishes on earth." This delicious sweet-and-sour dish is just one of the many tasty ways to serve this good-for-you vegetable. So here's to you, Louis!

1. Place ½ cup of the stock in a large skillet, and bring to a boil over high heat. Reduce the heat to medium-high, add the sausage and onions, and cook, stirring occasionally, for 5 to 10 minutes, or until the sausage is heated through and the onion is tender.

2. Transfer the sausage and onions to paper towels to drain. Then place in a covered dish, and set aside.

3. Wipe out the skillet with a paper towel, add the remaining cup of stock, and bring to a boil over medium-high heat. Reduce the heat to medium, and add the brown sugar, stirring until the sugar is dissolved. Add the apple slices, stirring to cover well, and cook uncovered for 5 minutes.

4. Remove the skillet from the heat, and stir in the sausage mixture. Transfer the mixture to a 2½-quart casserole dish, and toss in the sauerkraut.

5. Cover and bake in a preheated 350°F oven for 20 minutes, or until the apples are tender. Let sit, covered, for 5 to 10 minutes before serving.

NUTRITIONAL DATA (PER SERVING)

Fat: 1.8 grams   Calories: 200   % Calories from fat: 8%

Honey-Mustard Baked Beans With Sausage

This dish is what I call a "weekender," as you can assemble and bake it on Saturday morning, and then place it in the refrigerator, ready for the next hungry person. Warmed, it makes a satisfying snack or a one-dish meal.

1. Cut the sausage into 5 pieces, each 3 inches in length. Slice each 3-inch piece in half lengthwise. If using a microwave oven, arrange the pieces on a microwave-safe plate, cover with plastic wrap, and microwave on high for 3 minutes, or until heated through. If using a conventional stove, arrange the sausage pieces in a large nonstick skillet, and cook over medium to medium-high heat for 5 to 10 minutes, or until heated through.

2. Blot the sausages with paper towels to absorb as much fat as possible. Cut each piece into 3 pieces, and set aside.

3. Place all of the remaining ingredients in a 2½-quart casserole dish, and stir to mix well. Add the sausage, and stir to mix.

4. Bake uncovered in a preheated 375°F oven for 30 minutes. Allow to sit for at least 10 minutes before serving.

Quick Dish

Yield: *8 servings*

1 pound Healthy Choice low-fat smoked sausage, or other low-fat smoked sausage

3 cans (1 pound each) Van Camp's Vegetarian Style Pork and Beans, drained

¼ cup dark corn syrup

⅓ cup honey mustard-style barbecue sauce

2 tablespoons brown sugar, packed

1 teaspoon liquid smoke

1 small onion, chopped

NUTRITIONAL DATA (PER SERVING)

Fat: 2 grams	Calories: 190	% Calories from fat: 9%

Red Beans With Long Grain and Wild Rice

Yield: *6 servings*

¼ cup Vegetable Stock (page 96) or other fat-free stock

2 medium onions, chopped

1 large clove garlic, minced

2 cans (8 ounces each) tomato sauce

1 cup water

1 cup finely chopped green bell pepper

1 can (14½ ounces) Hunt's Choice-Cut diced tomatoes with roasted garlic, or other canned diced tomatoes, undrained

3 cans (1 pound each) dark red kidney beans, rinsed and drained

1 teaspoon crushed red pepper flakes

½ teaspoon dried thyme

1–2 tablespoons chili powder

1 large bay leaf

1 tablespoon sugar (optional)

Salt and freshly ground black pepper to taste

3 cups Chicken Stock (page 92) or other fat-free stock

1½ cups long grain and wild rice blend, or ¾ cup long grain rice plus ¾ cup wild rice

This is a new twist on a time-honored Southern dish. Adding a fresh green salad makes this a satisfyingly delicious meal!

1. Place the vegetable stock in a large, heavy skillet, and place over medium-high heat until hot. Add the onions and garlic, and sauté for 5 to 10 minutes, or until tender.

2. Reduce the heat to medium-low, and add the tomato sauce, water, bell pepper, and canned tomatoes to the skillet. Stir to blend well, and simmer, partially covered, for 15 minutes, stirring occasionally.

3. Stir the beans, crushed red pepper, thyme, chili powder, bay leaf, and sugar into the tomato mixture. Continue to cook, covered, for 45 minutes, stirring occasionally. Add salt and pepper to taste.

4. While the bean mixture is cooking, place the chicken stock in a medium-sized saucepan, and bring to a boil over high heat. Stir the rice into the stock, and return to a boil. Reduce the heat to medium-low, just to the point of a simmer; cover; and cook for 15 to 25 minutes, or until most of the stock has been absorbed. Do not stir or lift the cover during cooking. Remove the pot from the heat, and allow to sit, covered, for 10 minutes, or until the rice is fluffy and all of the stock has been absorbed.

5. Spoon the rice into a large serving bowl or casserole dish, making an indentation in the center. Spoon the beans into the center of the rice and serve hot, passing a bottle of hot pepper sauce.

NUTRITIONAL DATA (PER SERVING)

Fat: 2.1 grams   Calories: 455   % Calories from fat: 4%

Variation

To make Red Beans, Rice, and Sausage, cut up 1½ pounds of Healthy Choice low-fat smoked turkey sausage into ¼-inch slices, and then cut each slice into quarters. Bring ¼ cup of stock to a boil and add the sausage. Reduce the heat to medium, and cook for about 10 minutes. Add another ¾ cup of stock, and cook for 10 additional minutes. Stir both the sausage-stock mixture and the beans into the rice, and serve hot. Serves 10.

NUTRITIONAL DATA (PER SERVING)

Fat: 2.8 grams   Calories: 370   % Calories from fat: 7%

Italian Sausage and Peppers With Rice

This combination of sausage and peppers is wonderful with rice!

Yield: *6 servings*

1. Place ¼ cup of the stock in a medium-sized skillet, and bring to a boil over medium-high heat. Add the sausage, and cook uncovered for 10 minutes, stirring occasionally.

2. Remove the sausage from the skillet, and set aside to drain on paper towels, blotting the top of the sausage with additional paper towels. Allow the toweling to remain on the sausage to keep it warm.

3. Wipe out the skillet with paper towels, and add the remaining ¾ cup of stock. Bring to a boil over medium-high heat. Reduce the heat to medium, add the garlic and bell peppers, and sauté for 8 to 10 minutes, or until the pepper strips are crisp-tender.

4. Stir the wine into the skillet mixture, blending thoroughly. Add the drained sausage, and stir to mix well. Cover and cook over medium heat for 15 minutes, stirring occasionally.

5. Arrange the rice on a large serving platter, and spoon the sausage mixture over the rice. Serve hot.

1 cup Brown Beef Stock (page 90) or other fat-free stock, divided

1 pound Mr. Turkey Smoked Italian Sausage, sliced into ¼-inch-thick pieces

1 large clove garlic, minced

1 large green bell pepper, cut into thin strips

1 large red bell pepper, cut into thin strips

1 cup dry red wine

4 cups prepared fluffy white or brown rice

NUTRITIONAL DATA (PER SERVING)

Fat: 6.6 grams   Calories: 295   % Calories from fat: 20%

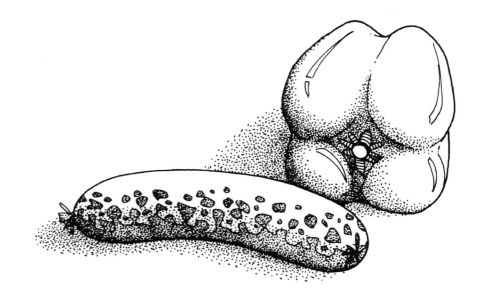

Great Northern Beans and Smoky Ham

Quick Dish

Yield: *8 servings*

4 cans (15½ ounces each) Great Northern beans, undrained

6 cups water

1 package (5½ ounces) Louis Rich Carving Board smoked ham, chopped

1 medium onion, chopped

1 large carrot, shredded

1 teaspoon liquid smoke

1 teaspoon ground dried summer savory

1 medium bay leaf

½ teaspoon onion salt

Freshly ground black pepper to taste

No need to cook this recipe for hours to get that authentic smoke-house flavor!

1. Place the beans and water in a large pot, and stir to mix. Bring to a boil over medium-high heat.

2. Reduce the heat to medium-low, and add the ham, onion, carrot, liquid smoke, and seasonings. Stir to mix, partially cover, and simmer for 45 minutes, stirring occasionally.

3. Serve hot, passing a bottle of hot sauce for those who like it hot and spicy.

NUTRITIONAL DATA (PER SERVING)

Fat: 2.4 grams   Calories: 228   % Calories from fat: 9%

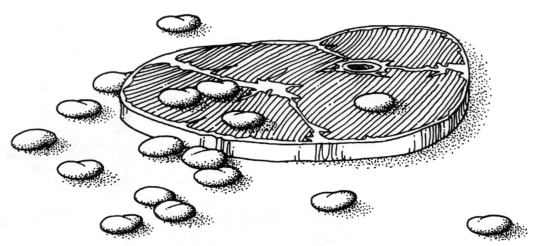

Baked Tuna Fish Cakes With Pickle Sauce

These savory tuna cakes may be served either hot or cold.

Yield: *8 servings*

1. To make the sauce, place all of the sauce ingredients, except for the relish, in a blender, and blend on high speed until creamy. Transfer the sauce to a small bowl, and stir in the pickle relish. Cover and chill until ready to serve.

2. Place the tuna, bread crumbs, and egg whites in a large mixing bowl, and stir to mix, breaking up any large pieces of the tuna.

3. Add the celery, onion, parsley, and lemon juice to the tuna mixture, adding onion salt to taste. Mix thoroughly.

4. Place the cereal in a large resealable plastic bag, and close the bag. Cover with a kitchen towel, and use a rolling pin to crush the flakes into fine crumbs. Transfer the crumbs to a shallow dish, and set aside.

5. Using your hands, firmly pat the tuna mixture into eight cakes of equal size. Press the cakes into the cereal crumbs, covering all sides.

6. Lightly coat a large baking sheet with cooking spray, and arrange the cakes on the sheet. Lightly spray the tops of the cakes with the spray, and bake in a preheated 350°F oven for 25 minutes, or until lightly browned, turning once during baking.

7. Serve hot, topped with a spoonful of the chilled sauce and garnished with fresh parsley.

NUTRITIONAL DATA (PER SERVING WITH SAUCE)

Fat: 1.7 grams	Calories: 165	% Calories from fat: 9%

2 cans (9 ounces each) chunk light tuna packed in water, drained

3 slices day-old whole wheat bread, made into fine crumbs

3 egg whites, slightly beaten

1 medium stalk celery, finely chopped

1 medium onion, finely chopped

1 heaping tablespoon dried parsley

1 tablespoon lemon juice

Onion salt to taste

1½ cups Wheaties cereal

Butter-flavored cooking spray

Fresh parsley sprigs (garnish)

SAUCE

1 cup 2% creamed or small curd cottage cheese

½ cup bottled fat-free French dressing

½ teaspoon lemon juice

Salt to taste

¼ cup sweet pickle relish

Garlic

For thousands of years, garlic has been greatly valued for its medicinal properties—and recently, scientific studies have proven that it deserves its reputation. It has been shown to lower blood pressure, to guard against infection, and to boost immune system function. It even may be a cancer preventive. But for the true garlic lover, all of this pales beside the fact that garlic, with its uniquely pungent flavor and aroma, can enhance an amazing variety of foods, from vegetables and meats to pastas and breads. Roasted, it can even be eaten on its own!

To the low-fat cook, garlic is an especially useful ingredient, as it adds glorious flavor, but no fat and few calories. But like any other ingredient, garlic will give you the best results when it is selected, stored, and used with care. Following are a few guidelines that will help you get the most out of this flavorsome bulb.

Choosing and Storing Garlic

At your supermarket, you are certain to find at least the common cloved garlic, which is what comes to mind when most people think of this vegetable. In addition, you may find elephant garlic. Although called "garlic," this is just a close cousin to garlic, and actually a wild ancestor of the leek. While its taste is quite pleasant, and although it can be used in much the same way as regular garlic, it is much milder, and is not a good substitute for true garlic.

Regardless of the type of garlic you're buying, choose heads that are fresh, firm, and without brown spots or sprouts. Then, once you get your garlic home, keep the heads intact, and store the garlic in a cool, dry, dark place—not in the refrigerator. Break off individual cloves only as the need arises. Depending on its age, properly stored garlic can last up to two months.

Cooking With Garlic

The way you cut—or don't cut—a clove of garlic will actually make a difference in the flavor of your dish. For the mildest of flavors, leave the clove whole. Slicing will give you a stronger flavor; mincing, even stronger; and crushing, strongest of all.

Another factor that can influence a garlic's flavor is the green "germ" that develops in the center of each clove as it ages. This germ—which, if the clove were planted, would become the stalk of the new plant—has a strong flavor, and can even be bitter.

If desired, slice each clove in half and the remove the bitter germ before adding the garlic to your dish.

The easiest way to peel a clove of garlic is to lay it on the countertop, place the flat side of a large, heavy chef's knife on top of it, and hit the blade with the side of your fist or the palm of your hand. Presto! A slightly smashed clove of garlic will easily slip out of its peel.

When sautéing garlic, do not let it get too brown, as it will lend a bitter taste to your dish. Rather, allow it to get only golden or lightly browned. When cooking garlic in liquids—in soups or stews, for instance—the flavor will actually become milder as the dish cooks.

To obtain the sweetest, mellowest flavor possible, roast your garlic before adding it to your dishes. To roast individual cloves of garlic, arrange the unpeeled cloves on a baking sheet or in a small baking dish. Cover with foil, and bake in a preheated 350°F oven for 15 minutes, or until soft and tender. To roast an entire head of garlic, wrap the intact head in aluminum foil, and place in the oven for an hour, or until soft. If using an outdoor grill, slice the top from a large head of garlic, and spray the top with I Can't Believe It's Not Butter spray. Place unwrapped on the edge of the grill, away from direct heat, for 30 minutes, or until very soft and tender. The roasted cloves may be squeezed out of the peel and used as a hot spread for bread; may be served as an accompaniment for meat dishes; or may be stirred into a variety of recipes.

Too Much of a Good Thing?

The distinctive odor for which the garlic is so prized becomes an annoyance to some people after they cook with or eat this delectable bulb. Fortunately, some simple measures can eliminate this problem.

To remove garlic odor from your hands, rub them with a cut lemon and rinse with water. Then rub your hands with salt and rinse once more. If the odor persists, wash with soapy water. In some kitchen stores and chef's catalogues, you can also find metal odor removers that can rub the odor from your hands.

If you want sweeter breath after eating garlic, try chewing fresh parsley, citrus peel, fennel, cloves, cardamom seeds, or fenugreek seeds. These foods should help remove the offensive odor, leaving just the memory of your divinely garlic-flavored meal!

Teriyaki Halibut Steaks

For added zest, accompany the steaks with Piquant Mango-Pineapple-Orange Relish (page 122).

Yield: *6 servings*

1. Rinse the halibut steaks with cool water, and pat dry with paper towels. Set aside.

2. Place a large resealable plastic bag in a bowl, with the bag's edges over the sides of the bowl so that the bag remains open. Pour in the teriyaki sauce.

3. Place the halibut steaks in the plastic bag and close the bag, expelling as much air as possible. Turn and press the bag until the fish is well coated, and lay the bag in a flat container for 1 hour in the refrigerator, turning once to evenly distribute the liquid.

4. Line a broiler pan with aluminum foil. Remove the steaks from the marinade, placing them on a rack in the broiler pan. Set aside.

5. Pour the marinade into a small saucepan, and bring to a fast boil over medium-high heat. Continue to boil for 1 minute. Reduce the heat just to the point of a simmer, and whisk in the margarine, butter-flavored sprinkles, and garlic, adding salt and pepper to taste. Continue to cook, whisking constantly, for 3 to 5 minutes. Remove from the heat and set aside.

6. Place the steaks in a preheated broiler, and baste the tops with the teriyaki mixture. Broil for 5 minutes. Turn, baste again, and broil for 5 additional minutes, or until the fish is opaque and flakes easily with a fork. Garnish with the parsley, and serve hot.

Six 5-ounce halibut steaks, ¾ to 1 inch thick

½ cup Kikkoman Teriyaki Marinade and Sauce or other bottled marinade

1½ tablespoons reduced-fat margarine

1 teaspoon butter-flavored sprinkles

1 medium clove garlic, crushed

Salt and freshly ground black pepper to taste

Chopped fresh parsley (garnish)

NUTRITIONAL DATA (PER SERVING)

Fat: 5 grams	Calories: 198	% Calories from fat: 22%

Atlantic Pollack and Rice With Tomato-Basil Sauce

Yield: *4 servings*

1¼ pounds fresh or frozen (partially thawed) skinless pollack fillets

Lemon pepper seasoning to taste

1 medium onion, thinly sliced and separated into rings

1 medium green bell pepper, cut into thin strips

1 cup long grain rice

2 cups cold water

½ teaspoon salt

Fresh parsley sprigs (garnish)

TOMATO-BASIL SAUCE

1 can (6 ounces) tomato paste

9–12 ounces water, according to desired thickness of sauce

1 can (8 ounces) tomato sauce

1 large clove garlic, minced

1 tablespoon crushed dried sweet basil

2 teaspoons crushed dried parsley

1 teaspoon sugar

Garlic salt and freshly ground black pepper to taste

This succulent dish is unbelievably light in fat and calories, but certainly not light in taste! If you don't have pollack available, you may substitute whiting, cod, haddock, or flounder without losing any of the delicious flavor.

1. To make the sauce, place the tomato paste and water in a medium-sized saucepan, and stir over medium-high heat until smooth.

2. Reduce the heat to medium, and stir in the remaining sauce ingredients, blending until well mixed. Bring to a slow simmer, cover, and cook for 5 to 10 minutes, stirring occasionally. Set aside.

3. Rinse the fish with cool water, and pat dry with paper towels. Arrange the fillets in a single layer in a 13-x-13-x-2-inch casserole dish, and sprinkle with the lemon pepper to taste.

4. Arrange the onion and bell pepper over the fish. Spoon all of the sauce over the fish and vegetables, completely covering the top.

5. Cover the casserole with a lid or aluminum foil, and bake in a preheated 400°F oven for 25 to 30 minutes, or until the fish flakes easily with a fork.

6. While the fish is baking, place the rice, water, and salt in a medium-sized heavy saucepan. Cover with a tight-fitting lid, and bring to a vigorous boil. Immediately reduce the heat to medium-low and simmer for 15 minutes. Do not stir or lift the cover. Remove the pot from the heat, and allow the rice to steam, covered, for an additional 10 minutes, or until the water has been totally absorbed and the rice is fluffy.

7. Transfer the hot rice to a large, shallow serving dish, and spoon the fish and sauce over the rice. Garnish with the parsley, and serve immediately.

NUTRITIONAL DATA (PER SERVING)

Fat: .6 gram   Calories: 325   % Calories from fat: 1%

Crab and Scallop-Stuffed Sweet Red Peppers

This is a beautiful main dish, full of tender, flavorful seafood.

1. Cut a slice from the top of each pepper, and remove the seeds and membranes.

2. Fill a large pot with water, and bring to a boil over high heat. Add the peppers, fully immersing them in the water, and cook for 5 minutes, or until slightly softened. Remove the peppers from the pot, drain, and set aside.

3. Place 3 cups of the chicken stock in a medium-sized pot, and bring to a boil over medium-high heat. Stir in the rice, cover, and remove from the heat. Let sit for at least 5 minutes without removing the lid.

4. Place the remaining ¼ cup of chicken stock in a large skillet, and preheat over medium-high heat. Add the scallions, garlic, and celery, and cook, stirring often, for about 5 minutes, or until tender.

5. Remove the skillet from the heat, and gently stir in the crab and scallops, blending well.

6. Place the cheeses in a large bowl, and stir to mix. Add the rice and the seafood mixture to the cheese mixture, and stir gently to blend thoroughly. Add the onion salt and pepper to taste.

7. Arrange the peppers, cut sides up, in a 13-x-13-x-2-inch baking dish. Divide the rice mixture among the peppers, cover, and bake in a preheated 350°F oven for 20 minutes, or until heated through. Serve hot, garnishing each pepper top with a sprig of parsley.

Yield: *6 servings*

6 medium-sized red bell peppers

3¼ cups Chicken Stock (page 92) or other fat-free chicken stock, divided

3 cups instant white rice

6 small scallions, finely chopped (include tops)

1 large clove garlic, minced

1 medium stalk celery, chopped

8 ounces flake-style imitation crab meat, finely chopped

8 ounces bay-style imitation sea scallops, cut into halves

½ cup shredded reduced-fat Cheddar cheese

½ cup shredded fat-free Cheddar cheese

¼ cup grated Parmesan cheese

Onion salt and freshly ground black pepper to taste

6 fresh parsley sprigs (garnish)

NUTRITIONAL DATA (PER SERVING)

Fat: 2.6 grams   Calories: 340   % Calories from fat: 7%

9

Viva Vegetables and Other Side Dishes

Lovely, lovely vegetables. Vibrant colors, a wealth of nutrients, *and* fabulous flavors. Who could ask for more? I have such a love of vegetables that my children have given me a large wicker basket in which nestles a collection of beautiful silk vegetables, adding color and warmth to my kitchen.

As interest in healthy eating has increased, so has interest in the vegetable. As a result, new and creative ways of cooking these wonderful foods have emerged, making it more pleasurable than ever to enjoy the vegetables we need for good health.

This chapter is the result of my love affair with the bounty of the garden. In it, you will find well over two dozen recipes for a wide variety of dishes using a wide range of fresh and frozen veggies. Potatoes are my all-time favorite, so you'll find several delectable potato dishes, including Roasted Rosemary and Garlic Potatoes, Best Ever Sweet Potatoes, and Baked Potato Pancakes. You'll also find such treasures as Gingered Baby Carrots, Roasted Chili Corn on the Cob, and more—dishes for every taste and every occasion. For those times when you're in a hurry and need to whip up a side dish in no time flat, you'll find plenty of Quick Dishes, too. And from Honey-Orange Peas to Simply Mushrooms, all are as high in flavor as they are low in fat.

When making any vegetable dish, I urge you to buy the best quality produce you can find. Always look for veggies with good bright colors and a firm texture. Besides looking and tasting great, these vegetables are higher in nutrients than produce that is past its prime. Then find a recipe that suits your fancy, and you'll soon become a vegetable lover, too!

Savory Pinto Bean Bake

Yield: *4 servings*

1 can (1 pound) pinto beans, rinsed and drained

¼ cup chopped sweet red bell pepper

½ cup Smoky Honey Barbecue Sauce (page 108)

¼ cup dark brown sugar, packed

2 tablespoons Oscar Mayer Real Bacon Bits

1 tablespoon dehydrated onion flakes

This easy side dish is a great accompaniment for sandwiches.

1. Place all of the ingredients in a 1½-quart casserole dish, and stir to mix well.

2. Bake uncovered in a preheated 350°F oven for 45 minutes, or until the sauce is thick and syrupy. Serve hot.

NUTRITIONAL DATA (PER SERVING)

Fat: 1 gram   Calories: 105   % Fat from calories: 8%

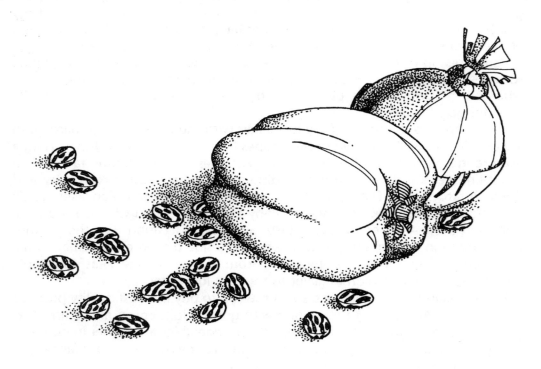

Healthy Refried Beans

In Mexico, refried beans are served at breakfast with eggs, as a side dish with lunch or dinner, and wrapped in a tortilla for between-meal snacks. The lard used in traditional Mexican refried beans makes this delicious dish very high in fat. Replace the lard with chicken stock, and the dish is just as delicious and much healthier.

1. Place the stock in a large nonstick skillet, and bring to a boil over medium-high heat. Reduce the heat to medium, and add the onion and garlic. Cook, stirring occasionally, for about 5 minutes, or until tender.

2. Drain the beans, reserving the liquid. Stir the beans and seasonings into the stock mixture, adding the chilies and/or salsa if a spicier dish is desired.

3. Using a sturdy metal or wooden spoon, mash the spices into the beans as they cook until the mixture is as smooth as desired. Add the drained bean liquid if needed to moisten the mixture.

4. Continue to cook, stirring often, for about 5 minutes, or until the beans are thick and smooth. If the mixture seems too dry, add more stock or any remaining bean liquid. Serve hot.

Quick Dish

Yield: *4 servings*

½ cup Chicken Stock (page 92) or other fat-free stock

1 small onion, minced

1 small clove garlic, minced

1 can (1 pound) red kidney beans or pinto beans, undrained

1–2 tablespoons chili powder

2 teaspoons ground cumin

Salt and pepper to taste

1 can (4 ounces) diced green chilies, drained (optional)

4 ounces salsa (optional)

NUTRITIONAL DATA (PER SERVING)

Fat: <1 gram   Calories: 125   % Calories from fat: 5%

Italian Baked Tomatoes

Quick Dish

Yield: *4 servings*

4 medium-sized firm ripe tomatoes, cored

2 slices day-old whole wheat bread

½ cup Brown Beef Stock (page 90), Chicken Stock (page 92), or other fat-free stock

1 small onion, finely chopped

1 large clove garlic, finely chopped

2 teaspoons dried sweet basil

½ teaspoon ground dried oregano

Salt and freshly ground black pepper to taste

1 tablespoon dried parsley

2 tablespoons grated Parmesan cheese (optional)

Butter-flavored cooking spray

Here is the Italian version of the perfect side dish to almost any entrée.

1. Slice the tomatoes in half crosswise, and arrange, cut sides up, in a broiling pan. Set aside.

2. Tear the bread into pieces, and place in a blender or food processor. Process until the bread turns into fine crumbs. Set aside.

3. Place the stock in a small nonstick skillet, and bring to a boil over medium-high heat. Reduce the heat to medium, and add the onion and garlic. Cook, stirring occasionally, for about 5 minutes, or until tender. Stir in the basil and oregano, and add salt and pepper to taste. Cook for 5 additional minutes.

4. While the onion mixture is cooking, place the bread crumbs, parsley, and, if desired, the Parmesan cheese in a small dish, and stir to mix.

5. Spoon the onion mixture over the tops of the tomato halves. Sprinkle the bread crumb mixture evenly over the tops, and spray each lightly with the cooking spray.

6. Bake in a preheated 450°F oven for 10 minutes, or until the bread crumbs are toasted and the tomatoes are soft, but not mushy. Serve hot.

NUTRITIONAL DATA (PER SERVING)

| Fat: .5 gram | Calories: 61 | % Calories from fat: 7% |

Gingered Baby Carrots

These sweet, gingery carrots can induce any child to eat his vegetables!

1. Place the water and butter-flavored salt in a medium-sized saucepan, and bring to a boil over medium-high heat. Add the carrots, cover, and reduce the heat to the point of a simmer. Cook for 10 to 15 minutes, or until the carrots are crisp-tender. Drain the carrots, and set aside.

2. Place the brown sugar, ginger, orange juice, and extract in a small mixing bowl, and whisk together until well mixed. Pour the mixture into a medium-sized skillet, and cook over medium heat, stirring constantly, for 3 to 5 minutes, or until the mixture becomes bubbly and thickened.

3. Increase the heat to medium-high, and add the carrots to the ginger glaze, gently tossing to cover well. Add the parsley, and continue to cook, gently tossing constantly, until the carrots are glazed and the liquid has been absorbed.

4. Spray the carrots lightly with the butter spray, gently toss to blend, and cook for 1 additional minute. Serve hot.

Yield: *4 servings*

1 cup water

¼ teaspoon butter-flavored salt

1 pound baby carrots

3 tablespoons brown sugar, packed

½ teaspoon ground ginger

½ cup orange juice

½ teaspoon butter-flavored extract

2 teaspoons dried parsley

I Can't Believe It's Not Butter spray

NUTRITIONAL DATA (PER SERVING)

Fat: 0 gram	Calories: 100	% Calories from fat: 0%

Minted Glazed Carrots

Yield: *6 servings*

1 cup water or Vegetable Stock
(page 96), divided

6 large carrots, peeled and cut
into 2-x-¼-inch strips

1 cup brown sugar, not packed

1 teaspoon butter-flavored
sprinkles

¼ cup chopped fresh mint, or 2
teaspoons dried mint

2 tablespoons reduced-fat
margarine

*This is a delightfully attractive dish that is as rich in nutrients as it is
in flavor!*

1. Pour ½ cup of the water or stock into a medium-sized saucepan,
and bring to a slow boil over medium-high heat. Add the carrots and
cook uncovered for 3 to 5 minutes, or just until crisp-tender. Drain the
carrots, and transfer to a 2-quart casserole dish. Cover and set aside.

2. Place the remaining ½ cup of water and the brown sugar, butter-flavored sprinkles, and mint in the medium-sized saucepan, and bring to
a boil over medium-high heat. Reduce the heat to medium, and whisk
in the margarine. Cook, stirring often, for 3 to 5 minutes, or until the
sugar has dissolved and the margarine is melted.

3. Pour the brown sugar glaze over the carrots, tossing to cover well.
Cover and bake in a preheated 350°F oven for 20 minutes, or until
thick and syrupy, occasionally spooning the glaze over the carrots.
Serve hot.

NUTRITIONAL DATA (PER SERVING)

Fat: 2 grams   Calories: 137   % Calories from fat: 13%

Quick Mesquite Chicken Rice

Quick Dish

Yield: *4 servings*

2 cups Chicken Stock (page 92)
or water

2 teaspoons mesquite chicken
seasoning

½ teaspoon poultry seasoning

½ teaspoon celery seed

Onion salt and freshly ground
black pepper to taste

2 cups instant brown or white rice

*In a hurry? Don't grab a high-fat side dish out of the frozen food
case. Instead, whip up this healthy dish in less than 15 minutes.*

1. Place the stock and seasonings in a medium-sized saucepan, and
stir to mix. Bring to a boil over medium-high heat.

2. Stir the rice into the stock mixture. Cover, remove from the heat,
and let sit, covered, for 5 minutes, or until the stock has been entirely
absorbed. Fluff and serve hot.

NUTRITIONAL DATA (PER SERVING)

Fat: 0 gram   Calories: 170   % Calories from fat: 0%

Mighty Parmesan Vegetables

All of the vegetables in this delicious Parmesan-flavored dish are packed with vitamins, minerals, and fiber. That's what makes these veggies so mighty!

1. Place the water or stock and the salt in a medium-sized saucepan, and bring to a boil over medium-high heat. Add the vegetables, stirring to mix. Reduce the heat to medium, cover, and simmer for 6 to 8 minutes, or until the vegetables are crisp-tender.

2. Drain the vegetables, and stir in the margarine and cheese. Serve hot.

NUTRITIONAL DATA (PER SERVING)

Fat: 1.5 grams   Calories: 59   % Calories from fat: 22%

Quick Dish

Yield: *6 servings*

1½ cups water or Vegetable Stock (page 96)

Salt to taste

½ pound snow peas, strings removed (optional)

½ pound broccoli florets (about 2 cups)

½ pound cauliflower florets (about 2 cups)

2 medium carrots, peeled and cut into julienne strips

1 tablespoon reduced-fat margarine

2 tablespoons grated Parmesan cheese

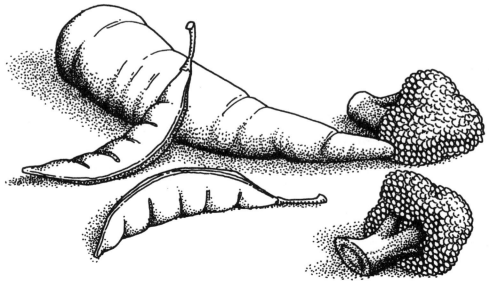

Mexican Rice With Tomato Sauce

Yield: *6 servings*

3 cups Chicken Stock (page 92) or other fat-free stock, divided

¼ cup chopped green bell pepper

1 small onion, chopped

1 medium clove garlic, minced

2 cups long-grain rice

2 cans (8 ounces each) tomato sauce

Salt and freshly ground black pepper to taste

This easy-to-make side dish is a great accompaniment to grilled fish or chicken.

1. Place ¼ cup of the stock in a large nonstick skillet, and bring to a boil over medium-high heat. Reduce the heat to medium, and add the bell pepper, onion, and garlic. Cook, stirring occasionally, for about 5 minutes, or until tender.

2. Stir the rice into the vegetable mixture, and cook, stirring constantly, for 3 to 5 minutes, or until well coated.

3. Stir the tomato sauce into the rice mixture, and cook for 3 to 5 minutes, or until the sauce is heated through.

4. Stir the remaining 2¾ cups of stock into the rice, and increase the heat to medium-high. Bring to a boil. Immediately reduce the heat to a slow simmer, cover, and cook for 15 to 20 minutes, or until the liquid has been entirely absorbed. Do not lift the pot lid during cooking.

5. Add salt and pepper to taste, and serve hot.

NUTRITIONAL DATA (PER SERVING)

Fat: 0 gram   Calories: 263   % Calories from fat: 0%

Green Pepper Rice

Looking for something different to serve on St. Patrick's Day? This fun, flavorful dish should be just the thing! If you want a little more bite, replace ¼ cup of the chicken stock with an equal amount of Tabasco jalapeño hot sauce.

1. Place the stock in large saucepan, and bring to a boil over medium-high heat. Boil for 1 minute. Then remove from the heat and allow to cool to room temperature.

2. Place ¼ cup of the cooled stock and the bell peppers, onion, garlic, and cilantro in a blender, and process on medium-high speed for 1 to 2 minutes, or until smooth. Set aside.

3. Place ½ cup of the cooled stock in a large skillet, and reheat over medium heat. Stir in the rice, and cook, stirring constantly, for about 5 minutes, or until the grains are well coated and consistent in color.

4. Stir the blender mixture into the rice, and cook, stirring constantly, for 5 minutes.

5. Stir the remaining 4 cups of stock into the rice, and increase the heat to medium-high. Bring to a boil. Immediately reduce the heat to a slow simmer, cover, and cook for about 20 minutes, or until the liquid has been entirely absorbed. Do not lift the pot lid during cooking.

6. Add salt and pepper to taste, and transfer the rice to a serving dish. Garnish with the parsley sprigs, and serve hot.

Yield: *6 servings*

4¾ cups Chicken Stock (page 92) or other fat-free stock

3 medium green bell peppers, chopped

1 large onion, chopped

1 large clove garlic, minced

2 teaspoons dried cilantro (optional)

2 cups long-grain rice

Salt and freshly ground black pepper to taste

Fresh parsley sprigs (optional)

NUTRITIONAL DATA (PER SERVING)

Fat: 0 gram   Calories: 273   % Calories from fat: 0%

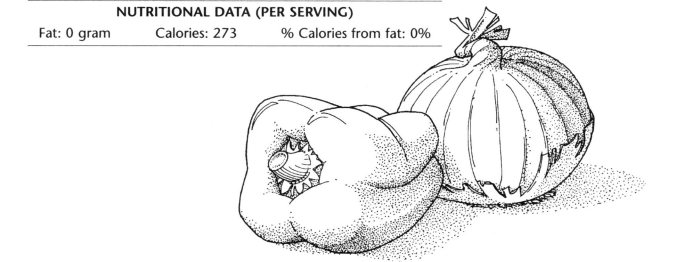

Rice Almandine With Mint

Yield: *8 servings*

4 cups Chicken Stock (page 92)
   or other fat-free stock

1 large clove garlic, minced

Salt and freshly ground black or
   white pepper to taste

4 cups instant long-grain rice

2 teaspoons crushed dried mint

2 ounces slivered almonds,
   toasted (page 77)

Fresh mint leaves (garnish)

Toasted almonds add a delightful crunch to this quick and easy dish.

1. Place the stock, garlic, and salt and pepper in a large saucepan, and bring to a boil over medium-high heat.

2. Stir the rice and the dried mint into the stock mixture. Cover, remove from the heat, and let sit for 5 minutes, or until the stock has been entirely absorbed.

3. Fluff the rice, and arrange on a serving dish. Sprinkle with the almonds, and garnish with the fresh mint. Serve hot.

NUTRITIONAL DATA (PER SERVING)

Fat: 3.7 grams   Calories: 223   % Calories from fat: 15%

Orange Blossom Rice

Yield: *6 servings*

1 cup long-grain rice

⅓ cup finely chopped celery

1 cup orange juice

1 cup fat-free stock, any type

2 tablespoons dehydrated onion
   flakes

½ teaspoon grated orange zest

¼ teaspoon butter-flavored salt or
   plain salt

1 tablespoon reduced-fat
   margarine

2 medium navel oranges, peeled
   and chopped into bite-sized
   bits

Slightly sweet and savory, this recipe makes a lovely pale orange side dish that will complement almost any meal.

1. Place all of the ingredients except for the orange bits in a medium-sized saucepan, and bring to a boil over medium-high heat.

2. Reduce the heat to the point of a slow simmer, cover, and cook for 15 to 20 minutes, or until all of the liquid has been absorbed. Do not lift the pot lid during cooking.

3. Add the orange bits to the rice, and toss gently to mix. Serve hot.

NUTRITIONAL DATA (PER SERVING)

Fat: 1 gram   Calories: 159   % Calories from fat: 5%

Hungarian Baked Potatoes

You might want to serve these potatoes with a bowl of paprika-sprinkled plain nonfat yogurt or Healthy Sour Cream (page 106). Any leftover potatoes are delicious reheated in a microwave or conventional oven.

1. Using a fork, pierce each potato 4 times. If using a conventional oven, place the potatoes on the center rack of a preheated 400°F oven for 45 minutes, or until soft. If using a microwave oven, microwave each potato on high for 7 to 8 minutes, or until soft.

2. While the potatoes are baking, place the cheeses in a small bowl, and stir to combine. Set aside.

3. Cut each potato in half lengthwise, and use a spoon to scoop out the pulp, leaving the skin intact. Transfer the skins to a baking dish, and set aside.

4. Place the potato pulp, yogurt, margarine, bacon, butter-flavored salt, 1 teaspoon of the paprika, ½ cup of the cheese, and the pepper in a medium-sized bowl. Using an electric mixer, whip on medium-low speed until fluffy and well blended.

5. Spoon the potatoes back into the skins, dividing the mixture equally. Top each with some of the remaining cheese and a sprinkling of the remaining paprika.

6. Return the potatoes to the oven, and bake at 400°F for 10 to 15 minutes, or until the cheese is melted and the potatoes are golden. Serve hot.

Yield: *8 servings*

4 medium unpeeled baking potatoes

¼ cup shredded reduced-fat sharp Cheddar cheese

½ cup shredded fat-free sharp Cheddar cheese

¾ cup plain nonfat yogurt

2 tablespoons reduced-fat margarine

2 tablespoons Oscar Mayer Real Bacon Bits

½ teaspoon butter-flavored salt

1½ teaspoons paprika, divided

Freshly ground black pepper to taste

NUTRITIONAL DATA (PER SERVING)

Fat: 2.6 grams   Calories: 166   % Calories from fat: 14%

The Popular Potato

One of the world's most popular and versatile vegetables—and certainly my personal favorite—the potato is also a great food for anyone who's following a healthy, low-fat diet. If you find this surprising, consider, first, that the potato is a virtual powerhouse of nutrition, with protein, fiber, vitamins B and C, and a wealth of minerals. At the same time, a medium-sized white potato contains only a trace of fat and about 120 calories. Why, then, does this wholesome vegetable have a reputation for being fattening? Because it's so often served fried or topped with butter, sour cream, or high-fat cheese! Prepared properly, though, potatoes can be a delicious and nutritious addition to your diet.

When using potatoes, you'll get the most satisfying results when you choose the best type for your dish, when you select the highest-quality produce available, and when you store and prepare your potatoes properly once you get them home. The following information should help you get the most out of each and every potato dish you make.

Knowing Your Potatoes

Although there are well over one hundred varieties of white potatoes, you're likely to find only a few types at your local supermarket. Each of these falls into one of two categories: mealy-textured potatoes, which are best for mashing and baking, or waxy potatoes, which are best for making potato salads. Then, of course, there's the sweet potato—which makes a delicious change of pace from the more common white varieties. The following potatoes are those that are most frequently called for in recipes and found in grocery stores.

Long white potatoes. These long, curved waxy potatoes have a thin, light tan skin, and make excellent boiled or roasted potatoes. Well-known varieties include White Rose and California News.

New potatoes. Not a variety in itself, the new potato is actually a young, immature version of any of the other types discussed here. Usually small, these firm and slightly sweet potatoes have thin skins, and are great for steaming or boiling, and for potato salads. As these potatoes don't keep as well as more mature potatoes, it is best to purchase only the amount you will use in a few days.

Round red potatoes. These waxy potatoes, which include Triumph and Pontiac, are best boiled or roasted with their "jackets" on.

Round white potatoes. Often referred to as all-purpose potatoes, these buff-colored veggies are perfect for making a lovely dish of fluffy, mashed potatoes. They are also excellent roasted or used in soups and casseroles. Round whites include Eastern and Maine potatoes.

Russet Burbank potatoes. Long or round with russet skins—rough brown skins that are heavily netted—these potatoes are the "standard" baking potatoes and the starchiest of the varieties, making them good for mashing and for use in soups. Idaho potatoes are among this group.

Sweet potatoes. While white potatoes and sweet potatoes are not botanically related, these two vegetables can be prepared in very similar ways and serve similar roles in meals. Thus, no discussion of the potato can be complete without a mention of this long, brown-skinned, sweet-fleshed veggie. It's worthwhile noting that although the terms "sweet potato" and "yam" are often used interchangeably, few true yams are grown in this country.

Yukon gold. Also referred to simply as Gold potatoes, these golden potatoes have a delicious buttery flavor. Try them mashed, roasted, or steamed.

Buying, Storing, and Using Potatoes

When selecting potatoes, choose well-shaped, firm ones with smooth, blemish-free skins. If you purchase your potatoes by the bag, be sure to open the bag as soon as you return home and to discard any soft or rotten potatoes. A single bad potato is quite capable of spoiling the whole bag!

Store your potatoes in a dark, cool, well-ventilated place—not in the refrigerator! Properly stored, most varieties will keep for two to three weeks.

If stored potatoes get too warm, they will sprout "eyes" and shrivel. Improperly stored potatoes may also begin to turn green. Any green, bitter portions should be cut away and discarded before the potato is cooked, as should the eyes. Do not wash potatoes before storing, and do not store with apples or onions, as this will make the potatoes spoil more quickly.

When making a potato dish, try to choose potatoes of equal size for even cooking results. If you are going to cook your potatoes with the skin on—a practice that helps retain nutrients—scrub them gently with a vegetable brush, dish cloth, or sponge under cold running water. Then pat them dry and use as desired. If your recipe calls for peeled potatoes, drop the whole peeled potatoes or cut pieces into ice cold water as you work to prevent the flesh from darkening. If a good deal of time may elapse before you cook the peeled potatoes, add some vinegar or lemon juice to the cold water to keep the potatoes white.

Whether boiled, mashed, baked, roasted, or made into a summer salad, potatoes make good nutritional sense—even when you're cutting excess fat from your diet. And by choosing these veggies wisely and preparing them with care, you can make sure that they will always be a welcome addition to your table.

Roasted Rosemary and Garlic Potatoes

When preparing this dish, try to use potatoes of uniform size so that they will finish baking at the same time. Or cut the potatoes to size as you cut them in half.

1. Arrange the potatoes, cut sides up, in a large baking pan. Add 1 inch of water to the bottom of the pan.

2. Place the rosemary, garlic powder, and salt and pepper to taste in a small dish, and stir to mix.

3. Spray the cut surfaces of the potatoes 4 times with the butter spray, and sprinkle with the rosemary mixture.

4. Roast uncovered in a preheated 350°F oven for 45 minutes, or until the potatoes are tender when pierced with a fork and are beginning to turn brown. Serve hot.

Yield: *4 servings*

6 medium unpeeled Gold or Yukon Gold potatoes, halved

1 teaspoon crushed dried rosemary

½ teaspoon garlic powder

Salt and freshly ground black pepper to taste

I Can't Believe It's Not Butter spray

NUTRITIONAL DATA (PER SERVING)

Fat: 0 gram   Calories: 180   % Calories from fat: 0%

Potatoes With Bacon Gravy

Yield: *4 servings*

4 medium red potatoes, peeled or unpeeled and cubed

½ teaspoon liquid smoke

3 tablespoons Oscar Mayer Real Bacon Bits

¼ cup water

1 tablespoon cornstarch

Salt and pepper to taste

2–3 tablespoons chopped fresh parsley (optional)

The potato is my favorite vegetable, and when I was growing up, I especially liked boiled potatoes seasoned with bacon. Here is a delicious low-fat version of that childhood dish.

1. Place the potatoes in a medium-sized saucepan, adding just enough water to cover. Stir in the liquid smoke and bacon bits.

2. Bring the potatoes to a boil over medium-high heat. Reduce the heat to the point of a simmer, cover, and cook, stirring occasionally, for 15 to 20 minutes, or until tender when pierced with a fork.

3. Drain the cooking water into a medium-sized skillet. Cover the potatoes to keep warm and set aside.

4. Place the skillet over medium heat. While the cooking water is reheating, place the ¼ cup of water and the cornstarch, salt, and pepper in a small dish, and whisk until mixed. Slowly blend into the cooking water.

5. Increase the heat under the skillet to medium-high, and bring to a boil, stirring constantly. Cook for about 5 minutes, or until the gravy is of the desired consistency.

6. Add the chopped parsley to the gravy, and cook for 1 additional minute. Pour over the potatoes, and stir to combine. Serve hot.

NUTRITIONAL DATA (PER SERVING)

Fat: 1.5 grams   Calories: 155   % Calories from fat: 8%

Best Ever Sweet Potatoes

When I asked my friend Judy to taste test this dish for me, her comment was, "These are the best sweet potatoes I have ever tasted! What did you put in them?" Was she ever surprised when I told her!

1. Place the potatoes in a large saucepan, adding enough water to cover. Bring to a boil over medium-high heat. Then reduce the heat to the point of a simmer, cover, and cook for 30 to 40 minutes, or until tender. Drain and allow to cool to room temperature.

2. Peel the potatoes and slice them into a large bowl. Add the butter-flavored sprinkles, and, using an electric mixer, whip on medium-low speed for 1 to 2 minutes to break up the potatoes. Add the remainder of the ingredients, and continue whipping on medium to medium-high speed until smooth and creamy.

3. Spoon the potatoes into a 2-quart casserole dish, cover, and bake in a preheated 400°F oven for 30 to 40 minutes, or until the mixture pulls away slightly from the edge of the dish. Serve hot.

Yield: *8 servings*

3 pounds unpeeled sweet potatoes

2 teaspoons butter-flavored sprinkles

¼ cup brown sugar, packed

¼ cup dark corn syrup

¼ cup coffee-flavored liqueur

1 teaspoon butter-flavored extract

NUTRITIONAL DATA (PER SERVING)

Fat: .5 gram   Calories: 256   % Calories from fat: 2%

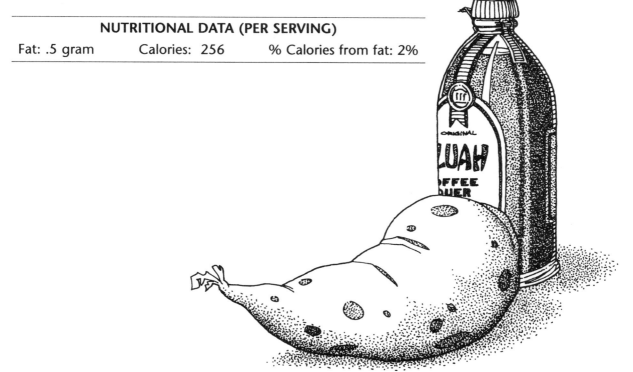

Oven-Baked Spiced Potato Slices

Yield: *4 servings*

4 medium unpeeled baking
    potatoes

I Can't Believe It's Not Butter
    spray

1 tablespoon crushed dried
    parsley

1 teaspoon chili powder

1 teaspoon garlic salt

These potatoes are so good, they will make you forget that French fries ever existed!

1. Peel the potatoes, and cut into ¼-inch-thick slices. Place in a large bowl or pot of cold water, and set aside for 5 minutes.

2. Drain the potatoes, and blot dry with paper towels or clean kitchen towels. Transfer to a medium-sized bowl, and spray with the butter spray, tossing until well coated.

3. Place all of the seasonings in a small dish, and stir until well blended. Sprinkle the mixture over the potatoes and toss, making sure the spices are evenly distributed.

4. Lightly spray a large baking sheet with butter-flavored nonstick cooking spray, and arrange the potatoes in a single layer on the sheet. Bake in a preheated 400°F oven for about 15 minutes, or until golden on the bottom. Turn and bake for 15 to 20 additional minutes, or until the potatoes are tender and golden. Serve hot.

NUTRITIONAL DATA (PER SERVING)

Fat: 0 gram   Calories: 145   % Calories from fat: 0%

Roasted Parmesan Potato Wedges

I am always on the lookout for new ways to fix my favorite vegetable. This is an especially flavorful dish!

1. Cut the potatoes lengthwise into equal-sized wedges. Place in a large bowl or pot of cold water, and set aside for 5 minutes.

2. Drain the potatoes, and blot dry with paper towels or clean kitchen towels. Transfer to a medium-sized bowl, and spray with the butter spray, tossing until well coated.

3. Place the onion flakes and onion salt in a small dish, and stir until well blended. Sprinkle the mixture over the potatoes and toss, making sure the spices are evenly distributed.

4. Lightly spray a large baking sheet with butter-flavored nonstick cooking spray, and arrange the potatoes in a single layer on the sheet. Bake in a preheated 425°F oven for 15 to 20 minutes, or until the potatoes are golden and tender.

5. Remove the potatoes from the oven, and sprinkle with the cheese. Serve hot.

Quick Dish

Yield: *4 servings*

4 medium unpeeled baking potatoes

I Can't Believe It's Not Butter spray

1 tablespoon dehydrated onion flakes

½ teaspoon onion salt

2 tablespoons grated Parmesan cheese

NUTRITIONAL DATA (PER SERVING)

Fat: .7 gram   Calories: 235   % Calories from fat: 3%

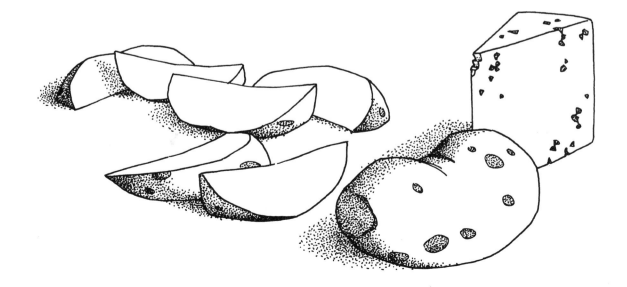

Baked Potato Pancakes

Yield: 8 servings

4 medium baking potatoes, peeled and shredded

1 small onion, finely chopped

½ cup soft bread crumbs

1 egg, slightly beaten

Salt to taste

Freshly ground black pepper to taste

I Can't Believe It's Not Butter spray

Yogurt-Dill Sauce (page 107) makes a delicious topping for these golden pancakes.

1. Place the potatoes, onion, bread crumbs, egg, and seasoning in a large bowl, and toss with a fork until well blended.

2. Lightly spray a large nonstick baking sheet with cooking spray. Divide the potato mixture into 8 evenly spaced mounds on the baking sheet, and use a spatula to flatten the pancakes to ½-inch thickness. Spray the top of each cake lightly with the butter spray.

3. Bake in a preheated 425°F oven for 10 minutes, or until the tops are golden brown. Turn, spray with the butter spray, and bake for an additional 10 minutes, or until the second sides are golden brown.

4. Serve hot, accompanied by a bowl of Yogurt-Dill Sauce, if desired.

NUTRITIONAL DATA (PER PANCAKE)

Fat: 1 gram   Calories: 97   % Calories from fat: 9%

Cheesy Garlic Mashed Potatoes

Here's a savory twist to an all-around favorite!

Yield: *6 servings*

1. Place the potatoes in a medium-sized pot, adding just enough water to cover. Add the garlic, and bring to a boil over medium-high heat. Reduce the heat to the point of a simmer, cover, and cook for 15 to 20 minutes, or until tender.

2. Drain the potatoes. Add the butter-flavored sprinkles and half of the milk. Using an electric mixer, begin to beat on medium-high speed until the potatoes begin to fluff up. Add the yogurt cheese, and continue to beat until well mixed. Whip in enough of the remaining milk to make the potatoes light and creamy, but not soupy.

3. Add butter-flavored salt and pepper to taste. Serve hot, garnished with a sprinkling of chives.

6 medium baking potatoes (about 3 pounds), peeled and cubed

2 large cloves garlic, finely chopped

1 tablespoon butter-flavored sprinkles

¼–½ cup evaporated skim milk

½ cup plus 1 tablespoon So-Simple Yogurt Cheese (page 53) or fat-free cream cheese

Butter-flavored salt to taste

Freshly ground black pepper to taste

Chopped fresh chives (garnish)

NUTRITIONAL DATA (PER SERVING)

Fat: 0 gram   Calories: 145   % Calories from fat: 0%

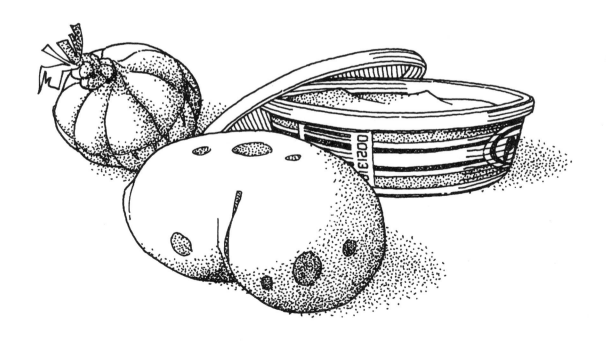

Cooking With Yogurt

Healthy, delicious, and amazingly versatile, yogurt well deserves its popularity. Not only can this creamy food be eaten on its own, straight out of the container, but it is also excellent as an ingredient in cold salad dressings and dips, dessert toppings, sandwich spreads, and marinades; and as a garnish for vegetables, chili, cereals, and so much more. It can even be made into a tasty fat-free cheese! (See page 53.)

While it's quite simple to use yogurt in cold dishes, a little know-how is needed when mixing yogurt into hot sauces. Cooking yogurt at a high temperature can cause it to separate. While this will not affect the flavor of the dish, it will spoil the dish's appearance and texture. Fortunately, you can easily stabilize yogurt by adding cornstarch to it before stirring it into your dish, as is done in Little Red Cottage Fries With Paprika Sauce (page 177). (Note that in this recipe, the Healthy Sour Cream contains some yogurt.) Once you master this simple technique, you can successfully use yogurt to replace higher-fat ingredients in a variety of cooked dishes.

Before adding the cold yogurt to your sauce, take 1 tablespoon of the yogurt and gently stir in 1 tablespoon of cornstarch. Then gently stir in the remaining yogurt and add this mixture to your dish, again stirring very gently to keep the yogurt from separating. Bring the mixture to a slow, gentle boil over low heat. Reduce the heat to the point of a slow simmer, and cook for 5 to 10 minutes, or until the desired consistency is reached. Then immediately remove the dish from the heat. Do not allow the sauce to come to a full rolling boil, as it may separate. Also avoid covering the saucepan with a lid, as a drop of moisture may fall into the yogurt mixture and spoil it.

Little Red Cottage Fries With Paprika Sauce

If possible, choose potatoes of equal size so that they all finish cooking at the same time. Then enjoy this delightfully saucy dish!

1. Place the potatoes in a medium-sized pot, adding just enough water to cover. Bring to a low boil over medium heat, cover, and cook for 10 to 15 minutes, or until only partially cooked. Remove the pot from the heat, and allow the potatoes to reach room temperature.

2. Slice the partially cooked potatoes ⅛ inch thick, and set aside.

3. Place the margarine in a large heavy nonstick skillet, and melt over medium-low heat. Add the potatoes, sprinkle with salt and pepper to taste, and cook, gently turning occasionally with a spatula, for 15 to 20 minutes, or until brown and tender.

4. While the potatoes are cooking, place the evaporated milk, paprika, sugar, if desired, and scallions in a small saucepan. Set aside.

5. Place 1 tablespoon of the sour cream in a small bowl, and slowly stir in the cornstarch. Gently stir the remaining sour cream into the cornstarch mixture, and add to the mixture in the saucepan, stirring in one direction only to blend.

6. Cook the sauce over low heat, bringing it slowly just to a low boil. Reduce the heat to the point of a slow simmer, and cook for 5 to 10 additional minutes, or until the sauce is of the desired consistency. Remove from the heat. Do not let the sauce reach a full boil, as it may separate.

7. Transfer the potatoes to a large serving dish, and allow to cool slightly for about 5 minutes. Add the sauce, gently turning the potatoes until well coated. Serve immediately.

Yield: *6 servings*

10–12 small red new potatoes (about 2 pounds)

2 tablespoons reduced-fat margarine

Salt and freshly ground black pepper to taste

PAPRIKA SAUCE

¼ cup evaporated skim milk

2 teaspoons paprika

1 teaspoon sugar (optional)

4 medium scallions, finely chopped (include tops)

1 cup plus 1 tablespoon Healthy Sour Cream (page 106), divided

1 tablespoon cornstarch

NUTRITIONAL DATA (PER SERVING)

Fat: 2 grams   Calories: 158   % Calories from fat: 11%

Parsley Potatoes

Yield: *5 servings*

5 medium all purpose potatoes, peeled and quartered

1½ cups Chicken Stock (page 92), Brown Beef Stock (page 90), or other fat-free stock

1 heaping tablespoon dried parsley

1 tablespoon butter-flavored sprinkles

Butter-flavored salt to taste

Freshly ground black pepper to taste

1 tablespoon chopped fresh parsley (garnish)

This is a simple, quick dish that beautifully accompanies virtually any meal.

1. Place the potatoes and stock in a medium-sized saucepan, and bring to a boil over medium-high heat.

2. Reduce the heat to the point of a simmer, and stir in the parsley. Cover and cook for about 20 minutes, or until tender. Remove from the heat; do not drain.

3. Add the butter-flavored sprinkles to the potatoes, and stir in butter-flavored salt and pepper to taste. Transfer the potatoes to a serving dish, garnish with parsley, and serve hot.

NUTRITIONAL DATA (PER SERVING)

Fat: 0 gram   Calories: 150   % Calories from fat: 0%

Whipped Orange Sweet Potatoes

Yield: *6 servings*

2 cans (1 pound each) sweet potato pieces, drained and mashed

¼ cup light brown sugar, not packed

1 cup orange juice

1 teaspoon vanilla extract

½ teaspoon grated orange zest

½ teaspoon cinnamon

Butter-flavored salt to taste

Easy, sweet, and yummy describe this dish. If desired, you may boil your own sweet potatoes for this recipe.

1. Place all of the ingredients in a medium-sized bowl. Using an electric mixer, whip the potatoes on medium-high speed until well mixed and fluffy.

2. Transfer the mixture to a 2-quart casserole dish, cover, and bake in a preheated 350°F oven for 25 to 30 minutes, or until heated through. Serve hot.

NUTRITIONAL DATA (PER SERVING)

Fat: 0 gram   Calories: 198   % Calories from fat: 0%

Simply Mushrooms

These versatile mushrooms may be used as a side dish or to top off pasta, potatoes, rice, chicken, or beef.

1. Place the stock, garlic, and salt and pepper in a large nonstick skillet, and cook over medium-high heat for 5 minutes or until the garlic becomes soft.

2. Reduce the heat to low, and stir in the mushrooms. Cover and cook for 5 to 10 minutes, or until the mushrooms are tender, tossing occasionally. Serve hot.

Quick Dish

Yield: *4 servings*

¼ cup Chicken Stock (page 92), Brown Beef Stock (page 90), or other fat-free stock

1 large clove garlic, minced

Salt and freshly ground black pepper to taste

1 pound fresh white mushrooms, sliced

NUTRITIONAL DATA (PER SERVING)

Fat: <1 gram   Calories: 28   % Calories from fat: 16%

Red Cabbage and Apples

This full-flavored sweet-and-sour dish reflects the versatility of that delicious vegetable, the cabbage.

1. Place the water, salt, nutmeg, and allspice in a medium-sized saucepan, and bring to a boil over medium-high heat. Add the cabbage and apples, and reduce the heat just to the point of a slow simmer. Cover and cook for 10 to 15 minutes, or until the apples and cabbage are crisp-tender.

2. Pour the excess water from the cabbage mixture, and stir in the vinegar and brown sugar, mixing thoroughly. Return the mixture to a slow simmer and cook uncovered for 15 to 20 minutes, or until the cabbage is wilted and the apples are soft, but not mushy. Serve hot.

Yield: *4 servings*

1½ cups water

Salt to taste

1 teaspoon ground nutmeg

½ teaspoon ground allspice

1 medium head red cabbage, shredded

4 medium Granny Smith apples or other tart apples, sliced

¼ cup apple cider or red wine vinegar

3 tablespoons brown or white sugar

NUTRITIONAL DATA (PER SERVING)

Fat: 0 gram   Calories: 121   % Calories from fat: 0%

Squash, Carrots, and Peppers With Onions

Yield: *4 servings*

¾ cup Vegetable Stock (page 96), Chicken Stock (page 92), or other fat-free stock, divided

1 medium onion, thinly sliced

1 medium clove garlic, minced

1 medium zucchini, cut into matchstick-sized pieces

1 small yellow summer squash, cut into matchstick-sized pieces

1 medium carrot, peeled and shredded

½ cup diced red bell pepper

1 teaspoon crushed dried basil

Salt to taste

This low-calorie dish makes a colorful addition to any meal!

1. Place ½ cup of the stock in a large, heavy skillet over medium-low heat. Add the onion and garlic, and simmer uncovered for 5 minutes, or until tender.

2. Add the zucchini, summer squash, carrot, bell pepper, and basil, and toss to mix. Cook uncovered for 5 minutes, tossing occasionally.

3. Add the remaining ¼ cup of stock, cover, and cook, tossing occasionally, for 5 to 10 additional minutes, or until the vegetables are crisp-tender. Salt to taste and serve hot.

NUTRITIONAL DATA (PER SERVING)
Fat: 0 gram   Calories: 30   % Calories from fat: 0%

Dilled Squash and Corn

Quick Dish

Yield: *4 servings*

½ cup Chicken Stock (page 92) or other fat-free stock

4 medium zucchini, thinly sliced

1½ cups frozen (unthawed) whole kernel corn

1 small onion, thinly sliced

½ cup chopped sweet red bell pepper

Salt to taste

1 teaspoon dried dill, or 1 tablespoon chopped fresh dill

Green zucchini, yellow corn, and red bell peppers make this a flavorful and colorful dish, as well as a healthful one.

1. Place the stock in a large nonstick skillet, and heat over medium heat.

2. Add the vegetables to the skillet, salt to taste, and stir to mix. Cover and cook, stirring occasionally, for 10 minutes, or until crisp-tender.

3. Stir the dill into the vegetables, and serve hot.

NUTRITIONAL DATA (PER SERVING)
Fat: <1 gram   Calories: 79   % Calories from fat: 6%

Roasted Chili Corn on the Cob

Try this taste-tingling, change-of-pace way of cooking corn on the cob.

1. Spray each cob of corn lightly with the butter spray. Set aside.

2. Place all of the seasonings in a small bowl, and stir to mix until well blended. Sprinkle the mixture over each ear of corn.

3. Wrap each ear of corn separately in aluminum foil. If using a conventional oven, place the corn on a baking sheet, and bake in a preheated 400°F oven for 15 to 20 minutes, or until a kernel is crisp-tender when pressed. If using a grill, place the corn over medium-hot heat for 10 minutes. Then turn and cook on the other side for 10 minutes. Turn once more, and cook until done. Serve wrapped in foil.

Yield: *6 servings*

6 whole ears of corn, fresh or frozen (thawed), husks removed

I Can't Believe It's Not Butter spray

1 tablespoon chili powder

¼ teaspoon garlic powder

½ teaspoon salt, onion salt, or garlic salt

1 tablespoon crushed dried cilantro

NUTRITIONAL DATA (PER SERVING)

Fat: 1 gram   Calories: 150   % Calories from fat: 6%

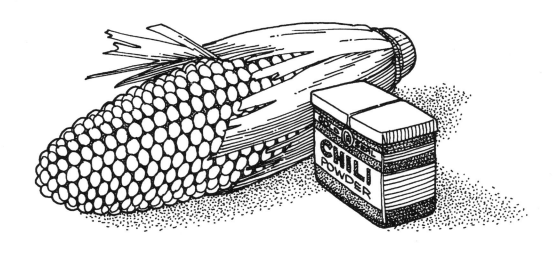

Mexican Skillet Corn

Yield: 6 servings

½ cup Chicken Stock (page 92),
Vegetable Stock (page 96), or
other fat-free stock

1 small onion, diced

1 large green bell pepper,
chopped

1 large red bell pepper, chopped

1 package (28 ounces) frozen
(thawed) whole kernel corn

1 tablespoon chili powder

2 teaspoons crushed dried
cilantro

½ teaspoon onion salt

This is a nice change from "plain ole" corn. In fact, once you try this Mexican-style dish, plain corn won't have quite the same appeal!

1. Place the stock in a large skillet, and bring to a boil over medium-high heat. Reduce the heat to medium, and add the onions and bell peppers. Cook, stirring often, for about 5 minutes, or just until crisp-tender.

2. Stir all of the remaining ingredients into the pepper mixture, mixing well. Cover and, stirring occasionally, simmer for 5 minutes, or until the corn is tender and heated through. Serve hot.

NUTRITIONAL DATA (PER SERVING)

Fat: .7 gram   Calories: 143   % Calories from fat: 4%

Popeye's Spinach

Yield: 6 servings

2 packages (10 ounces each)
frozen spinach

1 cup Red Wine Vinaigrette
(page 87), at room
temperature

3 tablespoons grated Parmesan
cheese

You can bet that Popeye didn't eat his spinach this way, but if you tell your children the name of this dish, maybe it will motivate them to eat it along with you!

1. Cook the spinach according to package directions. Drain well.

2. Transfer the cooked spinach to a large shallow serving dish, and drizzle the dressing over the top. Toss gently until well mixed.

3. Sprinkle the Parmesan cheese over the spinach, and toss lightly. Serve hot.

NUTRITIONAL DATA (PER SERVING)

Fat: <1 gram   Calories: 37   % Calories from fat: 17%

Peas With Mushrooms and Red Peppers

Sweet and colorful, this dish adds an elegant touch to any meal.

Yield: *4 servings*

1. Place ½ cup of the stock in a medium-sized saucepan, and bring to a boil over medium-high heat. Reduce the heat to the point of a simmer, and stir in the peppers, onions, and mushrooms. Cover and cook for about 5 minutes, or just until crisp-tender.

2. Add the remaining ¼ cup of stock to the pot, and return the mixture to a boil over medium-high heat. Add the peas, stirring to mix well. Reduce the heat to the point of a gentle simmer, cover, and cook for 10 additional minutes, or until the peas are tender.

3. Remove the pot from the heat, and allow to sit, covered, for 5 minutes, before serving.

¾ cup Vegetable Stock (page 96) or other fat-free stock, divided

1 medium red bell pepper, cut into thin 1-inch strips

1 small onion, finely chopped

4 ounces fresh white mushrooms, sliced (about 1½ cups)

1 bag (1 pound) frozen tiny green peas

NUTRITIONAL DATA (PER SERVING)

Fat: <1 gram   Calories: 115   % Calories from fat: 4%

Greek-Style Green Beans

These green beans are delicious whether served hot or cold.

Yield: *4 servings*

1. Place the stock in a medium-sized saucepan, and bring to a boil over medium-high heat. Reduce the heat to medium, and add the onions and garlic. Cook, stirring occasionally, for about 5 minutes, or until tender.

2. Add the tomatoes and cayenne pepper to the onion mixture, and stir to mix. Cover and cook, stirring occasionally, for about 15 minutes, or until the tomatoes are of a stewed consistency.

3. Stir the green beans into the tomato mixture, cover, and cook at the point of a gentle simmer for 10 minutes. Remove the cover and cook, stirring occasionally, for 5 additional minutes, or until the green beans are soft. Add salt to taste and serve hot, or chill and serve cold.

¼ cup Vegetable Stock (page 96) or other fat-free stock

1 large onion, chopped

1 large clove garlic, finely chopped

1 can (14½ ounces) diced tomatoes, undrained

¼ teaspoon cayenne pepper

1 package (1 pound) frozen French cut green beans

Salt to taste

NUTRITIONAL DATA (PER SERVING)

Fat: 0 gram   Calories: 52   % Calories from fat: 0%

Pop's Sweet and Sour Harvard Beets

Yield: *4 servings*

1 can (1 pound) sliced beets, undrained

¼ cup cider vinegar

¼ cup sugar

2 teaspoons butter-flavored sprinkles

½ teaspoon grated orange zest

⅛ teaspoon ground cloves

1 tablespoon cornstarch

I Can't Believe It's Not Butter spray

My father-in-law, who loves beets, counts this among his favorite dishes.

1. Drain the beets, reserving the juice. Set the beets aside.

2. Place the beet juice, vinegar, sugar, butter-flavored sprinkles, orange zest, cloves, and cornstarch in a small saucepan, and whisk until well mixed. Place over medium heat, and cook, stirring constantly, for about 5 minutes, or until the mixture has thickened.

3. Gently stir the beets into the sauce, blending well. Lightly spray the mixture with the butter spray, and gently stir to mix.

4. Continue to cook for about 5 minutes, or until the beets are heated through. Serve hot.

NUTRITIONAL DATA (PER SERVING)

Fat: 0 gram   Calories: 90   % Calories from fat: 0%

Top Left: Cranberry-Orange Twists (page 188)
Top Right: Viennese Coffee (page 204)
Center: Perfect Orange Cupcakes (page 190)

Top Left: Yummy Peach Cobbler (page 192)
Top Right: Strawberry Pound Cake (page 194)
Bottom: Chocolate Chip Cheese Cake
With Hot Fudge (page 198)

Honey-Orange Peas

Quick Dish

I eat my peas with honey—
I've done it all my life.
They do taste kind of funny,
But it keeps them on my knife!

Yield: *5 servings*

1 package (1 pound) frozen tiny green peas

1 tablespoon butter-flavored sprinkles

1 tablespoon reduced-fat margarine, melted

2 tablespoons honey

2 teaspoons grated orange zest

1. Fill a large saucepan with water, and bring to a fast boil over high heat. Add the peas and the butter-flavored sprinkles, cover, and return to a boil. Reduce the heat to the point of a slow simmer, and cook for 6 to 8 minutes, or until the peas are tender. Drain well, and transfer the peas to a serving dish.

2. Place the melted margarine, honey, and orange zest in a small dish, and stir to mix. Stir into the peas, and serve hot.

NUTRITIONAL DATA (PER SERVING)

Fat: 1 gram   Calories: 110   % Calories from fat: 8%

10

A Little Something Sweet

Many people fear that when they adopt a low-fat lifestyle, they will have to give up their much-beloved desserts. Certainly, most traditional-style cheesecakes, cookies, cobblers, puddings, premium ice creams, and other treats are made with lots of butter, eggs, cream, and other ingredients that have no place in a healthful diet. But with a little imagination—and a good deal of help from all the wonderful new low- and no-fat products that are now available—it's easy to create confections that are both luscious and low in fat.

In the following pages, you will find a variety of ways to satisfy your sweet tooth without straying from your low-fat lifestyle. Included are wonderful recipes for updated family favorites such as My Dad's Banana Puddin'; old-fashioned treats such as Chewy Coconut-Carrot Oatmeal Cookies; a sinfully luscious Chocolate Chip Cheese Cake With Hot Fudge; a bubbling Yummy Peach Cobbler; and delectable Cranberry-Orange Twists—to name just a few. In a hurry? Try one of the many Quick Dishes. Cookies'n Cream Sandwich Treats are both easy and fun to make, and are sure to be a hit on the next hot day. Or whip up Caramel Turtle Fudge Sundaes, a deceptively rich-tasting dessert that will have them asking for seconds—and thirds!

When choosing from among the many tantalizing offerings in this chapter, don't overlook the recipe for Purely Vanilla Extract. Believe it or not, it's simple to custom-make an extract—exactly suited to your tastes and needs—that will add rich, natural flavor to your desserts. The result? Luscious sweets that are as satisfying as they are low in fat.

Cranberry-Orange Twists

Yield: *40 slices*

2 loaves (1 pound each) honey-
wheat bread dough, thawed

¼ cup sugar

1 teaspoon ground cinnamon

1½ teaspoons grated orange zest

2 packages (3½ ounces each)
dried cranberries, chopped

2 egg whites, slightly beaten

1 tablespoon water

GLAZE

2 cups powdered sugar

2 teaspoons orange extract

2 tablespoons skim milk

These delicious twists make a lovely dessert or breakfast bread. They also make a great gift; just wrap in plastic wrap and finish off with a bright bow.

1. Cut each loaf in half lengthwise, so that you have 4 pieces of dough.

2. Place 1 piece of dough at a time on a lightly floured surface, and roll out with a rolling pin to form a 12-x-6-inch rectangle. Moisten the rectangle by lightly brushing it with water. (Do not get it too wet.)

3. Place the sugar, cinnamon, and orange zest in a small dish, and stir to blend. Sprinkle a quarter of the mixture over the rectangle. Sprinkle a quarter of the chopped cranberries over the sugar mixture.

4. Starting with the long end, roll up the rectangle, jelly roll-style, pressing the seams to seal. Repeat with the remaining pieces of dough, forming 4 rolls.

5. Lightly spray a large nonstick baking sheet with cooking spray, and arrange the rolls on the sheet, seam side down. Take 2 of the rolls and twist them together, pressing the ends together to seal and tucking the ends under the twist. Repeat with the 2 remaining rolls.

6. Lightly spray a large piece of plastic wrap with cooking spray, and place, sprayed side down, over the twists. Cover with a clean kitchen towel or tea towel, and put in a warm place for 45 minutes to 1 hour, or until the twists have doubled in size.

7. Place the egg whites and water in a small bowl, and stir to combine. Brush the egg mixture over the top of each twist.

8. Bake on the center rack of a preheated 350°F oven for 15 minutes. Cover the twists with aluminum foil, and bake for 10 to 15 additional minutes, or until the tops are golden brown. Remove from the oven and allow to cool to room temperature.

9. To make the glaze, place the powdered sugar and orange extract in a small bowl. Stir in just enough of the skim milk to get a smooth glazing consistency. Drizzle some of the glaze over each cooled twist. Cut each twist into 20 slices, and serve.

NUTRITIONAL DATA (PER SLICE)

Fat: <1 gram   Calories: 100   % Calories from fat: 9%

Orange Poppy Seed Loaf

This recipe makes a marvelous dense-textured bread that can be enhanced by spreading with warm orange marmalade, or enjoyed as is. When baking this and all other quick breads, you will get best results by first bringing all of the ingredients to room temperature.

1. Place the flour, sugar, baking soda, poppy seeds, and orange zest in a medium-sized bowl, and stir to blend thoroughly. Using a large spoon, make a well in the center of the ingredients. Set aside.

2. Place the 2 extracts in a measuring cup. Then add just enough orange juice to bring the level to the 1-cup mark, and stir to mix well.

3. Pour the orange juice mixture into the well of the dry ingredients, and stir just until the dry ingredients are moistened. Do not overstir, as this will toughen the loaf.

4. Lightly spray a 5-x-9-inch nonstick loaf pan with cooking spray. Spoon in the batter, spreading evenly.

5. Bake in a preheated 350°F oven for 45 to 50 minutes, or until a toothpick inserted in the center of the loaf comes out clean. Remove the pan from the oven, and allow to sit for 5 minutes before removing the loaf from the pan. Cool the loaf to room temperature on a wire rack before slicing and serving.

Yield: *14 slices*

2 cups whole wheat flour

½ cup sugar

1 teaspoon baking soda

1 tablespoon poppy seeds

1 teaspoon grated orange zest

2 teaspoons butter-flavored extract

1 teaspoon orange extract

⅞ cup (approximately) orange juice

NUTRITIONAL DATA (PER SLICE)

Fat: .5 gram   Calories: 88   % Calories from fat: 5%

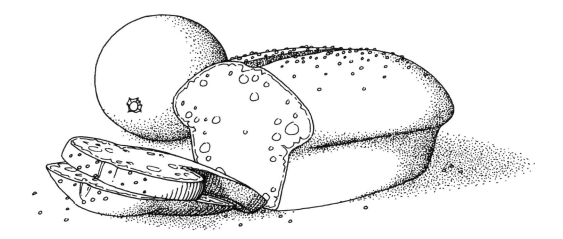

Perfect Orange Cupcakes

Yield: *12 muffins*

CUPCAKE BATTER

2 cups all purpose flour

⅓ cup sugar

1 tablespoon baking powder

1 tablespoon grated orange zest

½ teaspoon ground cinnamon

½ teaspoon butter-flavored salt

1 cup orange juice

2 egg whites, slightly beaten

¼ cup melted reduced-fat margarine, slightly cooled

1 teaspoon orange extract

1 teaspoon butter-flavored extract

ORANGE FROSTING

1 cup powdered sugar

1 tablespoon reduced-fat margarine

1 tablespoon orange juice

½ teaspoon grated orange peel

If practice makes perfect, these cupcakes deserve their name. The undisputed winners of the six or eight varieties I tried on my friends and family, these gems are bursting with flavor and are especially good with a cup of hot tea!

1. To make the cupcakes, place the flour, sugar, baking powder, orange zest, cinnamon, and butter-flavored salt in a medium-sized bowl, and stir until well blended. Using a large spoon, make a well in the center of the ingredients. Set aside.

2. Place all of the remaining batter ingredients in a medium-sized bowl, and stir until well blended.

3. Pour the orange juice mixture into the well of the dry ingredients, and stir just until the dry ingredients are moistened. The batter should still be lumpy.

4. Fill the cups of a 12-cup nonstick muffin pan two-thirds full with the batter. Bake in a preheated 400°F oven for 15 to 20 minutes, or just until a toothpick inserted in the center of a cupcake comes out clean.

5. Place the muffin tin on a wire rack, and allow the cupcakes to cool in the tin for 10 minutes. Remove the cupcakes from the tin, and allow to cool completely on the rack.

6. While the cupcakes are cooling, place all of the frosting ingredients in a small bowl. Using an electric mixer, beat the frosting for 2 to 3 minutes, or until the frosting is smooth and of a spreadable consistency.

7. Using a butter knife or small spatula, spread the frosting over the cooled cupcakes, swirling the frosting in an attractive pattern. Serve.

NUTRITIONAL DATA (PER CUPCAKE)

Fat: 2.6 grams   Calories: 160   % Calories from fat: 15%

Chewy Coconut-Carrot Oatmeal Cookies

These delightfully chewy cookies are rich with spicy flavor.

Yield: *48 cookies*

1. Place the butter, egg, sugars, and extracts in a medium-sized bowl. Using an electric mixer, beat the mixture on medium to medium-high speed until light and fluffy.

2. Add the carrots to the butter mixture, and beat on low speed until well blended. Set aside.

3. Place the flour, oats, baking powder, salt, cinnamon, and nutmeg in another medium-sized bowl. Stir to mix well.

4. Add the flour mixture to the butter mixture, and mix on low speed until well blended. Stir in the raisins until well coated.

5. Lightly spray a large nonstick cookie sheet with cooking spray. Using 2 teaspoons, drop spoonfuls of the dough onto the sheet, spacing the cookies 2 inches apart to allow for spreading.

6. Bake in a preheated 375°F oven for 10 to 12 minutes, or until the edges of the cookies turn slightly brown. Leave the cookies on the cookie sheet for 1 minute; then remove them from the sheet, and allow to cool completely. Store any leftovers in an airtight container.

⅓ cup light butter, softened

1 whole egg

¾ cup brown sugar, firmly packed

¼ cup sugar

1 teaspoon Vanilla Butter & Nut extract

1½ teaspoons coconut-flavored extract

1 cup finely shredded carrots (about 2 medium)

1 cup all purpose flour

1½ cups quick-cooking oats

1 teaspoon baking powder

¼ teaspoon butter-flavored salt or plain salt

1½ teaspoons ground cinnamon

½ teaspoon ground nutmeg

¾ cup dark or golden raisins

NUTRITIONAL DATA (PER COOKIE)

Fat: 1 gram   Calories: 50   % Calories from fat: 18%

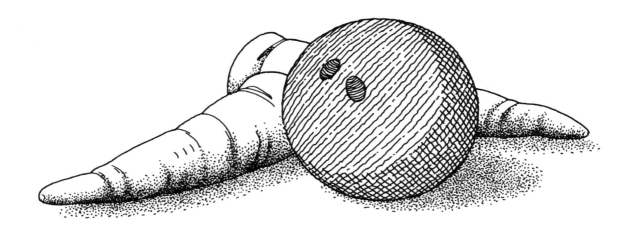

Yummy Peach Cobbler

Yield: *8 servings*

8 cups sliced fresh peaches
(12–14 medium)

2 tablespoons lemon juice

1 cup sugar

⅓ cup cornstarch

1 teaspoon ground cinnamon

½ teaspoon grated lemon zest

⅛ teaspoon ground ginger
(optional)

⅛ teaspoon butter-flavored salt or
regular salt

1 tablespoon Vanilla Butter & Nut
extract

2 flour tortillas (9-inch rounds),
99% fat-free

1 tablespoon sugar

½ teaspoon ground cinnamon

1 tablespoon reduced-fat
margarine

This cobbler is so deliciously full of flavor, it will vanish before your very eyes!

1. Place the peaches and lemon juice in a large saucepan, tossing to mix. Add the sugar, cornstarch, cinnamon, lemon zest, ginger, salt, and extract, and stir to blend well.

2. Place the pot over medium heat, and cook, stirring occasionally, for 10 to 15 minutes, or until the peaches are soft but not mushy.

3. Take 1 of the tortillas, and cut it into ½-inch strips. Stir the strips into the peach mixture.

4. Pour the peach mixture into a 9-inch pie pan or casserole dish. Cut the remaining tortilla into ½-inch strips, and arrange half of the strips over the peach mixture in one direction, spacing the strips as evenly as possible. Arrange the remaining strips so that they cross the first strips, forming a lattice pattern. Trim any strips that extend beyond the edge of the pan or dish, and set aside.

5. Place the sugar and cinnamon in a small dish, and stir to blend well.

6. Place the margarine in a small saucepan, and melt over low heat. Brush the margarine over the tops of the strips, and sprinkle the entire top of the cobbler with the sugar and cinnamon mixture.

7. Place the cobbler on a baking sheet, and bake on the center rack of a preheated 400°F oven for 20 minutes, or until the lattice top is golden brown. If the tortilla strips begin to brown too quickly, cover the top loosely with aluminum foil.

8. Transfer the cobbler from the baking sheet to a wire rack, and cool slightly before slicing. Serve warm or at room temperature.

NUTRITIONAL DATA (PER SERVING)

Fat: <1 gram	Calories: 229	% Calories from fat: 4%

Golden Peach Loaf

Here is a simple-to-make, luscious treat that will have your family coming back for seconds!

1. While the cake is still frozen, use a large serrated knife to cut it lengthwise into 3 equal layers. Set aside.

2. Place the peaches, sugar, and lemon juice in a large bowl, and toss to mix well. Set aside.

3. Place 1 of the cake layers on a flat surface. Spread half of the softened yogurt evenly over the layer. Spoon about a third of the peach mixture over the yogurt. Repeat with a second layer of cake, yogurt, and peaches. (Some peaches will be left over.) Top with the third cake layer, pressing all the layers together gently to form a tighter loaf.

4. Wrap the loaf first in plastic wrap and then in aluminum foil, sealing well. Place in the freezer for 10 to 15 minutes, or until the loaf seems firm and the yogurt has again hardened.

5. To serve, slice the loaf into 8 portions, and place each slice on an individual serving plate. Top with some of the remaining peaches, and serve immediately.

Yield: *8 servings*

1 loaf (13.6 ounces) fat-free golden loaf or pound cake, frozen

4 large peaches, peeled and thinly sliced

1 tablespoon sugar

1 teaspoon lemon juice

1 cup frozen nonfat peach yogurt, slightly softened

NUTRITIONAL DATA (PER SLICE)

Fat: <1 gram   Calories: 164   % Calories from fat: 3%

Variation

To speed preparation, replace the fresh peaches with a 24-ounce can of peach slices in juice. Drain the peaches, discarding the juice, and cut each slice lengthwise into thinner slices. Omit the sugar and lemon juice, and proceed with the recipe.

Strawberry Pound Cake

Yield: *8 servings*

1 pound (13.6 ounces) fat-free golden loaf or pound cake, frozen

4 ounces fat-free strawberry cream cheese, or 1 cup So-Simple Yogurt Cheese (page 53) mixed with 2 tablespoons strawberry jam

1 tablespoon powdered sugar

2 cups sliced fresh strawberries

2 tablespoons sugar

8 ounces light nonfat strawberry yogurt

4 large whole fresh strawberries, halved (garnish)

8 fresh mint leaves (garnish)

You will find it incredible that a serving of this scrumptious cake is virtually fat-free!

1. While the cake is still frozen, use a large serrated knife to slice it lengthwise into 2 equal layers. Set aside.

2. Place the cream cheese and the powdered sugar in a small bowl, and stir to mix well.

3. Lay the cake layers on a flat surface, cut sides up. Spread half of the cream cheese mixture on the top of each layer.

4. Place the strawberries in a large bowl, and sprinkle with the sugar.

5. Overlapping the strawberries, arrange a layer of strawberries over the cream cheese only on the bottom half of the cake. About 1 cup of strawberries should be left over. Set aside.

6. Reassemble the cake by placing the top half over the bottom half so that the strawberries are sandwiched between the 2 layers of cream cheese. Wrap securely in plastic wrap, and chill for at least 1 hour, or until ready to serve.

7. While the cake is chilling, place the yogurt in a small bowl, and stir in any remaining strawberry slices. Chill for at least 30 minutes, or until ready to serve.

8. To serve, slice the cake into 8 portions, and place each slice on an individual serving plate. Spoon some of the yogurt sauce over each slice, and garnish with a strawberry half and a mint leaf. Serve immediately.

NUTRITIONAL DATA (PER SERVING)

Fat: <1 gram   Calories: 175   % Calories from fat: 3%

Cinnamon-Yogurt Rice

I can attest to the fact that cinnamon is one of the most versatile of all spices. I love its distinctively sweet spiciness, and use it often in my recipes. This dish is a great way to use cinnamon and leftover rice.

1. Place the rice in a medium-sized bowl, and set aside.

2. Place the yogurt, sugar, and cinnamon in a small bowl, and stir to mix. Gently stir the yogurt mixture into the rice until well blended. If desired, fold in the raisins.

3. Cover the rice mixture and place in the refrigerator for at least 2 hours, or until the mixture is thoroughly chilled.

4. To serve, line 4 individual dessert dishes with the lettuce leaves, and spoon the rice over the lettuce. Sprinkle with cinnamon, and serve chilled.

Yield: *4 servings*

2 cups chilled cooked white or brown rice

8 ounces light nonfat vanilla yogurt

¼ cup brown sugar, not packed

½ teaspoon ground cinnamon

½ cup dark or golden raisins (optional)

Red leaf lettuce (garnish)

Ground cinnamon (garnish)

NUTRITIONAL DATA (PER SERVING)

Fat: 0 gram   Calories: 211   % Calories from fat: 0%

My Dad's Banana Puddin'

Yield: *10 servings*

6 cups skim milk

2 packages (4.6 ounces each)
    cook-and-serve vanilla pudding

1 teaspoon coconut-flavored
    extract

1 teaspoon butter-flavored extract

40 vanilla wafers

2½ tablespoons sugar

1½ teaspoons ground cinnamon

4 medium bananas

2 teaspoons lemon juice

My dad's all-time favorite sweet treat is banana pudding. For years, my mother often made it for him, using plenty of butter and eggs. Well, this pudding has evolved to keep up with the times—and the lighter version is just as appealing as the original. Judge for yourself!

1. Use the skim milk to prepare the pudding according to package directions. Just before removing the pudding from the heat, stir in the 2 extracts until well blended.

2. Remove the pudding from the heat, and allow to cool for 10 minutes at room temperature. Then cover with plastic wrap, and chill for about 45 minutes, or until cooled but not set.

3. Place the vanilla wafers in a plastic resealable bag. Lay the bag on a flat surface, cover with a clean towel, and use a rolling pin to roll the wafers into coarse crumbs. Set aside.

4. Place the sugar and cinnamon in a small dish, and stir until well mixed.

5. Peel the bananas, and cut into ¼-inch slices. Place the slices in a medium-sized bowl, sprinkle with the lemon juice, and gently toss to coat. Set aside.

6. Take about ⅔ cup of the wafer crumbs, and sprinkle over the bottom of a 2-quart casserole dish. Spoon 1½ cups of the cooled pudding over the crumbs. Arrange about a third of the banana slices over the pudding so that the slices touch one another. Sprinkle with 1 tablespoon of the cinnamon mixture. Repeat the crumb-pudding-banana-cinnamon layer.

7. Sprinkle another ½ cup of the crumbs over the last layer, and top with the remaining pudding. Arrange the remaining banana slices in a pattern of your choice over the pudding. Sprinkle with any remaining crumbs and cinnamon mixture.

8. Cover the pudding with plastic wrap, and chill for at least 2 hours, or until set. Serve chilled.

NUTRITIONAL DATA (PER SERVING)

Fat: 1.3 grams   Calories: 256   % Calories from fat: 4%

Orange Dream Cake

This cake was inspired by a favorite childhood ice cream treat called a Dreamsicle. It's a dream of a dessert served after any meal, and makes a refreshing treat on a hot summer day!

1. Place the slightly softened sherbet and the slightly softened yogurt or ice cream in a medium-sized bowl, and blend with a spoon until well mixed and of spreadable consistency. Do not allow the mixture to get runny. Set aside.

2. Using a large serrated knife, slice the frozen cake into 3 equal layers.

3. Place the bottom layer of the cake on a serving plate, and spread about half of the sherbet mixture over the cake. Place the middle cake layer over the sherbet, and spread with the remaining sherbet mixture. Top with the third cake layer, and smooth the outside of the cake by running a knife around it.

4. Wrap aluminum foil snugly around the sides of the cake. Then wrap the entire cake, including the serving plate, with additional foil or with plastic wrap, sealing it well. Place in the freezer for 45 minutes, or until the sherbet mixture is again frozen and firm.

5. While the cake is in the freezer, prepare the Fat-Free Whipped Cream, adding the orange extract along with the vanilla extract called for in the recipe. (If you're using a commercial frozen whipped topping, allow the topping to thaw before stirring in the orange extract.)

6. About 5 to 10 minutes before serving, remove the cake from the freezer so that it can soften a bit. (The sherbet mixture should remain frozen.) Slice while still frozen, placing each portion on an individual serving plate. Top with a spoonful of the whipped cream, and serve immediately.

Yield: *12 servings*

1 quart orange sherbet, slightly softened

1 quart frozen low-fat vanilla yogurt or low-fat vanilla ice cream, slightly softened

1 (10-inch) orange angel food cake, frozen

3 cups Fat-Free Whipped Cream (page 117) or frozen light nondairy whipped topping (thawed)

1 teaspoon orange extract

NUTRITIONAL DATA (PER SERVING)

Fat: 2 grams	Calories: 285	% Calories from fat: 6%

Chocolate Chip Cheese Cake With Hot Fudge

Yield: *8 servings*

2 cups So-Simple Yogurt Cheese
  (page 53)

½ cup plus 1 tablespoon
  powdered sugar

½ teaspoon lemon juice

½ teaspoon vanilla extract

1 (15 ounces) Entenmann's fat-
  free Golden Chocolatey Chip
  Loaf Cake or other fat-free
  chocolate chip loaf cake

½ cup nonfat fudge topping

Years ago, one of my favorite treats was a sinfully delicious cheese-cake brownie served at a neighborhood deli. This compares to that decadent confection in every way except for the fat and calorie counts!

1. Place the yogurt cheese in a medium-sized bowl, and sift the sugar over the cheese. Using an electric mixer, beat the cheese on medium-low speed until the mixture is smooth and creamy.

2. Add the lemon juice and vanilla extract to the cheese mixture, and continue to beat until well mixed and smooth. Set aside.

3. Slice the cake into 8 equal pieces, and place each slice on an individual dessert plate. Set aside.

4. If using a microwave oven, place the fudge topping in a glass bowl and microwave uncovered on high for 30 to 45 seconds, or until the topping is hot and spreadable, but not runny. If using a conventional stovetop, place the topping in a small saucepan and cook over low heat, stirring constantly, for 1 to 2 minutes, or until hot and spreadable.

5. Spread 1 tablespoon of the hot fudge over each cake slice. Top with ¼ cup of the cheese mixture, and serve immediately.

NUTRITIONAL DATA (PER SERVING)

Fat: 0 gram	Calories: 255	% Calories from fat: 0

Making Your Own Vanilla Extract

The strength of vanilla extracts varies from almost no flavor to very strong flavor. If you want to control the intensity of the extract you use, make it yourself in your own kitchen! By mixing up your own extract, you will be able to customize the strength based on your own preferences and needs. It really is a simple process, and so rewarding!

Purely Vanilla Extract

1. Split the vanilla bean lengthwise. Then cut each piece into 2-inch pieces. Set aside.

2. Pour the rum into a glass bottle or jar with a lid. Add the vanilla bean pieces, cover, and allow to sit at room temperature for at least 6 weeks, shaking the container every 3 or 4 days. The longer you leave the vanilla bean in the rum, the stronger the flavor will be.

3. When the extract has reached the desired strength, pour it through a cheesecloth-lined strainer into a glass container with a tightly fitting lid, and store in a cool dry place for 6 months or longer. Use as you would commercial vanilla extract.

Quick Dish

Yield: ¾ cup

1 vanilla bean
¾ cup 86-proof rum

NUTRITIONAL DATA (PER TEASPOON)

Fat: 0 gram   Calories: 12   % Calories from fat: 0%

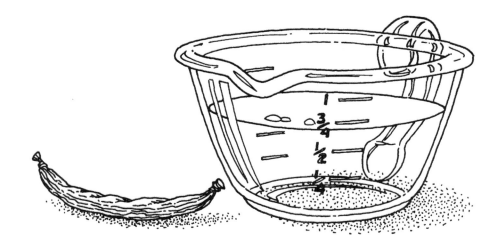

Cookies'n Cream Sandwich Treats

Quick Dish

Yield: *4 servings*

1 cup fat-free cookie chunk frozen
   yogurt or ice cream, softened

4 whole Honey Maid chocolate
   graham crackers or other
   chocolate graham crackers

Looking for a speedy treat? This is incredibly easy to make and delicious. If you don't have time to allow the frozen yogurt or ice cream to soften, try popping it into the microwave for a few seconds!

1. Place the softened yogurt or ice cream in a small bowl, and, if necessary, further soften with a spoon until of spreadable consistency. Do not allow the mixture to get runny.

2. Place 2 of the crackers on a flat surface, and spread ½ cup of the yogurt or ice cream on each, extending the filling to within ½ inch of the cracker's edges.

3. Top each cracker with 1 of the remaining grahams, and gently but firmly press each sandwich together, squeezing the filling to the edges of the sandwich.

4. Break each sandwich in half, and serve immediately.

NUTRITIONAL DATA (PER SERVING)

Fat: 1.5 grams   Calories: 115   % Calories from fat: 12%

Caramel Turtle Fudge Sundae

Quick Dish

Yield: *3 servings*

1 pint Healthy Choice Turtle
   Fudge Cake low-fat ice cream

3 tablespoons fat-free caramel
   sundae syrup

⅔ cup Kellogg's Honey Roasted
   Pecan Temptations cereal

This is deliciously rich and unbelievably low in fat. Maybe I should remind you that this recipe makes three servings, not just one!

1. Divide the ice cream evenly among 3 individual dessert dishes.

2. Top each serving of ice cream with a tablespoon of caramel syrup and ⅓ cup of the cereal. (Be sure to include some of the pecan pieces!) Serve immediately.

NUTRITIONAL DATA (PER SERVING)

Fat: 3.2 grams   Calories: 255   % Calories from fat: 11%

Praline and Caramel Ice Cream Cake With Butterscotch Sauce

The buttery caramel-and-pecan-crunch filling of this cake is wonderfully enhanced by the deliciously rich Old-Fashioned Butterscotch Sauce topping.

1. Leaving the paper wrapper around the cake, slice a ½-inch layer off the top. Reserve the top of the cake.

2. Using a serrated knife, cut a rectangular portion out of the center of the cake so that a ½-inch-thick shell is left on the sides and bottom. Reserve the cut-out cake for use in another recipe.

3. Spoon the softened ice cream into the cake shell, packing the ice cream tightly in the shell. Replace the top of the cake, pressing firmly. Wrap the cake well, first in plastic wrap and then in aluminum foil, sealing tightly. Place in the freezer for at least 1 hour, or until firm.

4. About 10 minutes before serving time, remove the cake from the freezer and allow to sit at room temperature.

5. To serve, remove the wrapper from the cake, and cut into 8 individual slices. Place each slice on an individual dessert plate, and top with some of the sauce. Serve immediately.

Yield: *8 servings*

1 loaf (13.6 ounces) fat-free golden loaf or pound cake

1 pint Healthy Choice Praline & Caramel low-fat ice cream, slightly softened

1 recipe Old-Fashioned Butterscotch Sauce (page 119)

NUTRITIONAL DATA (PER SERVING)

Fat: 2.5 grams   Calories: 250   % Calories from fat: 9%

Heavenly Mixed Berry Trifle

Yield: *12 servings*

3 packages (12 ounces each) frozen unsweetened mixed berries

12 ounces prepared angel food cake, torn into bite-sized pieces

1 cup fat-free cream cheese, softened

1 cup powdered sugar

12 ounces frozen fat-free nondairy whipped topping (thawed), divided

⅓ cup sugar

3 whole strawberries, sliced (garnish)

Fresh mint leaves (garnish)

This divine dessert may also be made with berries of just one type, such as strawberries, raspberries, blackberries, or blueberries.

1. Arrange the frozen berries in a single layer on a large cookie sheet. Allow to sit at room temperature for 20 to 30 minutes, or until completely thawed.

2. While the berries are thawing, place the cake pieces in a large bowl. Set aside.

3. Place the cream cheese in a medium-sized bowl. Add the powdered sugar, and, using an electric mixer, beat at low to medium-low speed until well blended.

4. Stir all but 1 cup of the whipped topping into the cream cheese mixture. Chill the remaining cup of topping for use as a garnish.

5. Pour the cream cheese mixture over the cake pieces, making sure that all of the pieces are well covered. Set aside.

6. Transfer the thawed berries to a medium-sized bowl. Sprinkle the sugar over them, and gently stir until well mixed.

7. Remove a third of the berries—about 1½ cups—and add to the cake mixture. Using a large spoon, gently mix the cake, cream cheese mixture, and berries together.

8. Spoon a third of the cake and berry mixture into the bottom of a 3-quart glass serving bowl. Gently spread a third of the remaining berries over the top of the cake mixture. Repeat the cake and berry layers twice, so that you have 3 layers of cake mixture divided by 3 layers of berries.

9. Cover the bowl with plastic wrap, and chill for at least 2 hours. To serve, arrange the reserved whipped topping in dollops over the top of the trifle. Garnish with the sliced strawberries and mint leaves, and serve immediately.

NUTRITIONAL DATA (PER SERVING)

Fat: 3.5 grams   Calories: 280   % Calories from fat: 11%

11

Bewitching Beverages

The most obvious purpose of a beverage is to quench thirst. But it can do so much more than that. When I was growing up, I spent many a magical summer's day relaxing on a wooden swing on my grandparents' southern-style front porch, sipping glasses of sweet lemony iced tea. Now, whenever I enjoy a tall glass of tea, it stirs these wonderful memories. For me, this beverage is comfort food. And other beverages perform other roles. They cool and refresh us. They warm us. They inspire celebration and conviviality. They help set the tone of a meal. And they allow us to relax over conversation at the end of a meal.

When glancing through the recipes that follow, think about the kind of magic you want your beverage to perform. Hawaiian Mint Tea, Raspberry Citrus Cooler, Fresh Lemonade, and, of course, Classic Iced Tea are the perfect choices when you want to cool off and relax on a hot summer's day. Garnished with Minted Ice Cubes, these drinks are as attractive as they are thirst-quenching. Chilled by a winter's night? Try Mexican-Style Hot Chocolate or Hot Frothy Butterscotch—soothing drinks that will warm the cockles of your heart, as well as the rest of you. For a deliciously light conclusion to a hearty meal, treat your guests to a cup of Viennese Coffee or French Vanilla Coffee. Or add sparkle to your next party with colorful Fruity Sangria Punch.

You'll be delighted to find that all of the beverages that follow are quick and easy to make. And, of course, all of them—yes, even Cinnamon-Vanilla Milk Shakes!—are low in fat. What a delicious way to enhance all of your low-fat meals!

French Vanilla Coffee

Yield: *1 serving*

1 tablespoon evaporated skim
   milk

2 drops vanilla extract

1 cup freshly brewed hot coffee

Sugar or sugar substitute to taste
   (optional)

It really isn't necessary to use fat-laden cream or nondairy creamers in your coffee to add flavor and body. This is a delicious fat-free coffee that won't make you feel guilty about having that second cup!

1. Stir the milk and vanilla extract into the hot coffee.

2. Add the sugar or the sugar substitute to taste, if desired, and serve immediately.

NUTRITIONAL DATA (PER SERVING)

Fat: 0 gram   Calories: 15   % Calories from fat: 0%

Viennese Coffee

Yield: *1 serving*

2 teaspoons sugar

1 mug freshly brewed hot strong
   coffee

2 cinnamon sticks

1 tablespoon frozen light
   nondairy whipped topping,
   thawed

The blended flavors and aromas of cinnamon and coffee are irresistible.

1. Add the sugar to the hot coffee, and use the cinnamon sticks to stir several times to blend the flavors.

2. Top the coffee with the whipped topping, and serve immediately, garnished with the cinnamon sticks.

NUTRITIONAL DATA (PER SERVING)

Fat: 1 gram   Calories: 50   % Calories from fat: 18%

Mexican-Style Hot Chocolate

Mexican hot chocolate is a delicious combination of chocolate and spices that is whipped just before serving. Instead of ending your next company meal with a traditional dessert, delight your guests with large earthenware mugs filled with this very special treat.

1. Place the cocoa, sugar, and cinnamon in a heavy medium-sized saucepan, and stir until well mixed.

2. Place the saucepan over medium heat, and slowly stir in ½ cup of the evaporated milk until the mixture is thick and smooth. Stirring constantly, slowly add the remainder of the evaporated milk and all of the skim milk. Cook, continuing to stir, for 5 minutes, or until well blended and hot. Do not allow the mixture to come to a boil.

3. Remove the saucepan from the heat. Stir in the extracts, and beat with a wire whisk or a rotary beater (egg beater) until the mixture is rich and foamy.

4. Divide the chocolate among 4 large mugs, and serve immediately.

Yield: *4 servings*

⅓ cup cocoa powder

½ cup plus 1 tablespoon sugar

1 teaspoon ground cinnamon

1 cup evaporated skim milk

3 cups skim milk

½ teaspoon vanilla extract

½ teaspoon almond extract

NUTRITIONAL DATA (PER SERVING)

Fat: 1 gram   Calories: 262   % Calories from fat: 3%

Hot Frothy Butterscotch

Yield: *2 servings*

1 cup skim milk

1 tablespoon brown sugar, packed

½ teaspoon butter-flavored extract

32 miniature marshmallows, divided

*T*ry this creamy, temptingly sweet drink on a wintry day or a sleepless night. It makes a nice change from hot cocoa.

1. Place the milk, brown sugar, and extract in a heavy medium-sized saucepan, and stir to mix.

2. Place the saucepan over medium-high heat, and, stirring constantly, heat until the mixture begins to reach a boil.

3. Reduce the heat to medium or medium-low, and add 20 of the marshmallows. Continue to heat, stirring constantly, until the marshmallows begin to melt.

4. Remove the saucepan from the heat, and whip the mixture with a wire whisk until it becomes frothy.

5. Place 6 of the remaining marshmallows in the bottom of each of 2 mugs. Pour the butterscotch mixture over the marshmallows, and serve immediately.

NUTRITIONAL DATA (PER SERVING)

Fat: <1 gram	Calories: 97	% Calories from fat: 2%

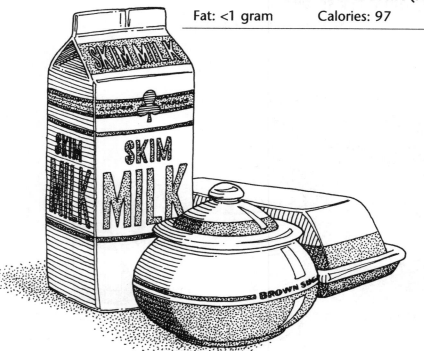

Tea Time

I often serve tea to friends, and am surprised by the number of compliments I receive. I am always hearing, "Mine never seems to turn out right. I don't know what I'm doing wrong." So, I offer this recipe for The Perfect Pot of Tea. Brew it for your own friends, and bask in the compliments.

The Perfect Pot of Tea

So many different teas are now readily available that you need never be bored at tea time. Try Earl Grey, Assam, English Breakfast, Jasmine—the list is almost endless. Or use your favorite herbal tea. Whatever type you choose, the following directions will help you make perfect tea every time.

Yield: 6 servings

6 tea bags or 6 teaspoons loose tea

4½ cups boiling water

1. Fill your teapot with hot water, and allow it to stand until the pot is warm.

2. Pour the hot water out of the teapot. If using tea bags, place the bags in the pot, leaving the paper tags on the outside for easy removal. If using loose tea, you may want to place the leaves in a metal tea ball. Do not fill the ball completely, as the tea leaves need room in which to swell. Alternatively, simply place the loose tea directly in the pot.

3. Pour the boiling water over the tea bags, tea ball, or loose leaves, and place the lid on the pot. Allow to steep for 3 to 5 minutes, or until the tea has reached the desired strength. (Be aware that brewing for more than 5 minutes may result in a bitter beverage.)

4. If using tea bags or a tea ball, remove and discard the bags or ball, and serve the tea immediately. If the loose leaves were placed directly in the pot, pour the brewed tea through a strainer as it is being served. Accompany with sugar, honey, milk, and/or lemon wedges.

NUTRITIONAL DATA (PER SERVING)

Fat: 0 gram   Calories: 2   % Calories from fat: 0%

Classic Iced Tea With Tea Cubes

Yield: *8 servings*

12 tea bags

12 cups boiling water

16 thin slices lemon (garnish)

One of America's favorite year-round drinks, this beverage has a way of evoking many fond memories of my childhood in the South. The easy-to-make tea cubes will keep your tea delightfully chilled without diluting it.

1. Place the tea bags in a large heatproof pitcher with a cover. Pour the boiling water into the pitcher over the bags, and stir well to saturate the bags. Cover and allow to steep for about 5 minutes, or until the tea has reached the desired strength.

2. Remove and discard the tea bags, and allow the tea to cool to room temperature.

3. To make the tea cubes, pour some of the cooled tea into 2 or 3 ice cube trays. Place in the freezer until frozen solid. Cover the remaining tea, and chill until ready to serve.

4. Divide the frozen tea cubes among eight 14-ounce glasses. Pour the chilled tea over the tea cubes. Make a tiny cut in each lemon slice, and place 2 slices of lemon on the edge of each glass. Serve immediately, passing a bowl of sugar or a pitcher of Sugar Syrup (page 211) for those who like their tea sweetened.

NUTRITIONAL DATA (PER SERVING)

Fat: 0 gram	Calories: 3	% Calories from fat: 0%

Fruity Sangria Punch

This delightfully fruity summer refreshment is a favorite at parties.

1. Place the wine, liqueur, orange juice, lemon or lime juice, and sugar in a 1-gallon pitcher or punch bowl. Stir until the sugar is completely dissolved. Cover and chill for at least 1 hour, or until the punch is cold.

2. When ready to serve, add the ice cubes and orange slices. Gently stir in the sparkling water, and serve immediately.

NUTRITIONAL DATA (PER 4-OUNCE SERVING)

Fat: 0 gram   Calories: 115   % Calories from fat: 0%

Variation

To speed preparation time, replace the sugar and the lemon or lime juice with 8 ounces of undiluted frozen lemonade or limeade concentrate.

Yield: *22 servings*

2 bottles (750 milliliters, or 23 ounces, each) sweet red wine or nonalcoholic wine

½ cup orange-flavored liqueur or nonalcoholic liqueur (optional)

1 cup orange juice

⅔ cup lemon or lime juice

1 cup sugar

36 ice cubes (do not use crushed ice)

2 small navel oranges, thinly sliced

1 bottle (12 ounces) sparkling water, chilled

Fresh Lemonade

Yield: *6 servings*

1½ cups Sugar Syrup (page 211)

3 cups water

Juice of 6 lemons (about 1¼ cups), strained of seeds

Ice cubes

6 sprigs fresh mint (garnish)

You will be ready for those long, hot, lazy days of summer with this luscious lemonade served in frosted glasses! To get the most juice from your lemons, before cutting and squeezing them, immerse them in hot (not boiling) water for about 10 minutes. Then roll each one on a flat surface, and continue with your recipe.

1. To frost your glasses, arrange six 14-ounce glasses on a tray, and place the tray in the freezer. Chill until the outsides of the glasses are coated with frost, or until ready to use.

2. Pour the Sugar Syrup into a 2-quart pitcher. Add the water and lemon juice, and mix until well blended.

3. To serve, remove the frosted glasses from the freezer, and fill with ice cubes. Pour the lemonade over the ice cubes and, if desired, garnish with a sprig of mint. Serve immediately.

NUTRITIONAL DATA (PER SERVING)

Fat: 0 gram	Calories: 205	% Calories from fat: 0%

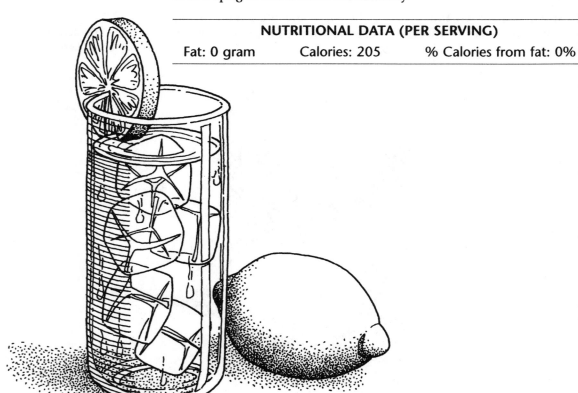

Making Summer a Little Sweeter

Most of us have, at one time or another, stirred a teaspoon of sugar into a glass of unsweetened iced tea, lemonade, or another summertime drink, only to have the sugar sink to the bottom of the glass. The result? An unsweetened beverage—until you reach its sugary end!

Fortunately, with a little preparation, you can easily sweeten even the chilliest of beverages. Just keep this easy-to-make Sugar Syrup on hand, and you'll have the sweetest summer yet!

Sugar Syrup

1. Place the water in a heavy medium-sized saucepan. Add the sugar, stir, and bring to a boil over medium-high heat, stirring constantly.

2. Reduce the heat to the point of a gentle simmer, and cook uncovered for 10 minutes, stirring constantly. Remove the pan from the heat, and allow the syrup to cool to room temperature.

3. Pour the syrup into a pitcher and use immediately, or place in a covered container and store in the refrigerator until needed.

Yield: 2 cups

2 cups cold water
2 cups sugar

NUTRITIONAL DATA (PER 1-TEASPOON SERVING)

Fat: 0 gram   Calories: 16   % Calories from fat: 0%

Raspberry Citrus Cooler

Yield: *14 servings*

2 cups water

⅔ cup sugar

4 cinnamon sticks

12 whole cloves

1 can (46 ounces) unsweetened
    pineapple juice

2 cups orange juice

½ cup lemon juice

12 to 14 Minted Ice Cubes
    (below)

24 ounces raspberry-flavored diet
    ginger ale

This is a deliciously refreshing way to get your vitamin C.

1. Place the water, sugar, cinnamon sticks, and cloves in a small saucepan, and bring to a boil over medium-high heat. Reduce the heat to a slow simmer, cover, and cook for 15 minutes, stirring occasionally.

2. Remove the saucepan from the heat, and allow to cool to room temperature. Remove and discard the cinnamon sticks and cloves, and set the sugar mixture aside.

3. Place all of the juices in a 3-quart pitcher or bowl, and stir in the sugar mixture. Chill for at least 1 hour, or until cold.

4. Just before serving, place the ice cubes in a punch bowl or a gallon pitcher. Pour the chilled juice mixture over the ice cubes. Then, pouring slowly to prevent the mixture from bubbling over, add the ginger ale. Stir gently, and serve immediately.

NUTRITIONAL DATA (PER 1-CUP SERVING)

Fat: 0 gram   Calories: 106   % Calories from fat: 0%

Adding Sparkle to Your Summer Drinks

Sometimes just a small touch can make even a simple drink look party-perfect. Use these ice cubes to add sparkle and color to almost any cold beverage. If planning a large party, start making these cubes days in advance and, as soon as each batch is frozen solid, transfer the cubes to a resealable plastic bag and store in the freezer until needed.

Minted Ice Cubes

Water

Fresh mint leaves

1. Fill your ice cube trays halfway with water, and place 1 small whole mint leaf in each compartment. Place in the freezer until frozen solid.

2. Add water to the trays until each compartment is full. Return the trays to the freezer until frozen solid, and use as needed.

Cinnamon-Vanilla Milk Shakes

Guiltless milk shakes? Who would have thought they could taste so good!

1. Place the milk, frozen yogurt, vanilla extract, and cinnamon in a blender, and process on medium speed until thick and creamy. Occasionally scrape the sides of the blender during processing.

2. Divide the shake among 4 tall chilled glasses. Top each with a tablespoon of the whipped topping and, if desired, a sprinkling of nutmeg. Serve immediately.

Yield: *4 servings*

1 cup skim milk, chilled

2 cups frozen nonfat vanilla yogurt

1 teaspoon vanilla extract

½ teaspoon ground cinnamon

¼ cup frozen light nondairy whipped topping, thawed

Dash ground nutmeg (optional)

NUTRITIONAL DATA (PER SERVING)

Fat: 1 gram   Calories: 152   % Calories from fat: 6%

Hawaiian Mint Tea

Cool and refreshing, this drink will make you feel as if you've been transported to one of the exotic islands of Hawaii!

1. Place the tea bags in a large heatproof pitcher with a cover. Pour the boiling water into the pitcher over the bags, and stir well to saturate the bags. Cover and allow to steep for about 5 minutes, or until the tea has reached the desired strength. Remove and discard the tea bags.

2. Drain the pineapple spears, reserving the juice. Set the spears aside.

3. Stir the pineapple juice into the tea, along with the sugar and lemon juice. Stir until the sugar is dissolved. Place the pitcher in the refrigerator for about 1 hour, or until chilled.

4. To serve, fill eight 12-ounce glasses with the Minted Ice Cubes. Divide the tea mixture among the glasses, and garnish each with a pineapple spear. Serve immediately.

Yield: *8 servings*

12 mint tea bags

8 cups boiling water

1 can (15¼ ounces) pineapple spears in juice, undrained

¾ cup sugar

⅔ cup lemon juice

32 Minted Ice Cubes (page 212)

NUTRITIONAL DATA (PER SERVING)

Fat: 0 gram   Calories: 107   % Calories from fat: 0%

Strawberry Cooler

Yield: 4 servings

Cold and luscious, this is the perfect drink to sip on the porch or patio, by the pool, or anywhere you can relax for a few moments and enjoy the delights of a summer day.

1½ cups liquid sweet and sour
    lemon bar mix

2½ cups frozen (unthawed)
    unsweetened strawberries

2 tablespoons powdered sugar

Mint sprigs (garnish)

1. Pour the bar mix into the blender.

2. Break the strawberries into medium-sized chunks, and add to the blender. Add the powdered sugar.

3. Process on medium-high to high speed until the mixture is thick and creamy. Divide among 4 tall chilled glasses, and serve immediately, garnishing each serving with a sprig of mint.

NUTRITIONAL DATA (PER SERVING)

Fat: 0 gram   Calories: 83   % Calories from fat: 0%

Index